Nelson's Navy
in 100
OBJECTS

Nelson's Navy in 100 OBJECTS

Gareth Glover

FRONTLINE BOOKS

Nelson's Navy in 100 Objects

This edition published in 2021 by Frontline Books,
An imprint of Pen & Sword Books Ltd,
Yorkshire - Philadelphia

Copyright © Gareth Glover, 2021

The right of Gareth Glover to be identified as the author of this work has been asserted by him in accordance with the Copyright, Designs and Patents Act 1988.

ISBN 978 1 52673 132 6

All rights reserved. No part of this publication may be reproduced, stored in or introduced into a retrieval system, or transmitted, in any form, or by any means (electronic, mechanical, photocopying, recording or otherwise) without the prior written permission of the publisher. Any person who does any unauthorized act in relation to this publication may be liable to criminal prosecution and civil claims for damages.

CIP data records for this title are available from the British Library

Pen & Sword Books Limited incorporates the imprints of Atlas, Archaeology, Aviation, Discovery, Family History, Fiction, History, Maritime, Military, Military Classics, Politics, Select, Transport, True Crime, Air World, Frontline Publishing, Leo Cooper, Remember When, Seaforth Publishing, The Praetorian Press, Wharncliffe Local History, Wharncliffe Transport, Wharncliffe True Crime and White Owl.

PEN & SWORD BOOKS LTD
47 Church Street, Barnsley, South Yorkshire, S70 2AS, England
E-mail: enquiries@pen-and-sword.co.uk
Website: www.pen-and-sword.co.uk

Or
PEN AND SWORD BOOKS
1950 Lawrence Rd, Havertown, PA 19083, USA
E-mail: Uspen-and-sword@casematepublishers.com

For more information on our books, please visit www.frontline-books.com, email info@frontline-books.com or write to us at the above address.

Printed and bound in India by Replika Press Pvt. Ltd.

Typeset in 10/14pt Adobe Caslon by SJmagic DESIGN SERVICES, India.

Contents

Foreword 7

1. Wind Direction Indicator or 'Tell Tale' in the Board Room of the Admiralty 14
2. Badge of the Royal Ordnance Department 17
3. The 'Nelson Staircase' which Ascended to the Navy Board Offices, Somerset House 19
4. A Contemporary Print of Haslar Hospital in Portsmouth 21
5. Flag of the Transport Board 23
6. Ships' Biscuit 25
7. Uniform of a Ship's Surgeon 27
8. Ship's Plans of HMS *Agamemnon* 30
9. Plan of the Dockyard and Defences of Portsmouth 33
10. Admiralty Model of the Hull of a 40-gun Frigate 37
11. A Copper Plate from the Sheathing of HMS *Victory* 40
12. Mast of HMS *Trincomalee* with Four Yards 42
13. Rigging on HMS *Victory* 45
14. Hemp Yarn 48
15. Sail from HMS *Victory* Used at Trafalgar, Showing Shot Holes 50
16. A Ship's Anchor at Greenwich 53
17. A 24-pounder Cannon dated 1807 on a Naval Gun Carriage, Fort Erie, Canada 56
18. Gunpowder Magazine and Filling Room, HMS *Victory* 58
19. The Figurehead of HMS *Ajax* built in 1809 60
20. Ship's Toilets, HMS *Victory* 62
21. A Cannonball Embedded in the Oak Timbers of HMS *Victory* at the Battle of Trafalgar 64
22. The Rope Walk at Chatham Dockyard 67
23. A Hand-Operated Seawater Pump, HMS *Victory* 69
24. 12-pounder Carronade 72
25. HMS *Trincomalee*, a Fifth Rate Frigate 74
26. The First Rate HMS *Victory* Afloat 76
27. French Prisoner of War Bone Model of HMS *Temeraire* 78
28. The Stern Gallery of the 74-gun HMS *Implacable* 80
29. Painting of HMS *Abergavenny* in 1801 82
30. HMS *Trincomalee*, a 46-gun Frigate 84
31. Model of the Hull of HMS *Carysfort*, 28 guns 87
32. The Reconstructed Brig HMS *Pickle* at Sea 88
33. Model of a British Gunboat circa 1800 91
34. Painting of the Battle of Basque Roads, 1809 93
35. A 12-pounder Naval Mortar 95
36. A 'Leaguer' Water Barrel used to Transport Nelson's Body Home 97
37. Sea Service Pistol 99
38. HMS *Victory* Firing a Broadside in Drydock in Portsmouth 102
39. The Red Ensign from 1800 104
40. Admiralty Commission for the Captain of HMS *Ramillies* 106
41. Original Lieutenant's Jacket circa 1805 109
42. Contemporary Painting of a Warrant Officer 111
43. Ship's Speaking Trumpet 1801 113
44. A Purser's Button 116
45. A 'Bosun's Start' – Rather a Fine Example Made out of Snake Skin 118
46. Carpenter's Workshop HMS *Victory* 120
47. Painting of Divine Service On Board a Frigate 122

48. Admiral's Barge HMS *Victory* 124
49. Ship's Wheel with Binnacle for a Light and Two Compasses, HMS *Victory* 127
50. Model of the Murray Shutter Semaphore System 129
51. Contemporary Chart of Halifax, Nova Scotia 133
52. Turner's Painting of the Wreck of HMS *Minotaur*, 1793 136
53. Midshipman's Fighting Sword circa 1805..139
54. The Royal Naval Academy, Portsmouth 142
55. Marine Compass 144
56. Recruiting Poster for the Royal Navy circa 1793 147
57. A Press Gang Cudgel 151
58. A Swatch of Cloth for the Royal Marine Uniform and the Lining Material sent by a Supplier to the Admiralty in October 1806 153
59. Ship's Bell, HMS *Victory* 157
60. A Seaman's Jacket 160
61. An Officer's Trunk 162
62. Sailors' Hammocks 164
63. A Chocolate Pot from HMS *Triton* ...166
64. Thomas Rowlandson Cartoon of a Ship's Cook...169
65. A Mess Table on HMS *Victory* 171
66. Skull Clearly Showing the Effects of Scurvy..174
67. Early Photograph of a Sailing Whaling Ship 176
68. A Barrel of Salt Pork 180
69. A Rum Cask 183
70. Congreve Rocket 185
71. HMS *Victory* Flying Nelson's Signal 'England Expects That Every Man Will Do His Duty' 188
72. Water Cask Captured from the Spanish *San Josef* at the Battle of Cape St Vincent, 1797 191
73. Powder Horn 195
74. Leather Tube for Carrying Powder Charges, HMS *Ganges* 197
75. Spanish Admiral Gravina's Personal Statement on the Battle of Cape Finisterre 199
76. Identifying Flags Flown by Each Ship at the Battle of Camperdown.....203
77. Naval Dockyard, Bermuda................207
78. Contemporary Print of the Main Deck of a Warship with Women On Board..211
79. Ship's Chronometer from Baudin's Expedition to Australia.....................214
80. Gravestones in the Naval Cemetery at Gibraltar.........................217
81. Contemporary View of the Naval Base at Halifax, Nova Scotia, in 1804..........222
82. Some of the Huge Treasure of Gold and Silver On Board the *Nuestra Senora De Las Mercedes* 225
83. Victorian Photograph of Three Hulks Moored at Plymouth 230
84. Stern Windows of HMS *Trincomalee* 234
85. Greenwich Royal Naval Hospital 238
86. Contemporary View of Port Royal, Jamaica..................................242
87. Admiralty House, Trincomalee, Purchased in 1810 245
88. An Original Bombay Marine Flag 249
89. Surgeon's Amputation Saw circa 1800..252
90. Death Mask of Richard Parker.........256
91. Superb Diorama of a 'Cutting Out' Expedition 260
92. A Pair of Slave Shackles 263
93. A Cat of Nine Tails 265
94. British Letter of Marque issued in 1813..268
95. Contemporary Depiction of the Landing at Aboukir Bay, 1801 272
96. A Patriotic Fund £100 Sword..........277
97. Contemporary Image of the Revenue Cutter *Greyhound* in Chase...............280
98. Naval Officer's Gold Medal 1794–1815 284
99. Staffordshire Ceramic Figurines of the 'Sailor's Farewell' and the 'Sailor's Return' 287
100. Colourised Photograph of Nelson's *Foudroyant* which Ran Aground at Blackpool in 1897..............................291

Index 296

Foreword

Born at Burnham Thorpe in Norfolk on 29 September 1758, Horatio Nelson was the sixth child of a village clergyman, but despite his humble beginnings he rose to become perhaps the most famous sailor of all time. He was sent to sea on a ship commanded by Maurice Suckling, his maternal uncle, at the age of only 12, but he survived his rough-and-ready apprenticeship and was the captain of his own ship by the time he was 20.

His small, weak frame did not augur well for Nelson's longevity at sea, but he survived serving a spell amongst the pestilential islands of the West Indies, the graveyard of many a British serviceman, and even returned home with Frances Nisbet whom he had married on the island of Nevis in 1787. His return was, however, to be a frustrating one. With Britain at peace, he took his wife to his father's house in Burnham and was forced to remain there on half pay, vainly hoping for a new command.

In 1793, his fortunes changed, with Britain joining a wide alliance of European monarchies against Revolutionary France, which had recently sent King Louis XVI to the guillotine, a British invention which had been adapted by the French.[1] Nelson was soon given a command in the Mediterranean, where he helped organise the capture of Corsica, although whilst in the trenches as they besieged the fortress of Calvi, a cannonball drove gravel into his right eye, the first of a number of injuries he was to suffer in his short life. Nelson did not lose his eye, but the retina had been damaged and he could only differentiate between light and dark through it. Despite popular mythology, Nelson never wore a patch over the eye, but he did arrange a sort of peak to his bicorn, which shaded his good eye, as it was susceptible to harsh sunlight.

He took a very a prominent part in the Battle of Cape St Vincent in February 1797. Having run his ship alongside the Spanish *San Nicolas* of 80 guns and captured her by boarding, he soon discovered that a larger Spanish warship, the *San Josef* of 112 guns was also alongside. As he prepared to board this second ship, she promptly surrendered. His exploit in capturing two larger

A miniature of Admiral Nelson.

---

1 The infamous Halifax Gibbet is only one example of earlier machines which closely resembled the guillotine, including the Edinburgh Maiden and another recorded to have been in use in Ireland as early as 1307.

A colourised photograph of HMS *Victory* in Portsmouth Harbour in the 1890s.

enemy ships was proclaimed throughout the country as 'Nelson's Patent Bridge for Boarding First Rates', astounding the British public. From this point on, Nelson was a superstar and was feted wherever he went.

However, whilst leading an armed boat attack at Santa Cruz at Tenerife that July, he was again severely wounded. This time he was shot in the right arm and the surgeons amputated it. However, he was soon mended, learnt how to scrawl like a spider with his left hand and was back at sea that autumn.

The following year found Nelson's squadron desperately seeking out the French Toulon fleet, which had broken out of their blockaded port during severe weather. It was known that the French fleet was carrying an army commanded by an up-and-coming general by the name of Napoleon Bonaparte, but he had no certain knowledge of where it was heading. Initially guessing that Egypt was their destination, he rushed there to find no sign of the French fleet and then fearing that they might have left the Mediterranean as part of an invasion of Britain, he sped back across the Mediterranean to Gibraltar, only to be informed that the French fleet had not passed through the Straits. Having been reinforced, Nelson sailed east again to Egypt only to find that the French had arrived after a far more leisurely crossing, with a stopoff to capture Malta on route and the French army was now safely ashore. However, sailing along the Egyptian coast, Nelson suddenly discovered the French fleet at anchor close inshore. Without a moment's hesitation, Nelson ordered his fleet to attack, and quickly realised that the French ships were only at single anchor. They therefore had to be far enough from the shore to avoid grounding as the tides turned the ships, far enough to allow his ships to pass on both sides of the French line, doubling up on each enemy ship. The gamble paid off spectacularly with almost the entire French fleet being destroyed or captured. The Battle of the Nile was to be the first of Nelson's three stunning victories. He was again wounded, being struck in the forehead leaving a skin flap dropping over his good eye. Nelson momentarily feared that he was mortally wounded but was eventually relieved to discover that it was a superficial wound.

The huge flag flown by the French *Généreux* at the Battle of Trafalgar.

Recuperating in Sicily following his glorious success, Nelson fell hopelessly in love with the young wife of the English ambassador, the septuagenarian Sir William Hamilton, and they began a clandestine affair. Three years later, having returned to England with the Hamiltons, Nelson was appointed second-in-command of a fleet sent into the Baltic, to break up a dangerous new alliance of Baltic states, known as the 'League of Armed Neutrality'. Arriving off Copenhagen, Sir Hyde Parker gave Nelson a large squadron with which to attack the Danish defensive line. The Danes fought heroically, but were eventually overcome by British gunnery and the Danish Reserve Fleet was decimated. The Danes remained defiant, with their main fleet still safe within the harbour, and tricky negotiations, led by Nelson himself, only succeeded with the fortuitous untimely death of Tsar Paul and the immediate collapse of the League. Nelson had won another great victory against strong opposition and he was again the darling of the nation.

The following few years saw Nelson commanding a flotilla of coastal craft which had been prepared to counter the threat of a French invasion across the English Channel and fathering a daughter named Horatia with Lady Hamilton. The year 1805 found Nelson in the Mediterranean again and as before the Toulon fleet under the command of Admiral Villeneuve escaped during bad weather. Guessing that they were headed for Egypt again, Nelson sped there with his ships only to find Alexandria quiet. Returning, he soon discovered that the French fleet had indeed sailed out of the Mediterranean towards the West Indies. Fearing that such a large fleet would cause havoc amongst Britain's sugar islands he pursued them as fast as he could. The Franco-Spanish fleet had achieved little in the West Indies, being anxious that Nelson might appear, so they sailed for Europe again with the intention of picking up the other French and Spanish squadrons as they passed northwards so as to arrive in the English Channel with superior numbers, giving Napoleon's army the window of opportunity to launch their invasion of Britain.

Messages sent home by Nelson had forewarned the Admiralty, so Villeneuve's fleet found itself facing another British squadron blocking their way under the command of Vice Admiral Calder and following a confused battle in thick mist, Villeneuve ordered his ships to Cadiz for repairs and resupply of provisions. The invasion scare was over, with Napoleon ordering his Army of England to march against Austria.

After a brief spell in England, Nelson was soon back with his fleet off Cadiz, waiting and hoping that Villeneuve's fleet would come out. Admiral Villeneuve heard the news that Napoleon had sent Admiral Rosily to relieve him of his command, but before he could arrive overland, Villeneuve sailed, intending to return to the Mediterranean. On 21 October, Nelson's fleet of twenty-seven ships of the line met the Franco-Spanish fleet of thirty-three of the line off Cape Trafalgar and destroyed them, Villeneuve losing

A fragment of HMS *Victory*'s Union Jack ripped up at Nelson's funeral as mementoes by his sailors.

twenty-two vessels in all. The victory did not save Britain from invasion, but it probably saved the Mediterranean from becoming a French lake. However, that was at the loss of their commander from a musket ball thought to have been fired from the tops of the French *Redoutable*, although who fired the shot will never be known. Having been mortally wounded, Nelson was taken below where he survived long enough to hear that he had gained a complete victory. Having died, he was not buried at sea as normal, but was transported home in a vat of brandy to help preserve him. The Royal Navy were never threatened again by a large-scale enemy fleet, its dominance of the sea remaining essentially unchallenged for over a century.

The news of the victory was received in England with raptures of delight, but it was also tinged with real sadness for the loss of their greatest admiral. Nelson was given a state funeral, being escorted by hundreds of river boats from Greenwich to St Paul's Cathedral where he was buried with great pomp at exactly the centre of the great dome.

The lead ball which mortally wounded Nelson, with flecks of his gold epaulette still embedded in it.

Nelson had already become a major war hero in Britain, but his death at the moment of his greatest victory, as the 'ideal romantic death' confirmed his place as Britain's greatest naval hero. His unorthodox tactics and style of command became an inspiration for generations of Royal Navy officers and remain so to this day. A number of massive monuments, including the famous column in Trafalgar Square, helped to further perpetuate his renown.

However, Nelson was not alone. Numerous other naval officers were imbued with a spirit of daring and a determination to succeed against any odds and a refusal to ever contemplate failure. The Royal Navy of this period was littered with many such men, all epitomising what was to become known as the 'Nelson spirit'. Men such as Hoste, Cochrane, Collingwood and Pellew continued his legacy, often achieving almost impossible things, refusing to give up and getting the best out of their subordinate commanders by bringing them into their plans, just like Nelson's captains, the original 'Band of Brothers'. Nelson's legacy was also very simple, 'duty' before all else; finesse in the battle plan was far less important than the simple premise of 'close with your enemy and defeat him'. Nelson augured in the era of spectacular naval battles where the capture of a handful of enemy ships was seen as useless; total annihilation was the only acceptable result.

The Royal Navy that Nelson knew was a huge and surprisingly efficient organisation, numerous Parliamentary inquiries into the running of every aspect of this giant operation having eradicated much waste, embezzlement and stiflingly over-bureaucratic systems. It is, however, difficult to visualize just how large an organisation the Royal Navy was at this time; at its peak it neared having 1,000 warships at sea, including well over 100 ships of the line and employing not only nearly 140,000 sailors and 30,000 Marines, but also tens of thousands more in building and repairing the ships, providing their armament, gunpowder and every other conceivable item needed to equip a warship at sea. But even beyond that, thousands more farmers supplied the beef, pork and wheat and thousands more prepared this food for immediate consumption or for long-term storage as salt provisions and ships' biscuit. Other produced barrels to store the provisions in at sea, whilst others brewed millions of gallons of ale for the men to drink each day. Hundreds of clerks kept huge ledgers of accounts, listing the expenditure of every farthing spent and paying this horde their wages regularly. Others were sent out to continuously recruit volunteers to fill the posts vacated by death, disease, accident and old age and when volunteers were in short supply, to round them up forcibly with the 'press gangs'. It was in fact the largest single organisation in the world at that time and the complexities of running such a huge and complex operation in every corner of the world in an age of wind propulsion and paper communications is little short of astounding.

For much of this period, the Navy was the last line of defence standing between Britain being overrun from the Continent. Therefore, every sinew was strained to maintain it at the peak of its power, often to the detriment of the Army which only rose to fame in the final decade of the wars under Wellington, when the Navy had already banished any lingering fear of invasion following their success in destroying their enemy's fleets. The character 'Jolly Jack Tar', who was the epitome of a 'devil may care' attitude to danger, fiercely loyal and patriotic, became the very embodiment of the general public's view of the men manning their fleets. However, the public were guilty of viewing life at sea through very thick rose-tinted glasses, as life in the Royal Navy of King George III was very hard, dangerous and very strictly disciplined, with extremely harsh punishments meted out routinely.

The uniform jacket worn by Nelson when he was shot. The bullet hole is still visible on the left shoulder.

This book is not about Nelson, but using a vast variety of images of contemporary items, it aims to explain the complex organisation, the ships, the bureaucracy, the men and their achievements; but more than anything else, to convey the systems and the routines, the challenges, the trials and tribulations of everyday life of a sailor in the navy of King George and to give a feel for the real essence of what it was like to serve in 'Nelson's Navy'.

FOREWORD

A commemoration piece for the death of Nelson.

Nelson's sarcophagus in the crypt of St Paul's Cathedral, directly under the centre of the dome. It had previously been made for Cardinal Wolsey but he had died before it was ready.

1
Wind Direction Indicator or 'Tell Tale' in the Board Room of the Admiralty

An indication of the importance of the Royal Navy was the fact that the First Lord of the Admiralty was a Cabinet minister and as such wielded great influence on matters of naval strategy and where the majority of its ships would be placed. Parliament voted a specific amount of money for its expenditure annually, known as the Navy Estimates, which came in three parts. The Ordinary Estimate covered the costs of the dockyards and the maintenance of the ships, the Extra Estimate was designed for the purchase of new ships and to cover any backlog of maintenance or debts and there was a Manpower Estimate. The Estimate for manpower was a crude and antiquated calculation which had not changed since the

The original Admiralty building on Whitehall, now the Department for International Development.

days of Oliver Cromwell. Parliament voted for a specific number of sailors and Marines and this was converted into a cash sum by assuming that each and every man would cost £52 per annum (£91 after the pay increases of 1797). This figure actually included money not only for their wages, but for wear and tear on ships' equipment, victualling and for the Ordnance Board to provide armament and this is how these departments were funded. The figure produced was pretty arbitrary and bore little actual resemblance to what the Navy actually spent each year. In fact the Navy was permanently in serious debt.

The First Lord of the Admiralty was sometimes a senior admiral (Earl St Vincent and Lord Barham) but just as regularly the post was filled by a politician (Viscount Melville, Earl Spencer and the Earl of Chatham). His Board consisted of five or six junior members, usually split reasonably evenly between politicians and naval officers and not all were particularly conscientious in their duties. The Board considered appointments and promotions, the movements of fleets and the orders for individual ships and the allocation of resources.

The Board met daily at the Admiralty Offices, the Board Room being fully fitted out with a 'Tell Tale' gauge which was linked to a weather vane on the roof and indicated the present prevailing wind direction, thermometers and barometers, as well as globes and roles of maps arranged above the chimney place. There was even a shutter telegraph station established on the roof to maintain communications with the main naval bases.

The staff of the Admiralty Offices then undertook the work of issuing their instructions and orders, but as most of the work was passed on to other departments to oversee, the Board

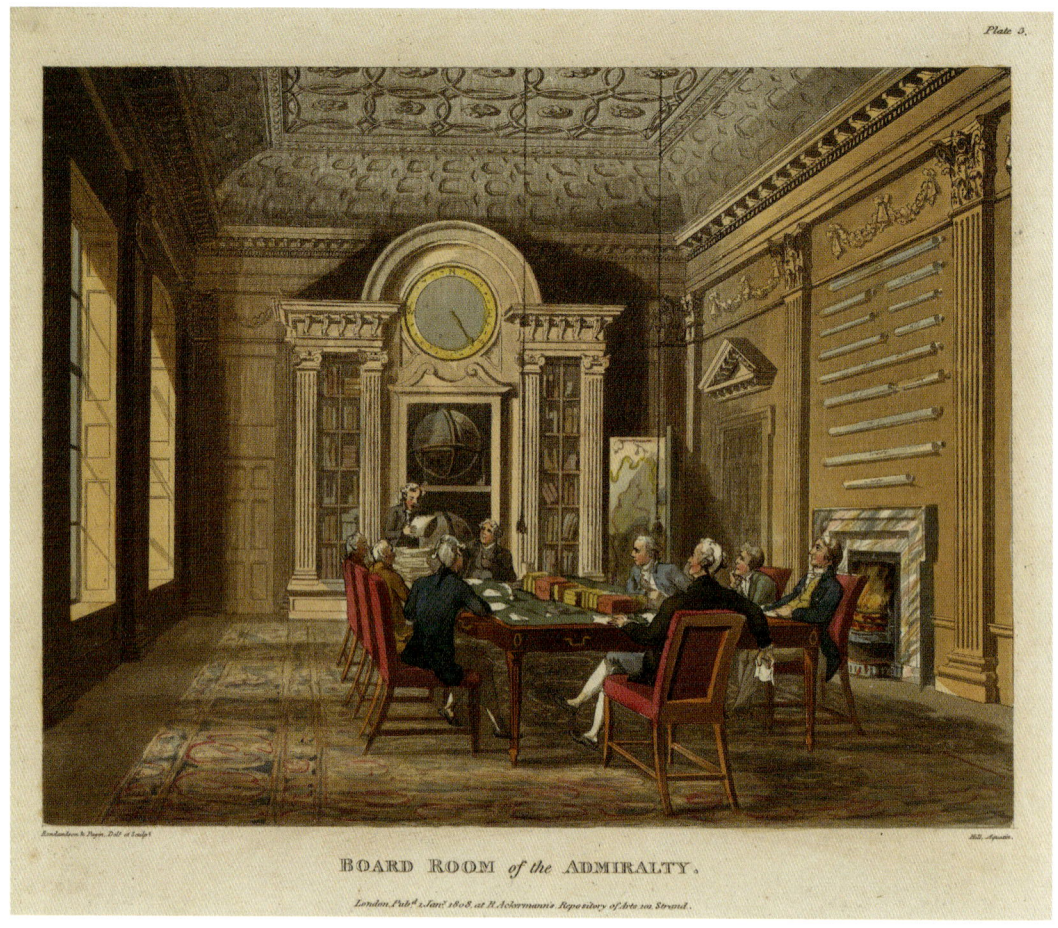

Admiralty Board Room.

only had a staff of twenty-eight men. Directly beneath the Board were two Secretaries who were quite considerable figures in their own right and on minor matters they often made decisions in their own right rather than bothering the Board. Sir Evan Nepean and John Croker were two well known First Secretaries and John Barrow was a very capable Second Secretary.

Another functionary of the Admiralty Offices was the Hydrographer, who was responsible for the production and distribution of Admiralty charts. This was a new permanent role brought in in 1795, when Alexander Dalrymple was appointed to the post. The Admiralty Offices also included the Marine Department, including the pay clerks.

2
Badge of the Royal Ordnance Department

The Admiralty was entirely responsible for their ships, crews and their general stores, but bizarrely they were not responsible for the supply of the armament carried by the ships or their ammunition: this was the prerogative of the Royal Board of Ordnance. The Board, centred on the Tower of London, had been established in Tudor times and they had supplied the armament and munitions to both the Army and the Navy ever since.

It was commanded by the Master General of the Ordnance, who was always a senior ranking Army officer, who sat in the government, but could also be deployed on active service. The Master General therefore dealt directly with the Army, while the Board of Ordnance dealt directly with the Navy. Although a broad arrowhead had been use since 1699 to denote Board of Ordnance stores of war, it was only in 1806 that the Board ordered that all items of

Board of Ordnance arrow.

Ordnance stores would bear the well-known mark. In the same year, the Board became too large to be housed within the Tower and they purchased Cumberland House, Nos 85–87 Pall Mall, to house their clerks, eventually taking over further properties (Nos 83 and 84) next door.

So as to be able to readily supply weapons and ammunition for ships proceeding to sea and to enable ships to be disarmed before major dockyard repairs, a series of gun wharfs were established at the primary naval dockyards under the Board's control at Woolwich, Sheerness, Chatham, Portsmouth and Devonport, with a smaller one at Yarmouth.

Despite this awkward division of responsibilities, it does seem to have generally worked quite efficiently during the Napoleonic period. The Board oversaw the production of high-quality gunpowder at Waltham Abbey and Faversham which they purchased from private ownership and did much to scientifically improve. Indeed during the Napoleonic Wars their gunpowder was deemed far superior to any other nation's. They also oversaw the safe storage of gunpowder in purpose-built magazines constructed near the naval bases, but far from population centres, in case of explosions. The Board also oversaw improvements to the designs of weapons, Thomas Blomefield, Inspector of Artillery, redesigned the cannon, simplifying them by removing much of the decoration and thinning the barrel, reducing the overall weight and yet retaining their strength. He also introduced a metal loop at the rear of the barrel. This was a huge improvement, particularly for naval gunnery, as it allowed the rope to pass through the loop rather than having to wrap it around the knob at the rear of the barrel and by 1794, his cannon were the standard pattern for the Navy. Blomefield also introduced a system of test firing for all new barrels and in the early years up to a quarter of cannon delivered were rejected. This drastically reduced the number of barrels bursting, saving many thousands of sailors from death or maiming. The Board also encouraged the development and eventual introduction into the navy of new weaponry, such as carronades and rockets.

The Board also oversaw the building, maintenance and arming of fortifications throughout the country, including the fortifications defending the various dockyards at both home and abroad.

Board of Ordnance crest at the Tower of London.

3

The 'Nelson Staircase' which Ascended to the Navy Board Offices, Somerset House

The Navy Board (previously known in Tudor times as the Council of the Marine) was responsible for much of the financial and technical administration of the Navy and consisted of a mixture of naval officers, shipwrights and civilians. The Board examined and appointed the boatswains, carpenters and cooks to each ship. Other warrant officers, such as the masters, surgeons and pursers, were not examined by the Board but were allocated to ships by them. The Board also oversaw the maintenance of ships and of buildings within the Royal Dockyards. It also supervised the work of both the Victualling and Sick and Hurt Boards.

The Board was headed by the Comptroller of the Navy, an experienced naval officer, and supported by the Surveyors who were responsible for ship design, both building and maintenance. The Navy Board also put out contracts for everything from building entire ships to ordering stocks of individual items of equipment and awarding these contracts.

The Navy Board moved into the western half of the brand-new Southern Wing of Somerset House, overlooking the Thames, in 1789. It was soon joined by the Victualling Commissioners, Sick and Hurt Commissioners and the Navy Pay Office who all moved into the adjoining West Wing. The terrace to the west of the quadrangle also provided dwellings for the Comptroller of the Navy, the Treasurer of the Navy (who got the mansion at the river end including a coach house and stables for ten horses in the vaults), the Secretary to the Board and five Commissioners.

The Board had been regularly criticised, with claims of inefficiency and corruption on a huge scale. Because of this, the department endured Parliamentary enquiries and was completely restructured in 1796. The Board was normally seen as highly conservative, but it did see through the implementation of a number of major improvements in ship design. The Board also held the examinations for midshipmen to gain promotion to lieutenant and granted their commissions. It was eventually disbanded and its duties taken into the Admiralty itself in 1832.

NELSON'S NAVY IN 100 OBJECTS

Southern Wing of Somerset House overlooking the Thames in 1817.

Pennant of the Navy Board.

4
A Contemporary Print of Haslar Hospital in Portsmouth

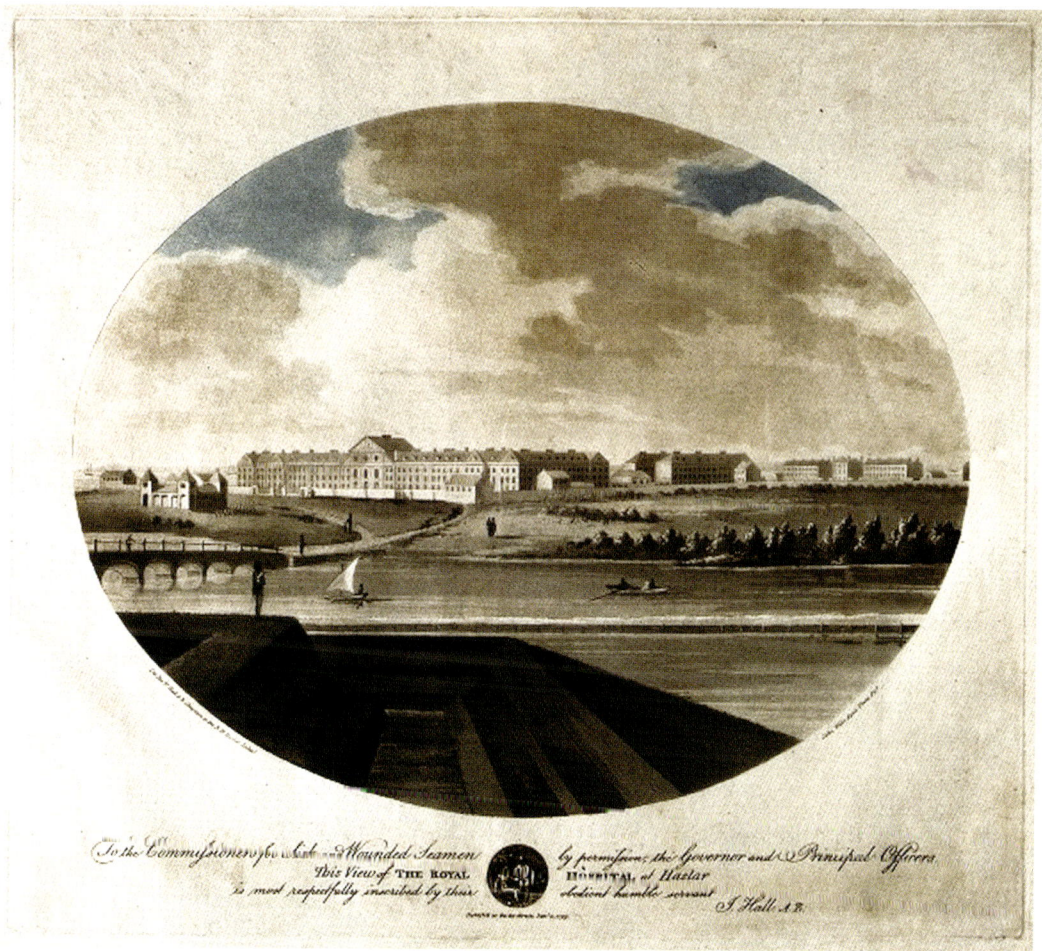

Before 1715, the provision of commissioners to oversee the medical needs of the fleet were sporadic, only coming into effect when the Navy was at war. However, the need for permanent commissioners was recognised and in 1715, the Sick and Hurt Board was established, separate but subordinate to the Navy Board. The full title of the commissioners by the 1740s certainly explained their role; as they were 'The Commissioners for taking care of sick and wounded seamen and for the care and treatment of prisoners of War'.

The medical care available for seamen was initially very poor, although surgeons had begun to be employed on warships, but with few checks on their qualifications and at times of crisis, hulks lying in harbour were used as hospital ships, although their suitability was very questionable. On major deployments 'hospital ships' were also assigned to accompany the fleets. During the Anglo-Dutch wars, it was also found necessary to utilise temporary shore hospitals near the ports but these closed immediately on peace being declared.

The Board took over responsibility for ensuring that the surgeons afloat were supplied with equipment and stocks of medicines, but it was not until 1796 that they took over the examination and appointment of ships' surgeons, the same time that they handed over responsibility for the care of prisoners of war to the Transport Department.

However, the Commissioners were responsible for the gradual introduction of permanent shore-based Royal Naval hospitals, and their equipment, staffing and management, which improved the naval medical service dramatically. The Commissioners are also given credit for the introduction of lemon and lime juice to treat scurvy, but its introduction was very slow after the discovery of the cure, leading to many unnecessary deaths.

The first naval hospitals were established abroad, where the ravages of fever highlighted their urgent need. The first to be established was at Mahon in Menorca in 1711, when the island was in British hands, and additional permanent hospitals were established in Gibraltar in 1741, Port Royal, Jamaica in 1743 and Madras in 1745. Other foreign stations established hospitals at Antigua in 1763, Halifax, Nova Scotia in 1782 and Simon's Town in the Cape of Good Hope in 1813.

Providing permanent naval hospitals in Britain took a little while longer, but when they were built, they were on a much larger scale. The first to be completed in Britain was the Royal Naval Hospital Haslar in 1753, which was sited away from the dirty, crowded streets of Portsmouth, being built in the far more healthy open countryside on the Gosport side of the harbour. The hospital at Stonehouse in Plymouth followed quickly in 1760, but it was not until 1793 that a hospital was established at Great Yarmouth. Two further hospitals were established at Deal and at Paignton in 1800 to cover ships in the Downs and Torbay respectively. Chatham did not receive a permanent hospital until the establishment of Melville Hospital in 1828. The Sick and Hurt Board was wound up in 1806 and all of its medical duties were transferred to the Transport Board.

Royal Naval Hospital, Great Yarmouth.

5
Flag of the Transport Board

The Transport Board was re-established in 1794, having previously been disbanded in 1724, and was given responsibility for all military transportation overseas, which meant that the Army also required their services for movements of troops abroad. Indeed, a committee set up to review its operations in 1806 stated that the Board was responsible for:

> The hiring and appropriating of ships and vessels for the conveyance of troops and baggage, victualling, ordnance, barrack, commissariat, naval and military stores of all kinds, convicts and stores to New South Wales and a variety of miscellaneous services such as the provision of stores and a great variety of articles for the military department in Canada and many articles of stores for the Cape of Good Hope and other stations.

All ship hiring was open to tender, but there was strong evidence that bribes changed hands to ensure preferential treatment in the receipt of contracts and of increasing the public expense.

The Board is often described as a subsidiary of the Admiralty, but it was actually directly responsible to the Treasury and took orders directly from the Secretary of State for War, bypassing the Admiralty. The Transport Board officers wore naval uniform, but as they were not sea officers, they were not subject to naval discipline. The Board set up a network of resident agents at British ports and at overseas ports which the Transport ships used regularly. Other agents travelled with the transport ships when required. Each agent (normally a lieutenant) was provided with a small staff of a purser, gunner, boatswain and carpenter who received Navy pay. In the case of a number of transports sailing together, a 'Principal Agent' would be appointed of captain's rank and he would fly a blue pennant at the mast. In the absence of an armed naval escort, he commanded. The Transport Board hired merchant vessels to carry out its tasks and at times of major deployments, such as in 1808 when a British army was sent to Portugal, it was necessary to hire a staggering 40 per cent of the entire British merchant fleet. Peak requirement for transports was in 1814 when the war ended and the army required transports to bring it home, over 200,000 tons of merchant shipping was hired that year as transports.

In 1795, the Transport Board took over the care of prisoners of war and in 1806 it subsumed the responsibilities of the Sick and Hurt Board entirely. The Board managed prisoner of war camps at Portsmouth, Plymouth, Yarmouth, Greenock, Stapleton, Norman Cross, Dartmoor and Greenlaw (near Edinburgh) and twenty-one

British troops disembarking from transports in Portugal.

Prison hulks at Portsmouth.

prison ships at Chatham, Plymouth and Portsmouth housing a further 11,000 prisoners. It also oversaw the parole of enemy officers at sixteen 'parole towns' and prisoner of war camps abroad. Due to the continued claims of embezzlement, the Transport Board was disbanded in 1817, its responsibilities being taken over by the Admiralty.

6

Ships' Biscuit

The supply of food and beverages to the Navy was the responsibility of the Victualling Board, which had originally been established in 1550. The Board consisted of seven members, who each oversaw a specific area. The chairman oversaw the cash books whilst the others controlled the Brewhouse Department, the Cutting House Department, the Dry Goods Department, the Cooperage Department, the Hoytaking (shipping) Department and the Stores Department.

As the Navy grew in size and demand for supplies increased exponentially, the Board began to set up dedicated victualling yards at the main Royal Dockyards (Portsmouth, Plymouth and Deptford, the latter also covering Chatham) and also at Dover. Smaller yards were established later at Chatham, Sheerness, Deal, Hull, Newcastle, Leith, Whitehaven Falmouth and Cobh near Cork in Ireland. A major base was set up at Gibraltar and other facilities at Halifax, Bermuda, Malta, the Cape of Good Hope, Jamaica and Antigua. The yards had their own dedicated deep-water wharves where ships could come alongside to be completely victualled for sea from the warehouses and slaughterhouses on site. The goods loaded would be mainly the preserved foodstuffs, including ships' biscuits (otherwise known as hard tack), salt beef and pork, pease, oatmeal, butter, cheese and small beer (lower alcohol) which were largely supplied in wooden casks which were themselves manufactured by the Victualling Board, which was by far the largest purchaser of foodstuffs and beverages in Britain, if not the world.

In 1793 Deptford Wharf could accommodate four ships alongside its wharf at one time and it could deal with 260 oxen per day in the slaughterhouse and 650 pigs in the hog-hanging house. It had twelve ovens to bake ships' biscuit and spirit vats holding 56,000 gallons (254,581 litres). By 1810 this one victualling yard alone covered 20 acres. The slaughterhouses only operated in the cooler months of the year (October–April).

In an effort to ensure the quality of food supplied, the Victualling Board set up manufacturing processes at each yard and they became major food manufacturers as well. The quality of the food produced might be indicated by the fact that less than 1 per cent of the food supplied was condemned for going off, despite long-term stowage. Use was made of all by-products possible, using hides to make leather, tallow to make soap and candles and the shins and bones to make portable soup. Deptford specialised in the production of other foodstuffs on a smaller scale, such as mustard, pepper, oatmeal and chocolate (each prepared in a dedicated milling area). There were also separate storehouses for rum, coffee, sugar, tea, rice, raisins, wine and tobacco, all of which were purchased in London and stored in Deptford prior to being distributed for use in the other depots as required. Fresh water supplies had also to be secured to fill the ships' barrels.

With the huge quantities of food required to be prepared, seasonal restrictions and the difficulties of getting it to numerous far-flung destinations despite the vagaries of wind power, it is not merely the sheer scale of the operation that astounds, but the fact that it actually worked pretty efficiently throughout the period.

In 1817 the Victualling Board took over responsibility for medical services when the Transport Board was abolished, but was itself abolished in 1832, its duties transferring to the Admiralty.

The gates to Deptford Victualling Yard.

7
Uniform of a Ship's Surgeon

of ship to which the Navy should appoint him, and served for a period in this capacity before becoming a fully-fledged surgeon. The numbers of surgeons in the Navy rose throughout the wars as the number of ships grew. In 1793 there were 550 surgeons in the fleet, but this had grown to 850 by 1814, with a further 500 surgeon's mates.

Surgeons had the entire charge of the sick and wounded on board his ship, his duties being virtually independent of any other officer, as they were generally not connected to any other branch. He was of course overseen in his role by the captain of the ship who he was required to report to. Surgeons provided their own medical instruments and medicine chests, which were checked before each voyage to ensure they were well stocked. Their role was twofold: dispensing medicines and generally looking after the sick on board, and also carrying out surgical operations on the wounded as deemed necessary to save lives.

He was required to maintain a journal, recording the numbers of sick, their diagnosis, treatments administered and operations undertaken and their outcomes, which was regularly inspected. In serious cases, he would also liaise with shore hospital establishments regarding the removal of patients from the ship and their return. He was also responsible for the general health of the entire crew and acted as an advisor to his captain on how best to maintain the good health of the crew. He carried out at least two medical rounds per day and also had to be able to deal with dental issues and even with those showing mental incapacity. In the case of infectious diseases the surgeon was also tasked

Surgeons had usually completed an apprenticeship before going to sea, but the training ashore was often far below what was required and an oral examination, held at the Surgeons' Hall in London, had to be passed before they were appointed to a ship. The examination covered anatomy, diseases and surgery in detail. He was normally appointed as a surgeon's mate initially, the universities recommending the rate

Surgeons' Hall, London.

with seeking out the source and taking steps to stop its further transmission, a very important issue on warships packed with men. Typhus and yellow fever were the most prevalent of these diseases, which once brought on board could rapidly decimate a crew. Unfortunately these diseases and their transmission was not well understood and surgeons were unable to do much beyond offering a little comfort to the dying.

Previous to the war beginning in 1793, naval surgeons were not highly regarded, often being described as incompetent drunkards who only served at sea having failed to run a successful practice ashore. However, efforts were made during the early years of the war to improve the surgeons' pay and allowing them half pay when not serving on a ship and therefore giving them greater stability. The biggest pay rise came in 1805 at the same time that surgeon's mates were renamed assistant surgeons. The surgeons were aided on board by unqualified assistants taken from the crew, to carry out the menial tasks including cleaning down, who were known as 'loblolly boys'

This change of attitude towards the health of crews and the abilities of surgeons was summed up by Admiral Nelson when he wrote: 'The great thing in all military service is health; and you will agree with me that it is easier for an officer to keep his men healthy, than for a physician to cure them.'

Many naval surgeons at this period were Scottish, having received their medical training at the universities of Edinburgh, Glasgow and Aberdeen. A small number of surgeons with a prestigious medical education or having made a significant contribution to naval medicine, were appointed as physicians, who usually oversaw the work of a number of surgeons at a hospital. The Navy had fourteen physicians in 1814.

UNIFORM OF A SHIP'S SURGEON

Surgeon's medicine chest.

8

Ship's Plans of HMS Agamemnon

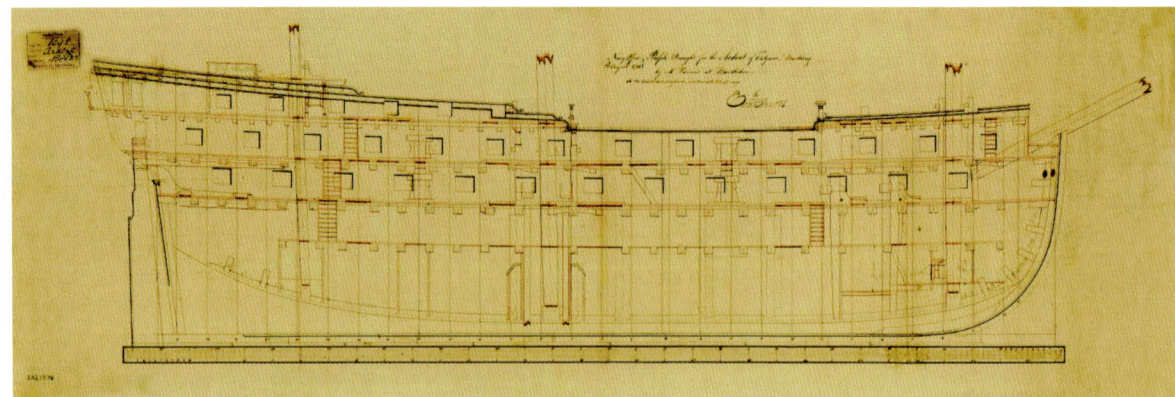

During the period known as the French Revolutionary Wars (1792–1802), Royal Navy shipbuilding was not at a particularly high level, with just over 110,000 tons of shipping being produced during that decade, of which 75 per cent came from private yards. Large warship production was a very specialised business and was often beyond the capabilities of private yards, although a small number, such as Perry's at Blackwall on the Thames, were capable of doing so. The Admiralty were clearly cautious regarding the use of private yards as it is particularly noticeable that the shipyards chosen to construct warships were either on the Thames and Medway, where they could be easily overseen by the Board, or in Hampshire, where the Surveyor at Portsmouth Dockyard could visit to ensure quality. There were still, however, a number of problems with bankruptcies and poor-quality workmanship which dogged the reputation of privately-produced ships, particularly after the loss of the 70-gun HMS *Temple* when only three years old and the need to repair the 74-gun HMS *Ajax* after only four years at sea. Indeed, with Lord St Vincent becoming First Lord of the Admiralty in 1801, orders to private dockyards virtually ceased.

There was a marked change, however, during the Napoleonic Wars (1803–15) when Napoleon's France underwent a huge expansion in shipbuilding in a determined effort to out-build the Royal Navy and to gain naval supremacy. French naval production during this period increased to an impressive 300,000 tons in those 12 years, whilst the warships Napoleon was able to draw in from allies totalled another 170,000 tons.

It was therefore imperative for the British warship programme to increase significantly to match this threat and with Lord Barham taking over at the Admiralty in 1805 huge orders flowed out, many to civilian yards never previously used, all over the country. These contracts were perhaps made easier to fulfil for these inexperienced yards, as the need for the largest warships was now less, following the virtual demise of great fleet battles after Trafalgar. The Royal Navy's superiority in large battleships was now so great that it would be

SHIP'S PLANS OF HMS *AGAMEMNON*

Blackwall shipyard from the Thames with at least seven hulls on the slipways and another just launched.

Launch of HMS *Impregnable*, Devonport 1810.

decades before Napoleon could build up a force to challenge them. The Royal Navy's problem was now an acute shortage of small, handy ships, capable of convoy work and other such duties and these smaller warships were ideal for civilian shipyards to build. In those 12 years, Britain actually out-built France, constructing an incredible 355,000 tons of shipping or 567 ships. With the additional capture of 100,000 tons of enemy warships during the period, the Royal Navy actually succeeded in expanding at a faster rate than Napoleon's entire empire could.

It is also interesting to note where the increased production of warships actually took place. The dominance of Thames-based yards was now ended, although they still produced eighty-four ships during the period, while Hampshire and the Isle of Wight exceeded them with eighty-seven ships and the Medway produced fifty-one. New areas now also showed up strongly, with seventy-one built in Devon and Cornwall, twenty-five in the north-east, eleven at Hull and seven in the north-west, amongst others. The Royal Dockyards had also greatly expanded, producing eighty-two ships. There was, however, one other very significant new producer of ships and that was foreign dockyards, especially in India where they were often built from local teak. They contributed an impressive fifty-two ships.

To produce the ships to a specification, the Admiralty designers produced line drawings of the exact design and construction of the ships and accurate copies were produced from the originals by pushing pins through the plans to mark it out. These were then sent to the shipyards to produce the ships exactly to the drawings.

HMS *Magicienne* of 36 guns being launched at Fishbourne, Isle of Wight, in 1812.

9

Plan of the Dockyard and Defences of Portsmouth

The Navy required a number of bases to accommodate its large and growing fleet. Some of these had been established many hundreds of years ago and were not really ideal for the larger ships now being built and required a great deal of dredging to keep the channels open. These bases were also centred around the English Channel, the area most threatened from invasion from France and to protect London. So there was a dual policy of improving and enlarging the existing bases and establishing a number of new ones in other parts of the country as the threat widened.

Because of the difficulties of getting in and out of narrow waterways and the dependence of the correct wind direction to achieve it, ships were kept at sea unless required to enter the port for dockyard repairs, remaining in the large anchorages outside, where they could be re-supplied but could also sail out again in most winds, so did not become trapped in harbour.

Two major anchorages existed for ships bound for London or the Medway, these were at The Nore just off the mouth of the Medway and was traditionally used for warships based at Chatham and had in the past been heavily used as the best anchorage for assembling ships blockading Holland and also protecting the Thames Estuary. Further along the coast, between Dover and the Medway, were The Downs. This anchorage was used by merchant ships awaiting entry into London and by the Navy, being the rendezvous for ships patrolling the North Sea and had now become the base for blockading Dutch ports. Its main disadvantages were that there was no port along this coastline for support, having to

Chatham Dockyard.

PLAN OF THE DOCKYARD AND DEFENCES OF PORTSMOUTH

still use Chatham or Sheerness (for small ships only), and the ever-present danger of running onto the shifting Goodwin Sands, the cause of many shipwrecks. Chatham struggled with a constantly silting river, a difficult navigation out to sea and the river was not deep enough for ships fully armed to proceed up and down, their guns having to be removed and replaced at a spot known as Sea Reach.

The main anchorage for the naval forces defending the English Channel was at Spithead, which lay off Portsmouth, the other long-established dockyard, which was now the primary dockyard and because of its importance it underwent rapid expansion at this time. The landward defences of both Chatham and Portsmouth were also improved greatly during the Napoleonic Wars to protect them from a successful invasion force attacking them in the rear.

For ships patrolling the English Channel further to the west, the large protected anchorage of Torbay was used and ships here could watch the French fleet at Brest without the problems of sailing against the prevailing winds. The anchorage was, however, very dangerous in an easterly wind and there were no harbours in the

Devonport Dockyard.

Deptford Dockyard.

vicinity to be able to get supplies; ships were forced to move to Plymouth Sound in such circumstances. Plymouth Sound was reasonably protected from westerly or easterly winds, but was very open and therefore highly dangerous in southerly winds. To combat this, construction of the breakwater began in 1812, but it was not completed until 1840. Once finished, however, Plymouth became a very good anchorage in all winds and Torbay anchorage became obsolete. The dockyard had been begun in 1690 and it was established on land to the west of Plymouth at Devonport as the original harbour was totally inadequate for naval purposes.

Yarmouth Roads was also a popular rendezvous for fleets destined for the Baltic, Milford Haven began to be developed for ships patrolling the Irish Sea and Cobh near Cork also became a very important port for fleets destined for the West Indies and America.

Deptford was another example of an outdated dockyard, built when control of the mouth of the Thames was vital. With naval supremacy now established, it became of much less value and suffered from the fact that the larger warships could not lie there fully rigged. Therefore, once new hulls were completed they had to move to the new docks at Woolwich to complete with masts and coppering, but even here they could not fully complete their stores, needing to proceed down to Sheerness, before there was ample depth of water.

10

Admiralty Model of the Hull of a 40-gun Frigate

Good ship design is a balance between a number of competing factors. Wooden ships steadily grew larger over time, but their size was always dictated by the shipbuilding techniques available in the period, therefore there were gradual and incremental improvements rather than radical change. However, advances in ship design and construction techniques did allow progressively larger ships to be launched as they found better ways to stiffen the hull structure, to avoid movement of the ship's joints. During this period ships of up to 130 guns were built, but this was pushing contemporary shipbuilding to its limits.

Warships needed to be sleek and fast, yet also capable of carrying very heavy loads of armament and stores and also remaining stable, despite the problems with topweight caused by a heavy mast structure. Ship design was therefore a very skilled business. In the early years of the Revolutionary and Napoleonic Wars, the French certainly had the best designs and captured French ships were eagerly sought as commands by Royal Navy officers. However, a number of French naval architects escaped to Britain during the Revolution and helped advise British designers, whilst the construction techniques and fine lines of captured warships were studied in great detail. British ship design therefore soon caught up and their designs were deemed as good if not better than anyone else's, until they came up against American designs later in the war.

Ships' hulls were usually constructed of oak, although teak was also used in the Far East, but the size of the Royal Navy and their incessant demands far exceeded the supply of oak from the traditional producers in the New Forest and the Forest of Dean. They could produce only 4,000 tons of mature oak per annum when the Royal Navy in 1812 required 74,000 tons. Supplies were therefore sourced from Southern Russia, Turkey and Austria while mahogany was sourced from Africa and teak from India, all in vast quantities, while mast timbers came from the Baltic. Attempts at building warships in pine were not a success, the wood deteriorating at a greatly advanced rate.

The difficulty of obtaining the very large curved timbers, which came from 100-year-old oaks, to construct the frames of the largest warships grew steadily worse throughout

HMS *Agamemnon*, 64 guns.

ADMIRALTY MODEL OF THE HULL OF A 40-GUN FRIGATE

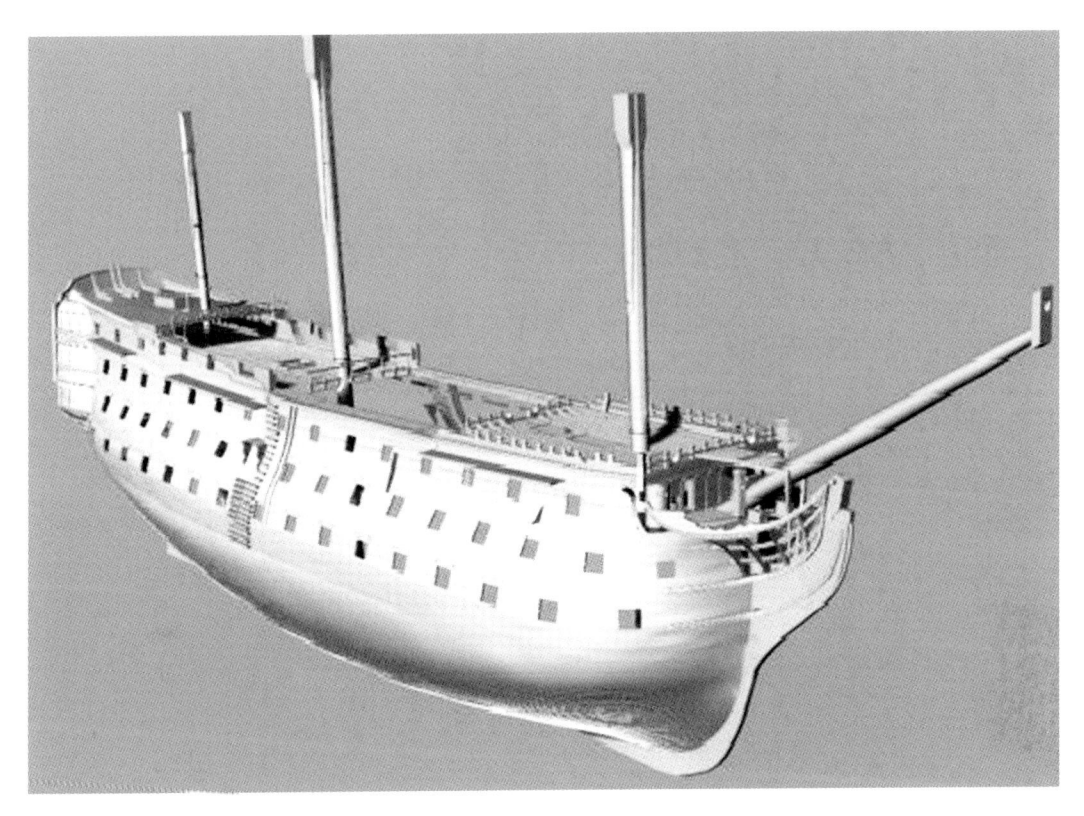

3D image of the hull shape of HMS *Victory*.

the period. Eventually Robert Seppings, one of the Surveyors of the Navy, saw through a number of major improvements, including the introduction of iron joints instead of the wooden ones which were so difficult to find. Seppings is also credited with the radical use of diagonal bracing to strengthen the rigidity of the hull, allowing much larger wooden ships to be built, although this largely happened after the war. It has, however, been established that the Americans had used diagonal bracing already and he may well have learnt of this method from them.

The wooden frame of the ship was held together by huge iron bolts or copper alloy ones for the underwater section so as not to react with the copper sheathing. Once the frame was complete the outer planking of the hull, normally 2in (5cm) thick was applied and the deck timbers fitted.

It is estimated that some 2,000 oak trees were required to construct a Royal Navy 74 gun vessel, while the *Victory* took over 3,000.

11
A Copper Plate from the Sheathing of HMS Victory

As the Royal Navy ventured further abroad during the seventeenth century, they discovered that when in the warm tropical waters of the Caribbean, Africa and India, the unprotected wooden hulls of their ships were subject to attack from the Teredo worm, which could seriously reduce the strength of the timbers, which led to a number of ships being lost at sea.

In 1761 the frigate HMS *Alarm* was the first warship in the world to have her underwater hull clad in copper sheets to protect against these burrowing worms. The Ancient Greeks had previously recognised the problem and had utilised lead sheathing to prevent this, but this added significant weight to the hull. It was soon found to be a success in preventing or at least seriously limiting the problem. Another advantage of copper sheathing, which had not been anticipated, was the significant reduction of the fouling of the hull with other sea life such as barnacles and seaweed. This both improved the ships' speed at sea and reduced the amount of time ships spent out of commission having to be dry-docked or careened on a beach to remove the crustaceans and weed growth.

Copper nails were initially used to fix the sheets to avoid any corrosion issues with using iron, but they soon changed to using brass nails which were much stronger and harder, having less tendency to bend. However, the Navy still found that there were problems with the copper causing corrosion to the iron bolts which held the ship's hull together and experiments continued. It was only in 1778 that the Royal Navy finally ordered that the entire fleet be fitted with copper sheathing, when it had been discovered that by applying a thick layer of treated paper or tarred

A COPPER PLATE FROM THE SHEATHING OF HMS *VICTORY*

cloth to the hull underneath the copper sheathing corrosion of the iron bolts was prevented.

The copper sheets were usually 4ft (1.2m) long and 14in (36cm) wide and each sheet overlapped with their neighbours. For a hull the size of HMS *Victory* nearly 4,000 copper sheets were needed to cover it fully, weighing some 15 tons (15.2 tonnes). Copper sheathing usually lasted about 20 years before it was necessary to completely replace it. It was fortuitous that Britain had only recently begun the mass extraction of copper via mining, the largest being Parys Mountain on Anglesey. The term 'copper bottomed', as used to this day for a plan or investment that is certain to succeed, comes from this process

A fragment of sheathing and copper nails used to attach to the wooden hull.

Copper sheathing on HMS *Trincomalee*.

41

12
Mast of HMS Trincomalee with Four Yards

Most warships had three masts named the foremast, mainmast and mizzen mast (although a few smaller ships had two [no mizzen] or even one), plus a bowsprit which extended the sails beyond the bow of the ship. The mast is not actually a single entity although the whole thing can be called a mast. It really consists of three separate mast sections, which became progressively thinner with height to reduce topweight, each section being a mast in its own right. Hence the mainmast actually consisted of the mainmast, the main topmast and the main topgallant mast. The lower mast, which ran through the ship right down to the hull, was the thickest and was often comprised of a number of timbers (between seven and nine) held together by thick iron bands known as a 'composite mast', a process invented by the French. This mast rested on a 'step' on the base of the hull and passed up through each deck, where wooden wedges held it firmly in place. The maximum thickness of the mast was at about the level of the upper deck and it then began to taper higher up. The upper masts were made from single trees. Near the top of each mast were the 'hounds' where there was a joint attaching the top

MAST OF HMS *TRINCOMALEE* WITH FOUR YARDS

Masts and Yards of a Sailing Warship

1. Mizzen boom
2. Mizzenmast
3. Crossjack yard
4. Mizzen gaff
5. Mizzen topmast
6. Mizzen topsail yard
7. Mizzen topgallant mast
8. Mizzen topgallant yard
9. Mizzen royal yard
10. Mainmast
11. Main yard
12. Main topmast
13. Main topsail yard
14. Main topgallant mast
15. Main topgallant yard
16. Main royal yard
17. Foremast
18. Fore yard
19. Fore topmast
20. Fore topsail yard
21. Fore topgallant mast
22. Fore topgallant yard
23. Fore royal yard
24. Bowsprit
25. Spritsail yard
26. Jib boom
27. Sprit topsail yard

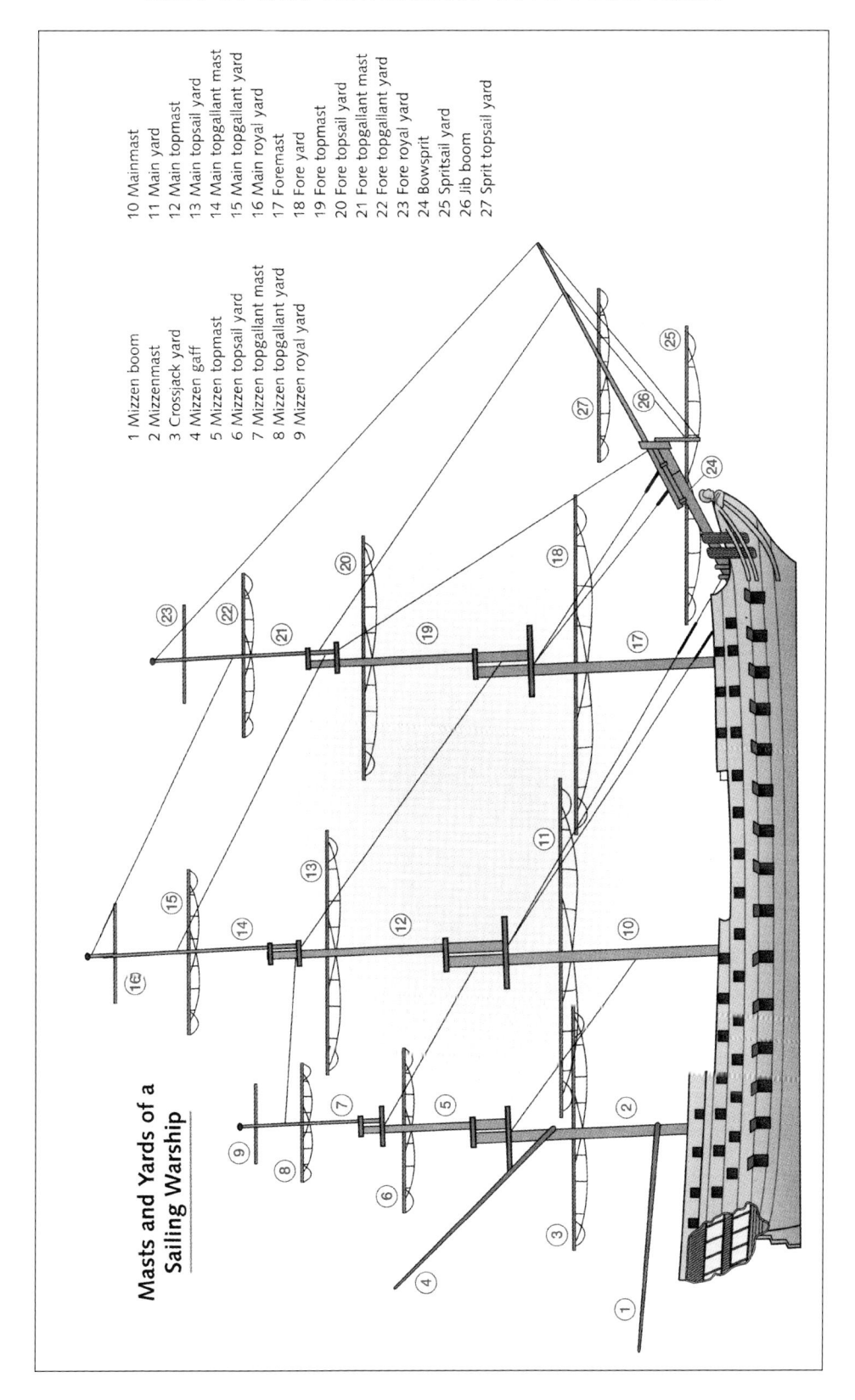

of the mast with the base of the next section and this was surrounded by a flat D-shaped platform to make it easier for the sailors when working aloft. This platform could be used by the Marines during battles, to fire down onto the upper deck of enemy ships and was therefore also called a 'fighting top'. It was not, as it is often popularly called, a 'crow's nest' which was an earlier round structure with high sides.

The function of the masts were of course to hold the huge area of canvas sails that would be hoisted up them. The shorter foremast was set as far forward as possible and with as big a gap as possible from the mainmast to avoid the mainmast blocking its wind. The mizzen mast was the shortest, again so as not to block the wind for the mainmast. The standing rigging consisting of stays and shrouds were attached to the masts to prevent their movement. To give some idea of the height of these masts, the top of HMS *Victory*'s mainmast stands some 205ft (62.5m) above the waterline.

Fir, pine or spruce trees were used for the masts as this wood is both light and quite flexible, so does not break easily under the normal stresses of ship movement and winds. These timbers were largely sourced from the Baltic countries including Russia, hence Britain's demands to maintain free access into the Baltic for her merchant ships.

A section of HMS *Victory*'s mast.

13
Rigging on HMS Victory

Anybody who has ever been on board a large sailing vessel cannot help but be taken aback by the incomprehensible confusion of ropework which connects with every yard or sail, but to a sailor in Nelson's Navy, they were the lifeblood of a ship and everyone would know exactly which one did what. There were two main differences between the functions of different types of rigging, which makes it a little easier to understand.

A Ship's Standing Rigging

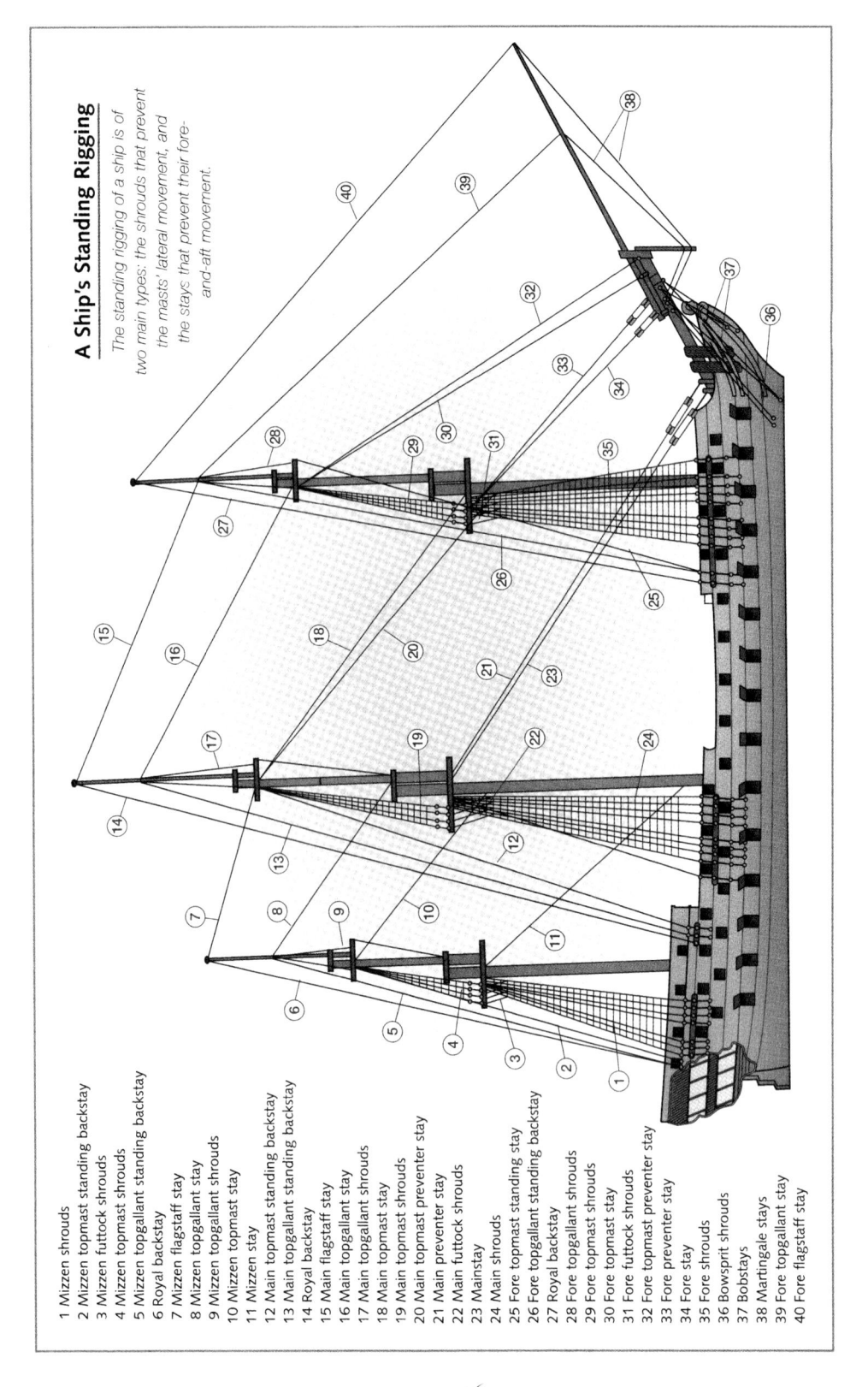

The standing rigging of a ship is of two main types: the shrouds that prevent the masts' lateral movement, and the stays that prevent their fore-and-aft movement.

1 Mizzen shrouds
2 Mizzen topmast standing backstay
3 Mizzen futtock shrouds
4 Mizzen topmast shrouds
5 Mizzen topgallant standing backstay
6 Royal backstay
7 Mizzen flagstaff stay
8 Mizzen topgallant stay
9 Mizzen topgallant shrouds
10 Mizzen topmast stay
11 Mizzen stay
12 Main topmast standing backstay
13 Main topgallant standing backstay
14 Royal backstay
15 Main flagstaff stay
16 Main topgallant stay
17 Main topgallant shrouds
18 Main topmast stay
19 Main topmast shrouds
20 Main topmast preventer stay
21 Main preventer stay
22 Main futtock shrouds
23 Mainstay
24 Main shrouds
25 Fore topmast standing stay
26 Fore topgallant standing backstay
27 Royal backstay
28 Fore topgallant shrouds
29 Fore topmast shrouds
30 Fore topmast stay
31 Fore futtock shrouds
32 Fore topmast preventer stay
33 Fore preventer stay
34 Fore stay
35 Fore shrouds
36 Bowsprit shrouds
37 Bobstays
38 Martingale stays
39 Fore topgallant stay
40 Fore flagstaff stay

Standing Rigging

Once the huge wooden masts were inserted through the decks and the base fixed to the hull, fixed rigging was required both to the hold the masts in position, but also to serve as the means for the crew to ascend the masts quickly and safely. Standing rigging denoted that it was fixed and remained static and it could be tarred to help preserve it, hence its usual black and oily appearance. Most warships carried two or three tall masts to accommodate the huge area of canvas required to propel the ship at speed. However, masts actually comprised of three separate sections, each of differing thickness, one above the other (the narrower and lighter forming the topmast). The shrouds ran to the top of each of these masts to hold them firmly in position (not needed on the topmast) with horizontal ropes, known as ratlines, used to form a ladder for the crew to ascend and descend easily. Other rigging running forwards or backwards (known as forestays and backstays respectively) stopped the mast moving forward or back. There were also lashings fixing the bowsprit securely to the main bow structure. All of this constituted the standing rigging.

Running Rigging

This rigging controlled the yardarms and the direction of the sails. They comprised both the ropes attaching the yardarms to the mast and others which allowed the yardarms to be raised or lowered. Other lines held the yards in a horizontal position and others allowed the yardarms to swing horizontally to position the sails so as to maximise the wind energy. Sails were tied on to the yardarms and rigging was attached to each corner of the sails to allow them to be hauled tighter or loosened.

Other rigging provided footropes for the men whilst they worked the sails on the yardarms high above the deck and ropes known as clewlines and buntlines allowed the area of canvas to be reduced by shortening the amount of sail out.

Other ropework could be rigged for the use of booms when using fore-and-aft sails, for putting up awnings in excessive sunshine, for boarding nets and stowing hammocks, to haul casks up the side, to provide ladders to the waterline or for boat work.

A sailing ship was provided with many miles of rigging, as without it the entire vessel would be uncontrollable and hence it took many years of experience before both officers and seamen fully understood this incredibly complex system of ropes and pulleys. The largest vessels such as HMS *Victory* carried nearly 27 miles (43.5km) of rigging and utilised nearly 800 pulley blocks.

14

Hemp Yarn

Hemp was a vital part of the construction of a warship and the Royal Navy required huge quantities of the material to maintain their ships. Much of the hemp they used came from Russia and when Britain was at war with Russia, it was so vital that the Navy was forced to scour the world for alternative supplies.

The planks on the hulls of ships was laid tight up to each other, but it was impossible to make them waterproof. Therefore, the gaps between each plank was filled with hemp fibre, driven in hard by a mallet. When the gaps were tightly filled, they were sealed with hot pitch which protected the hemp from the water, sealing the hull watertight. The process was known as caulking.

Ships would find that the caulking would begin to fail over time and many ships suffered from minor leaks in the hull. Caulking could be replaced during service, but it was hard, backbreaking work and was very unpopular. A team of men were constantly employed in checking and repairing the caulking on ships. Indeed, it was a common punishment for sailors to be set to caulking the decks. Major leaks in the hull required dry-docking or careening on a beach to re-caulk the ship.

Hemp is a species of the cannabis plant, which grows extremely fast and its fibrous stalk can easily be converted into fibres for use in caulking. This variety of the cannabis plant contains much lower concentrations of the THCs which are associated with the plant and do not seem to have caused any issues with its use.

A caulking mallet and chisels.

A field of hemp.

15
Sail from HMS Victory Used at Trafalgar, Showing Shot Holes

Being totally reliant on wind power, warships required vast areas of canvas to move them at any speed. Almost all warships were square rigged, meaning that they were hung from yards which were perpendicular to the ship, although the arms could be angled to gain the maximum wind. On these ships the only sail running fore and aft (i.e. parallel to the ship) was the mizzensail which hung from a yard stretching from the mizzen mast to the stern. Other sails which could be rigged fore and aft were supplied but rarely used.

These huge sails hung from the yards and were pulled taught by ropes attached to the lower corners, called sheets. Such vast sails could not be produced in one piece, in fact sails were produced from strips of canvas 2ft (61cm) wide sewn together with a 1½in (4cm) overlap. The edges of the completed sails were hemmed (called tabling) and then a rope run around the edge with hoops incorporated to facilitate attaching the various control ropes – see the picture above.

The sails were produced in different thicknesses of canvas for different weather conditions. The thickest canvas, used in stormy weather and very strong winds, was known as No. 1 and weighed 44lbs (20kg) for every 38-yard (35m) strip of canvas, whereas the lightest, known as No. 6,

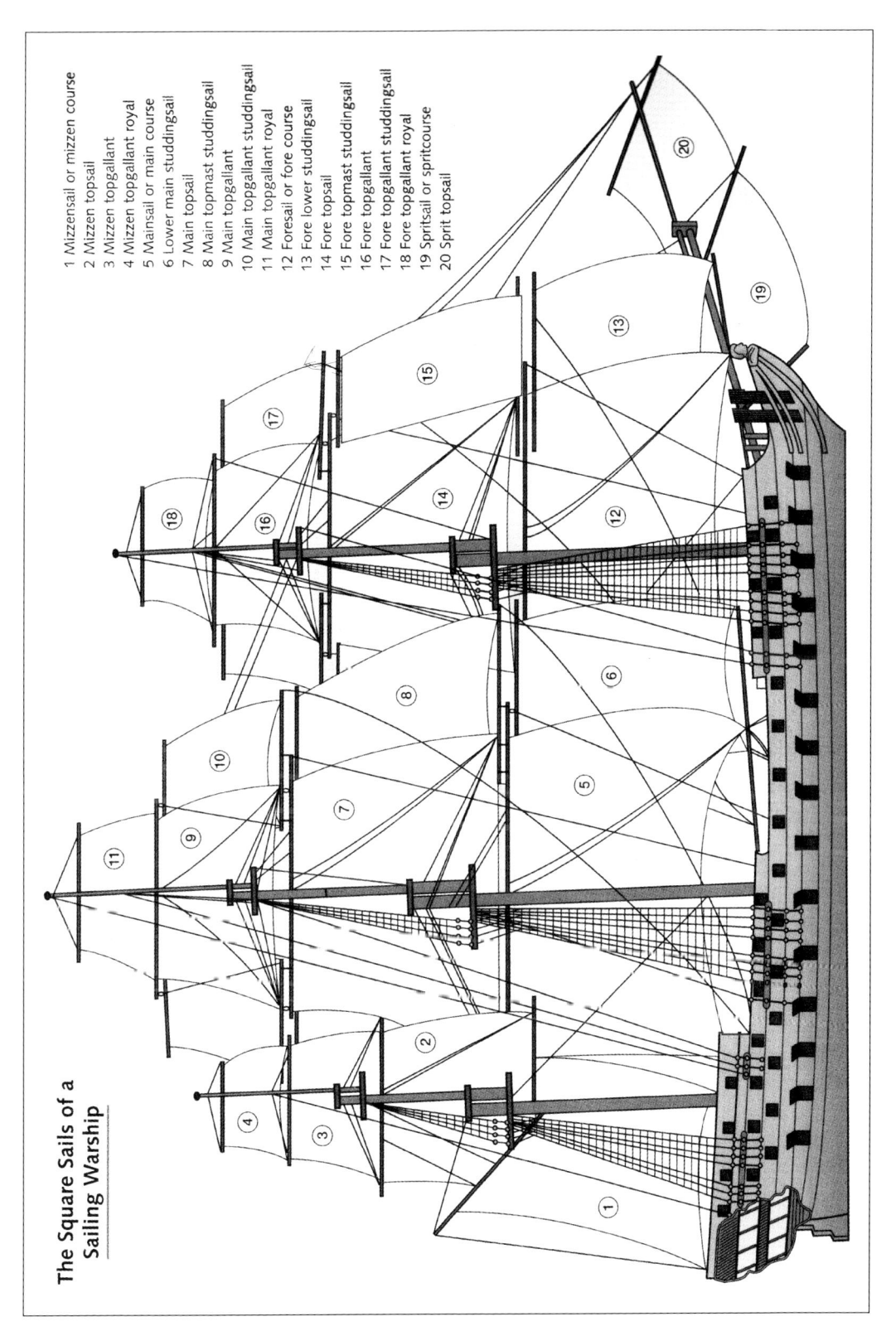

SAIL FROM HMS *VICTORY* USED AT TRAFALGAR, SHOWING SHOT HOLES

The Square Sails of a Sailing Warship

1 Mizzensail or mizzen course
2 Mizzen topsail
3 Mizzen topgallant
4 Mizzen topgallant royal
5 Mainsail or main course
6 Lower main studdingsail
7 Main topsail
8 Main topmast studdingsail
9 Main topgallant
10 Main topgallant studdingsail
11 Main topgallant royal
12 Foresail or fore course
13 Fore lower studdingsail
14 Fore topsail
15 Fore topmast studdingsail
16 Fore topgallant
17 Fore topgallant studdingsail
18 Fore topgallant royal
19 Spritsail or spritcourse
20 Sprit topsail

51

weighed only 29lbs (13kg) for the same size strip. Some sails even had double thicknesses of canvas in areas where they received the greatest stresses, further increasing the weight. Even a main topmast studding sail for a 20-gun ship required no less than 141 yards (129m) of canvas which in No. 1 canvas would weigh 163lbs (74kg). The main topsail of a 100-gun ship like the *Victory* would use 765 yards (700m) which in the lighter No. 6 canvas would weigh in excess of 590lbs (270kg). As can be seen, very large sails were excessively heavy and doubly so when wet, making it very hard work indeed to handle them. Most sails were not, however, rectangular, rather tapering in towards the top, as the yards above were invariably shorter than the ones below the sail. Sails were not meant to be hauled so tight as to form a solid wall of canvas, but were designed to billow in the centre to hold the wind: this was called 'the belly' or 'bunt'.

Smaller warships could be fully rigged fore and aft which was rarely used by the Royal Navy for anything beyond the size of a cutter with a single mast, not dissimilar to a modern-day yacht.

The need to repair the canvas sails was continuous, their being susceptible to damage by high winds tearing the fabric, shot holes in battle which needed to be patched and rot from the incessant dampness when stored between decks. Every warship carried a sailmaker who often had a number of assistants under him. Sail making and repairing was a highly skilled job and extremely hard work, many of the tools used to penetrate the thick canvas often serving as ad hoc weapons during fighting at close quarters. Stitching seams with waxed twine could only be done by hand and required a minimum of 108 stitches per yard. To completely stitch just one of the smaller top sails for HMS *Victory* required 1,200 man-hours.

The *Victory* had a set of thirty-seven sails covering a total area of 6,500 square yards (5,428m^2) and also carried twenty-three sails in reserve.

A frigate under full sail.

16
A Ship's Anchor at Greenwich

Anchors have always been necessary so that a ship at sea can fix itself in one position, but in the age of sail, the use of anchors was much more varied and hence major warships carried a number of anchors for different purposes.

The anchors used during Nelson's time were virtually identical to those used for centuries before as there had been very little development in their design. The traditional design incorporated an iron shank running through a heavy wooden stock. The iron shank had two arms at its base with large pointed flukes, designed to bury themselves deep into the seabed and to help hold it there. At the top of the shank was a large iron hoop for the purpose of attaching the cable. However, as with all anchors, the weight of the anchor

Ship's capstan.

alone was insufficient to hold a ship in position and it relied on the additional weight of the anchor cable to help it retain its hold.

Small warships generally carried only three large anchors and a 74-gun ship carried four. The two carried either side of the bows were for anchoring in deep water, while the third was used as a 'sheet anchor' which could be deployed to the rear of the ship, to help haul it off a bank when it ran aground. If a fourth large anchor was carried, it was a spare in case of loss or damage. These large anchors on major warships could weigh up to 4 tons (3,269kg) each without the heavy cable attached. Even on small warships these anchors weighed 20 cwt (1,016kg).

Lighter anchors were carried in addition as a 'stream anchor' to help hold the ship in a steady position rather than swinging with the tide or swinging into the wind. A 'kedge anchor' was also carried, which could be taken forward of the ship by boat (slung underneath ready to cut free) and dropped, allowing the ship to haul in on it in restricted waters or shallows. Larger warships had two kedge anchors of differing sizes.

Anchors were attached to extremely thick and heavy cables made of rope of up to 21in (53cm) in circumference of 120 fathoms in length (720ft/219m) and two or more such cables could be joined together in very deep water.

As can be seen, the weight of an anchor and its sodden cable would be a very serious weight to raise and capstans were used to bring the anchors in. The capstan was a huge winch which the cable was wrapped around. Placing twelve bars designed to accommodate six men each, in the slots, the cable could be wound in and then stowed below decks on special ventilated boards. Hauling in the anchors could often require the entire crew including the Marines to accomplish it: it was backbreaking work. Just as the war was coming to an end, experiments began on using iron chain link for anchors rather than rope.

A SHIP'S ANCHOR AT GREENWICH

Contemporary depiction of the use of a capstan to haul in a cable.

17

A 24-pounder Cannon dated 1807 on a Naval Gun Carriage, Fort Erie, Canada

A striking example of the power of a major warship of the Napoleonic Wars is to compare the weight of shot capable of being fired by Wellington's army at the Battle of Waterloo in comparison with HMS *Victory*'s broadsides. Although Wellington deployed 156 cannon at Waterloo firing a combined weight of 1,116lbs (506kg), in comparison *Victory*'s 104 guns could fire an incredible combined weight of 2,300lb (1,043kg) of shot or over double the weight. When *Victory* went into battle at the Battle of Trafalgar, her first broadside was treble-shotted, hence her opening broadside from just half of her guns fired a simply staggering weight of 3,240lbs (1,473kg), three times Wellington's total capability at Waterloo.

As guns at sea remained virtually static, their weight was not of such importance as it was to the Army who had to drag them through muddy fields and over rough terrain. Ships therefore invariably carried iron cannon rather than brass ones, because although heavier and less manoeuvrable, they did not suffer such issues as 'barrel droop' when they got too hot from excessive firing. It also meant that the average cannon at sea could be of a much greater calibre and therefore much more destructive than those used on land.

Because of the fear of having too much topweight and the consequent danger of heeling over too far and sinking, warships mounted their heavier guns near the waterline and progressively reduced their weight in each tier above. Smaller single deck warships were rarely armed with anything heavier than 18-pounder cannon, whereas two-decker frigates were often armed with 24-pounders on the main deck and 9-pounders on the forecastle and quarterdeck. Two-decker 74s commonly carried 32 or 24-pounders on the lower deck, 18 or 24-pounders on the upper gundeck and 9-pounders on the upper deck. The largest warships such as HMS *Victory* carried 32-pounders on the lower deck, 24-pounders on the next and 12-pounders on the upper deck. These could all be supplemented by larger carronades, which will be dealt with in another article.

A 32-pounder weighed 55 cwt (2.8 tonnes) and an 18-pounder 42 cwt (2.1 tonnes), therefore it can readily be seen that warships were required to carry a vast amount of weight in armament.

All of the guns were supplied by the Ordnance Board, which had them privately manufactured in iron foundries in England and Scotland, the most famous being the Carron Iron Works in Stirlingshire and Samuel Walker of Rotherham. All cannon at this time were smoothbores, the barrels being cast solid and the bore machined out to ensure the maximum strength of the barrel. All barrels were proof tested on receipt at Woolwich by firing a charge well in excess of anything they would ever normally fire. If the barrel survived without any sign of weakness it was accepted.

Much work during the latter half of the eighteenth century was centred around standardisation. The previous 'Armstrong' design was officially superseded by the 'Blomefield' pattern in 1794 and no other type was then manufactured. However, as late as 1808 records show ships still carrying the Armstrong cannon. The gun or 'truck' carriages were produced by the Ordnance Board and standardised although of differing dimensions because of the different sizes of cannon, wheels on ship were generally made of wood.

The gun deck of HMS *Victory*.

18
Gunpowder Magazine and Filling Room, HMS Victory

Warships were required to store vast quantities of gunpowder safely in dry conditions and to achieve this, great pains were taken to try to avoid explosions. The magazines were built in the hold or 'hanging' below the orlop deck where they were below the waterline and therefore were less vulnerable to enemy roundshot crashing through the walls, but well above the keel to avoid water ingress. The greatest dangers, however, were of course, fire or sparks and everything possible was done to try to avoid such disasters. The magazines were provided with a lead floor and copper sheeting on the plaster walls (a fire-retardant material) and deck head, to keep the magazine dry, prevent damage from vermin and to avoid sparks. All equipment in the room was also made from wood, copper, lead or leather, again to avoid any possibility of static and sparks. Lighting was provided by candlelight, held within a safety lamp and placed behind a thick glass partition outside the magazine to shed light within. Even the men were required to be extremely careful not to cause a spark. They wore only linen and leather goods and they even wore wicker shoes or leather slippers. Charcoal was also stored in the room as this drew any moisture out of the air.

The gunpowder was delivered in wooden casks with wood or copper banding, each containing 100, 50 or 25lbs (45, 23 or 11kg) of gunpowder and these were stored within the grand magazine in the hold, larger warships having one or two other small magazines for ready-use cartridges. HMS *Victory* for example carried 784 100lb barrels, which totalled over 35 tons of gunpowder. As the more powerful 'cylinder' powder began to be issued, it was necessary to distinguish it from the old, weaker powder as different measures were needed for the charges. The cylinder powder was marked in red letters rather than blue to avoid confusion. When delivered to the vessel, the ship's gunner informed the captain and every candle in the ship and even the galley fire was extinguished. To be used in the cannon, the gunpowder had to be emptied out of the barrels into a lead-lined bath and charges made up of varying amounts of gunpowder for the different sizes of cannon. The loose gunpowder was scooped into linen sacks using copper or wooden hand shovels and these ready-made charges were placed in the wooden racks, each rack being clearly marked for the calibre of gun. During an action these would be handed out one at a time in their wooden boxes, through a leather screen to the 'powder monkeys' to convey them to their individual gun. It was normal to have each gun loaded ready to fire and two cartridges in a ready-use wooden box nearby, so as to be able to fire rapidly when needed. Paper cartridges were also produced on board to be used for priming the cannon.

Every three months all of the barrels of gunpowder had to be turned to avoid the nitrate separating to the bottom. Empty barrels were eventually returned to the Ordnance Storekeeper and the gunner received 1 shilling for each one, a very nice incentive.

At the Battle of Trafalgar, HMS *Victory* used about 8 tons of gunpowder, close to a quarter of her total stock.

Gunpowder barrels.

19

The Figurehead of HMS Ajax built in 1809

Figurehead of HMS *Implacable* with simple gilding.

The use of a figurehead was an ancient practice, with the Egyptians, Romans, Vikings and Phoenicians using a figure on the bow of their ships. By the 1700s large warships had become symbols of the strength of the monarch and they were heavily gilded on the stern and had very ornate figureheads, again gilded. Figures popularly used were unicorns, saints or royal personages, but most warships of the Royal Navy invariably had a lion figurehead.

By the end of the century, as the wars against Revolutionary France began, the gilding had largely disappeared and in 1796 the Admiralty attempted to abolish figureheads on new ships. Sailors are, however, a superstitious lot and many felt that a ship without a figurehead would be unlucky, therefore it was decided to carry on with the tradition.

With the end of gilding, it became normal around 1800 and onwards to paint the figurehead in vibrant or realistic colours. Most ships had a carved animal or a mythological figure which represented the name of the ship. Initially they were full length, but this soon changed to a figure from the waist up only. Figureheads were not official and in the architectural drawings the position of the figurehead was denoted by a plain block, it was down to the carpenters of the construction dockyard, perhaps in agreement with the new captain, what the carving would be of. Smaller naval vessels were not designed to carry a figurehead and they now sported a simple leaf motif around the bow. Larger warships often portrayed the Royal crest rather than a figurehead as such (see the photograph of HMS *Victory* below).

Figureheads really died out with the age of sail, as steam warships saw their bow as a ramming weapon and the very last Royal Navy ship to sport one was HMS *Cadmus* in 1903.

Figurehead of HMS *Victory*.

20
Ship's Toilets, HMS Victory

With up to a thousand men on board a ship for lengthy periods of time, the issue of toilets and sanitation becomes a very important matter. For some level of privacy, to eradicate evil, obnoxious smells and also for ease of effluent removal, the toilets for the crew were placed right up at the bow of the ship. Men requiring to urinate were expected to do so out to sea, but only in this vicinity. To do so elsewhere would attract severe punishment. New sailors soon learnt that it was best to do so on the downwind side of the ship, for obvious reasons.

Those requiring to defecate used the seat on the boxes as shown, the *Victory* having two seats either side of the bowsprit, but most smaller ships only had single-seat units on each side. Here the user was clearly fully at the mercy of

The admiral's private toilet, HMS *Victory*.

The admiral's toilet with folding door for privacy.

the elements and in stormy weather it might become far too dangerous to use them, when they were forced to resort to a simple bucket. The effluent dropped down directly into the sea and the waves crashing onto the bow were very useful in continually scouring the bow of the ship clean. Because of their position right forward, ship's toilets were known as 'heads', a tradition that is retained by the Navy to this day. At night, buckets were often provided for the men below decks for urgent calls of nature.

Officers were not expected to use the same facilities as the men and they utilised one of the private cubicles towards the ship's rear quarter. The other was reserved for the admiral when on board or the captain in his absence.

21

A Cannonball Embedded in the Oak Timbers of HMS Victory at the Battle of Trafalgar

As was the case with the Army, the solid iron cannonball or roundshot was by far the most common type of projectile, fired by the Navy in action. These of course varied in weight from 9lbs to 32lbs (4kg to 14.5kg), depending on the calibre of the cannon which the ship was supplied with. Cannonballs were extremely destructive to anything they struck, particularly human flesh, and fired at very close range they could penetrate right through the oak hull and were often powerful enough to pass through the other side of the ship as well. A well-aimed, or more often a very lucky, shot could bring down a mast or destroy the rigging, making the ship much less manoeuvrable, or strike the hull below the waterline causing serious flooding. Anyone unlucky enough to be struck by a cannonball would be killed outright or have one or more limbs mutilated, but at sea there was a much greater threat to personnel from these iron balls. The simple act of smashing through the wooden hull, caused huge numbers of razor-sharp splinters of wood which sprayed out in all directions, killing and horrifically maiming many more than those in the direct line of the roundshot.

Apart from cannonballs, other projectiles could be fired from the ship's iron cannon, either as anti-personnel weapons or designed for reducing the ability of the enemy ship to manoeuvre. Iron guns, which were heavier than the brass cannon used by the Army, meant that these other odd-shaped shot could be fired without causing damage to the barrel. The softer brass barrels would have suffered badly as the iron would have scoured the bore and caused it to quickly become unserviceable.

Against enemy personnel on the upper deck, the standard weapon used at sea was grapeshot, which contained a number of small cannonballs tied up within a canvas bag and therefore

Grapeshot.

Bar shot.

Expanding bar shot.

resembling grapes. On firing, the bag broke open and the iron balls spread out in a wide arc, devastating large numbers on deck. Canister was also used, although far less frequently at sea. This consisted of a tin can filled with small iron balls, a little larger than musket balls, hence a very large number could be packed in.

When fired, the can split and the balls flew out in an arc, with an effect similar to the spray of bullets from a modern machine gun. Large versions fired from 32-pounder and 64-pounder carronades could effectively sweep the entire deck clear with a single discharge. These two rounds were quite different, but are often mixed up, although grape shot was not fired from brass (Army) guns.

Chain shot.

Multiple bar shot.

Another type of ammunition was designed specifically to damage canvas sails and the multitude of ropes that were required to work the ship, which would slow the enemy significantly and make them far less manoeuvrable and therefore very vulnerable. There were many versions of these weapons produced in an effort to find the most effective at destroying rigging. Simple bar shot rotated as they flew through the air, smashing anything that came into its path. An adaptation of this was the elongated or extended bar shot, in which the two lengths of iron bar could be compressed whilst in the barrel, but was pulled out to their full extent when they left the barrel and spun through the air.

Chain shot linked the two half-spheres of a cannonball, which again spread out on leaving the barrel to tear through canvas sails and ropework. Another design was the multiple bar shot, which were linked together by an iron hoop, the three bars scything through the air at tremendous speed to cut through anything in its path.

It seems needless to say that all of these weapons were also particularly lethal to humans and there are many graphic accounts of the terrible injuries they caused, almost all of which were fatal.

22
The Rope Walk at Chatham Dockyard

Warships of the Napoleonic Wars were dependent on rope for everything from standing rigging to the huge anchor cables as the use of iron chain was only beginning to be introduced as the war ended. Being a natural product, which will deteriorate from regular contact with salt water and damaged with constant use, there was therefore a continuous demand for rope. A First Rate ship of war required over 31 miles (50km) of rope to complete it.

A huge long building known as a 'ropewalk' simply because of its vast length, was constructed at each of the major naval bases to manufacture vast quantities of various thicknesses of rope, from half an inch (1cm) to 24in (61cm) circumference. Chatham ropewalk, originally constructed in 1790 (shown above), has an internal length of 1,135ft (346m), allowing it to produce complete ropes in standard Royal Naval lengths of 1,000ft (305m).

Raw hemp, manila hemp or sisal was broken down into individual long strands or fibres in a process called 'hatchelling', then spun into yarn and tarred. Only then was it brought to the rope walk to be twisted into rope. With the thickest anchor cables a number of ropes were twisted together to produce one extremely thick cable, as can be seen clearly in the photograph below of the *Victory*'s anchor cable. Because of their extreme weight, it required hundreds of men to form the largest ropes. A 20in (51cm) rope took over 200 men and the largest of all would require over 300. It is therefore not surprising to learn that hauling in the anchor and cable required the entire crew to handle it. All Dockyard rope was produced with a single coloured strand woven through it to identify it as government property, to prevent pilfering: the custom continues to this day.

Every seaman required the knowledge and ability to work rope, including splicing ropes together, using a fid to open up the strands to pass the strand of the connecting rope through it. The ability to tie knots was essential, so essential in fact that it was simply expected. The numerous knots essential to know were divided into bends, which tied two ropes securely together, and hitches which attached ropes to another object. Many of these knots are rarely known today, such as the Blackwall and Magnus Hitch or the Matthew Walker but many modern knots tell of their nautical beginnings. The reef knot was used to reef sails, and the bowline to attach the bowline bridles to the sails.

A highly decorative ivory awl or 'fid' for separating the fibres in a rope.

Thick anchor cable on HMS *Victory*.

23
A Hand-Operated Seawater Pump, HMS Victory

Water was needed to scrub the decks regularly and also to fight fires, but fresh water was too valuable to waste on such work and therefore a number of hand-operated pumps were installed which could raise sea water to deck level for this task.

All wooden ships leak to some degree and this was often exacerbated in rough seas when the movement of the frame allowed the joints to open further. This was a particular problem for ships which had not seen their caulking renewed for a considerable period, often causing them to take in a significant amount of water each day, which collected in the bilges.

To combat this ingress of sea water, a number of bilge pumps were installed and were worked daily to keep the level of water down, but the ships hulls were rarely if ever free of some water. Working the bilge pumps was backbreaking work and was an unpopular duty and therefore

Bilge pump on HMS *Victory*.

A HAND-OPERATED SEAWATER PUMP, HMS *VICTORY*

sand which might well have interfered with the working of the bilge pumps.

Despite generally being hated, the bilge pumps could often be seen as a lifesaver, when ships were taking on excessive amounts of water from underwater shot holes or storm damage when the ship was in danger of foundering. In such situations the pumps were often required to run continuously night and day, until the ship arrived in shallow waters and could commence repairs, or the crew became too exhausted to continue, when a watery grave was the almost inevitable conclusion.

Coles & Bentinck Chain Pump

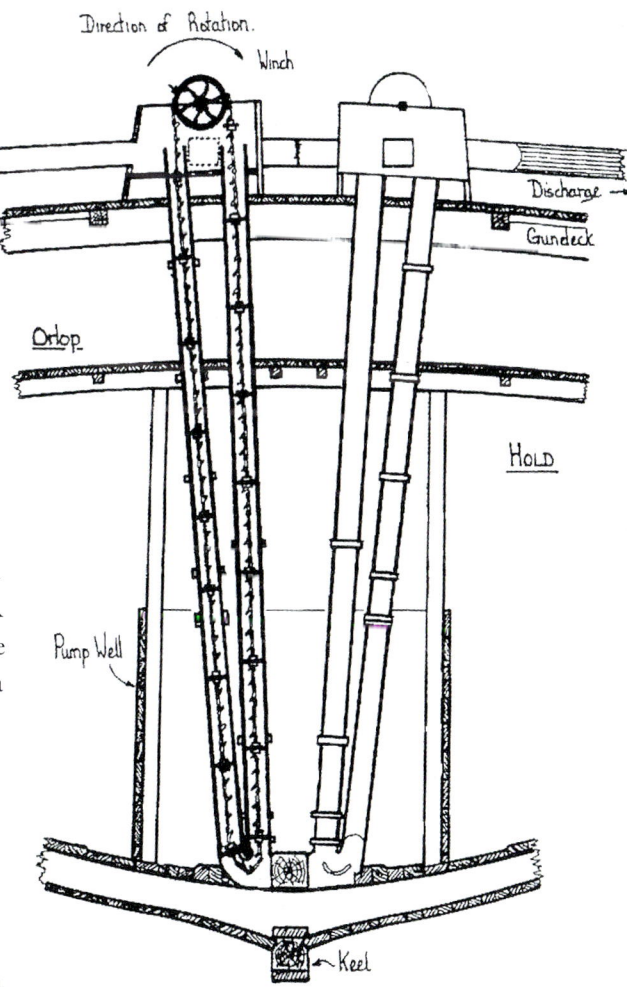

A Navy fire bucket.

sometimes used as a punishment. All warships were fitted with a minimum of two bilge pumps, in case of the failure of one, and ships over 70 guns had four.

A basic bilge pump had existed since the fifteenth century and its design had not changed radically since then. The system saw a continuous chain with leather discs attached to form a reasonably watertight seal, which ran through a cast iron tube from the deck above the waterline, down through all the decks to the bilge and then returned to the deck. Long iron crank handles which could accommodate a large number of men together (later changed to a wheel) were attached to a cog system which rotated the chain, trapping water in the tube above the discs and then raised to the deck, where it was discharged over the ship's side. The four pumps were capable of lifting 120 tonnes of water per hour. Part of the ballast of warships was carried as shale at the bottom of the ship. This was used rather than

24

12-pounder Carronade

The true armament of a warship during the Napoleonic Wars is invariably confused by the introduction (often unofficially) of carronades to the upper deck guns by ship's captains.

The gun, developed by the Carron Iron Works established at Falkirk in Scotland in 1759, was born out of desperation. The standard cannon produced in the early years for the Admiralty was often found to be defective or of poor quality and in 1773 the company lost its contract to supply standard cannon to the Royal Navy and all of its cannon were removed from warships.

One of the owners, John Gascoigne, put forward a new type of cannon, originally known as a 'Gasconade' or 'Mellvinade' as possibly invented by Lieutenant General Melville, but it soon became better known as the 'Carronade'. The gun had a considerably shorter barrel although it could still fire the same size ball, therefore they had a very considerable weight advantage over traditional cannon. By 1778 carronades had become a huge success and they were manufactured until 1850.

The carronades were initially designed for merchant vessels because of their ease of use and ability to be mounted on pivoted sliders for ease of aiming. Designed as a close-quarters weapon, requiring a smaller charge was also an advantage as well as the smaller crew required. However, being only a third of the weight of traditional cannon was a real advantage, avoiding topweight issues.

The Royal Navy was initially sceptical due to the poor reputation that the Carron Works had gained and they were not counted within the traditional armament of the ship. However, carronades began to be fitted on the upper deck as anti-personnel weapons at which they proved to be very adept indeed. By the time of Trafalgar, the *Victory* sported two huge 68-pounder carronades on the forecastle and they were used to great effect in clearing the gun deck of the French *Bucentaure* with the single discharge of a single roundshot and a keg of 500 musket balls fired through her stern windows and causing sheer carnage along the entire length of the ship. Royal Navy sailors often referred to them as 'smashers'. They certainly proved to be very effective in decimating enemy boarding parties (a particular favourite tactic of the French) or completely sweeping the upper deck of enemy personnel, allowing them a decided advantage when they boarded the enemy ship.

Soon almost every warship carried a few carronades, causing the Navy to experiment with arming a warship entirely with them. Two ships, HMS *Glatton* and *Rainbow*, were armed purely with carronades, *Glatton*, officially only carrying 56 guns, thereby actually carrying a heavier broadside than *Victory*. The ships proved successful in battle at close quarters, but were vulnerable to an opponent who kept their distance, where their long guns outranged the carronades. Smaller carronades were fitted to boats and proved to be a fearsome weapon in boat actions.

The French captured carronades early on but struggled to produce a similar gun because of their poorer-quality iron. They preferred to use a short brass weapon called an '*obusier de vaisseau*' which fired an explosive shell or grenade rather than solid ball. It was not anywhere near as effective.

A 68-pounder carronade aboard HMS *Victory*.

25

HMS Trincomalee, *a Fifth Rate Frigate*

As the Navy grew ever larger, it had become necessary to put each ship into a category, termed the rating system, to indicate their size and power. Previous versions of the system had existed in the Stuart Navy, where ships were classed, depending on the number of cannon carried, as either Royal ships (over 42 guns), Great ships (38–40 guns) Middling ships (30–32) and Small ships (less than 30). The system was soon modified to subdivide the smaller ships into three and these six classes became ranks. In 1626 Charles I had a table of the ships of the Royal Navy and for the first time, the ships were divided into six 'rates' (by size of crew).

As ships had become larger and the variations in size of ship and numbers in the crew grew, it was decided in 1660 to rate ships by the number of cannon they carried rather than the size of the crew. These rates helped to make the work of the different Boards a little easier, as the supplies required for ships within each 'rate' became standardised.

HMS TRINCOMALEE, A FIFTH RATE FRIGATE

During the eighteenth century, it became standard that only ships of a certain number of cannon were allowed to appear in the formal fighting line of battle and these were termed 'ships of the line'. Only ships of the First, Second and Third Rates were officially classed as ships of the line.

By 1800, the rates had been altered slightly to accommodate the largest of warships (above 100 guns in the Royal Navy) and the different rates were set as follows:

First Rate   100 or more guns
Second Rate   90–82 guns
Third Rate   64–80 guns
Fourth Rate   50–62 guns
Fifth Rate   32–48 guns
Sixth Rate   20–30 guns
Unrated   Below 20 guns

However, during the Napoleonic Wars, the rating system only indicated the ship's 'Established Armament' because many ships carried additional guns or carronades, which were not counted. In 1817 the rating system was amended to counter this issue and all cannon including carronades were counted in setting a ship's rating. The system of rating by number of cannon ended in 1856.

Painting of a Third Rate and a Fifth Rate frigate.

26
The First Rate HMS Victory *Afloat*

The largest warships of the Royal Navy of the Napoleonic Wars were the First Rate ships of over 100 cannon on three decks (plus guns on the upper deck) displacing from 2,000 to 2,500 tons, the broadside of these huge ships firing a weight of shot greater than the Duke of Wellington's army could fire at the Battle of Waterloo.

The Royal Navy had six 100-gun ships in this period, *Victory*, *Royal Sovereign*, *Britannia*,

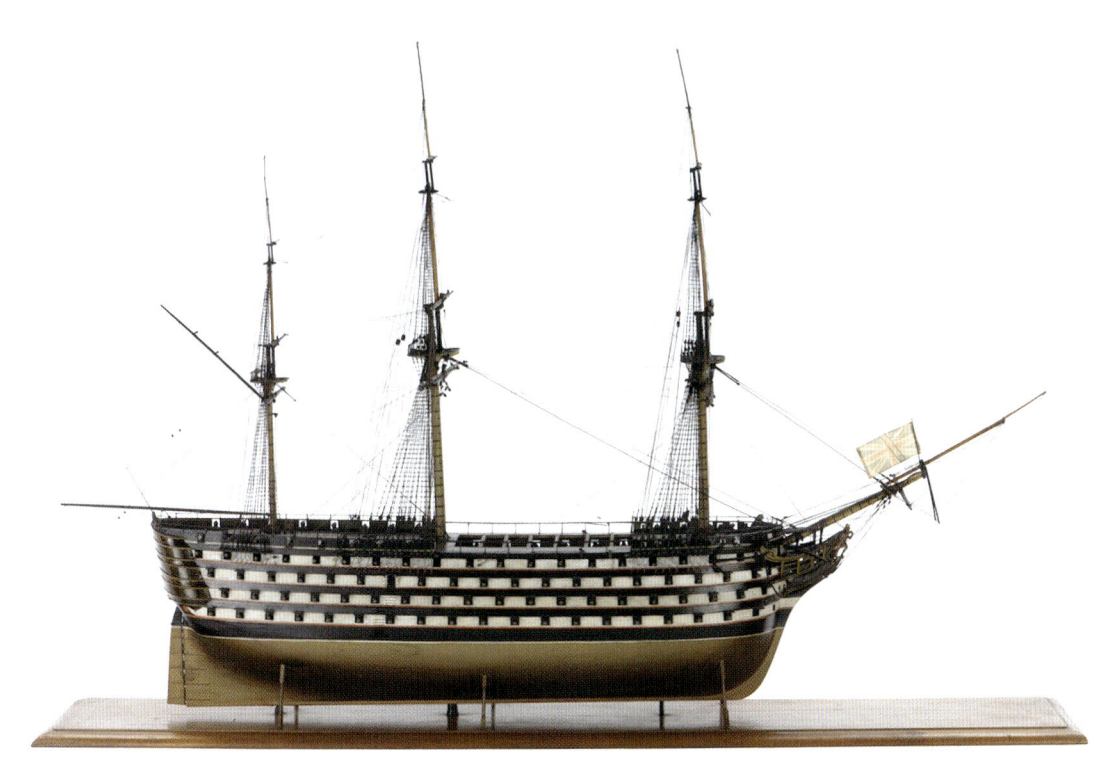

Model of HMS *Kent* circa 1810.

Royal George and two *Queen Charlotte*s (the first was destroyed by fire in 1800 and the second replaced her in 1810), but these were not the largest ships the Navy had. During the war, it began building larger vessels, having seen how difficult it was to defeat the Spanish 130-gun *Santissima Trinidad*, with the construction of the *Impregnable* of 104 guns, two 110-gun ships copying the design of the captured French *Ville de Paris*, named *Hibernia* and *Neptune*, the 112-gun *St Lawrence* which sailed on Lake Ontario and four 120-gun ships, *Caledonia*, *Nelson*, *St Vincent* and *Howe*, although all but *Caledonia* were only completed as the war came to an end.

Although extremely powerful, they were very slow and cumbersome because of their weight of armament and were poor sailers, so they were limited to the role of flagships for the admiral commanding battle fleets. They were also very expensive to build (up to £61,000 each – £3 million in today's terms) and required huge crews to man them. However, plans were made for a four-deck, 140-gun ship in 1809, to be called HMS *Kent*, but it never went beyond the model stage.

27
French Prisoner of War Bone Model of HMS Temeraire

During the Napoleonic Wars, the Navy only had twenty-five Second Rates in total as they were not a popular type of ship. The Navy had a number of older two-deck 90-gun ships in service (*Blenheim*, *Ocean*, *Barfleur*, *Prince George*, *Princess Royal* and *Formidable*), which had been developed as a cheaper option to the First Rate ships, but a few had ended their service or had foundered before the end of the war. A small number of 98-gun ships were constructed during the war to add to the older ones that were still in service (*Duke*, *St George*, *Glory*, *Atlas*, *Prince*, *Impregnable*, *Windsor Castle*, *Boyne* and *Prince of Wales*, the newer-built being the *Dreadnought*, *Neptune*, *Temeraire* and *Union* and a replacement *Boyne*) simply by adding more guns on the forecastle and quarterdeck. These ships were generally armed with 32-pounders on the lower deck, 18-pounders on the middle deck and 12-pounders on the upper deck. These ships were short and high sided and therefore were found to have poor sailing abilities. They acted as flagships for admirals, but they generally preferred First Rates and therefore they usually served as the flagship of the second or third in command of a fleet or as flagships of the port admirals.

During the mid-eighteenth century, the Navy had also experimented with 80-gun ships but very few of these were built. Only four of these vessels (*Caesar*, *Foudroyant*, *Rochfort* and *Cambridge*) were built during the Napoleonic Wars. They were very powerfully armed, carrying 32-pounders on the main deck and 24-pounders on the upper deck, but the Admiralty preferred the far more manoeuvrable 74.

Turner's poignant 'The Fighting *Temeraire*', showing the warship being towed to the scrapyard by a steam tug.

28

The Stern Gallery of the 74-gun HMS Implacable

The Third Rate ship was the smallest of the warships included in the line of battle but were also by far the most numerous in the Navy. The French had developed the idea of a 74-gun battleship in the 1740s and the Royal Navy quickly came to admire their combination of speed and manoeuvrability while carrying very heavy firepower. Having captured a few French ships the construction was immediately studied and the Navy was very quick to produce large numbers of copies of the design, alongside producing even larger numbers of the modified British 70-gun design. By the 1790s 74s accounted for well over half of all line of battle ships in the Royal Navy. Falconer's *Marine Dictionary* of 1769 went so far as to state that 'the ships of 74 cannon . . . are generally esteemed the most useful in the line of battle, and indeed in almost every other purpose of war'.

The ships carried 32-pounders on the lower deck and 24-pounders on the middle deck and even 12- or 18-pounders on the upper deck, giving them a very formidable broadside for their size. The ships were well built and weathered the seas well, they were manned by around 600 men and fully loaded were able to achieve speeds of up to 6 knots. Around sixty-nine 74s were in the fleet when the Revolutionary Wars began, many of which foundered or were broken up before 1815, but an incredible further seventy-nine were launched by 1815, with more still on the stocks.

The Third Rate also included the less popular 64-gun warship, developing from the older 60. These ships had experimented with 32-pounders on the lower gun deck but it had not proven a success and they generally carried 24-pounders as standard. They were exactly what they seemed, a much cheaper option to the 74, but they could not sail as well, nor could they carry anything like the same firepower. In fact their only benefit was that they were cheaper to build when the Navy was desperate for more ships in the 1770s.

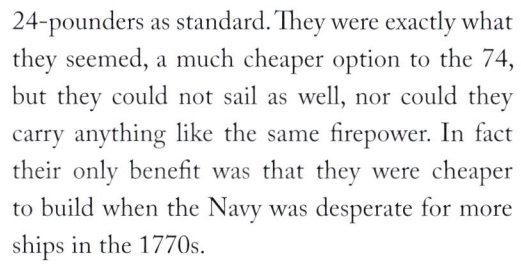

A 74 at sea.

After the end of the War of American Independence, no more of these ships were built, being regarded as obsolete, but thirty-seven remained in service in 1793, making them the second largest class of line of battleship in the Navy. At least a third had been broken up by 1803.

The 64-gun HMS *Asia* in Halifax harbour, 1797.

29
Painting of HMS Abergavenny in 1801

Fourth Rate ships of between 46 and 60 guns had been a common type of warship in the early eighteenth century, but the larger 60s had all but disappeared by 1793, with only the *Panther* still in service.

The 50-gun ship had a much more chequered existence, as it fell in and out of favour at different times, with sixteen of these ships still on the Navy's books in 1793 but very few of them were still operational in 1812. Six new 50s were built during the wars, three between 1798 and 1802 (*Antelope*, *Diomede* and *Grampus*) and three more in 1813–15 (*Salisbury*, *Romney* and *Isis*).

They had been seen as the ideal size to be a patrol ship or a flagship for frigate squadrons in peacetime. They were also found to be of some use when operating in shallower waters, such as the North Sea and Baltic. They carried 24-pounders on the main deck and 12-pounders on the upper deck. Unfortunately, their sailing qualities were very poor and they were unpopular commands. Nine East India Company ships were purchased in 1795 by the Navy and converted to 54 or 56 guns (*Calcutta*, *Grampus*, *Hindostan*, *Abergavenny*, *Malabar*, *Glatton*, *Coromandel*, *Madras* and *Weymouth*) and two

HMS *Leopard*, 1790.

more were purchased in 1804 (*Malabar* and *Hindostan* – bought to replace the earlier ship of the same name that had been lost in 1804) but they were generally seen as a poor man's warship and many served in distant stations, such as the East Indies.

30
HMS Trincomalee, *a 46-gun Frigate*

The Fifth Rate was dominated by the warship known as a frigate. The frigate was the most glamorous and quite often the most lucrative command in the Royal Navy. It was large enough to carry a significant broadside, but was also fast and highly manoeuvrable, allowing it to usually escape larger warships. The gun deck was specifically designed to be high above the waterline to allow it to safely heel over in strong winds in sharp turns under a lot of canvas to maintain speed while still able to use its guns. It was not unknown for frigates to achieve speeds of 15 knots. Frigates generally displaced in the region of 800 to 1,000 tons. Frigates also cost half the price of a 74-gun ship to produce, so unsurprisingly large numbers were kept in service.

They were often used in independent roles as they were too weak to be in the line of battle, being more often utilised as lookouts for the main

HMS *Pomone*, a 38-gun frigate.

battle fleet, convoy escort duties, patrolling and commerce raiding, including attacking enemy installations along the coast. By convention large battleships did not usually engage frigates, because of their overwhelming firepower which could easily destroy them, unless they provoked them and then they were fair game.

This sort of independent command was highly sought after and the greatest frigate captains, such as Cochrane and Hoste, became household names and were feted like superstars. The constant patrolling of enemy coastal waters gave the opportunity for single combat against enemy frigates, but also the opportunity of capturing numerous enemy merchant ships and gaining prize money. Many frigate captains became very wealthy and a number of naval dynasties were established on the riches earnt during this period.

Frigates varied greatly in size from the largest 44- or 46-gun frigates like the *Trincomalee*, which although launched in 1817 was built to the classic dimensions of a frigate during the Napoleonic Wars. In the early years of the war, they were routinely armed with 12-pounders, but following a number of actions where enemy frigates outgunned the British ships, the 18-pounder became the norm. Even so, when fighting the Americans in the War of 1812, whose frigates routinely carried 24-pounders, the British vessels again found themselves outgunned and from 1813 the Navy began designing frigates with 24-pounders to match the new threat, although the *Trincomalee* and many others were still fitted out with 18-pounders.

The 32-gun ship had been the standard size of British frigate until about 1790, when the larger

Model of HMS *Indefatigable* after she had been cut down.

French 38s forced the Royal Navy to increase the size of their frigates, but even in 1812 there were still thirty-five of these 32s armed with 12-pounders still on the Navy List, while there were another twelve 32s of a later design with 18-pounders instead. A larger 36-gun frigate had also been popular since 1750, armed with 18-pounders, and large numbers of this ship continued to be constructed during the war, there were no less than 70 of them in service in 1812.

As the French had introduced the 38-gun frigate, the Royal Navy similarly began to produce very large numbers of these and in 1812 there were eighty of these ships on the list. A later development, the 40-gun frigate, never really became popular and there were only thirteen of them in service in 1813, but five more were rapidly ordered in 1813, built of pine, to counter the new American frigates. Only a few 44- and 46-gun frigates began to appear towards the end of the war.

One other method of producing Fifth Rates was the Razée. This was a long-established practice whereby decks were removed from ships of the line. Three 64s (*Anson*, *Magnanime* and *Indefatigable*) were cut down in the early years of the war to 38- and 40-gun frigates, with mixed success however, as this caused the gun decks to be too close to the waterline.

31
Model of the Hull of HMS Carysfort, *28 guns*

The Sixth Rate of between 20 and 30 guns was effectively a scaled-down frigate, the most common being the 28-gun ship. It was a form of frigate, but was very lightly armed, usually with only 9-pounders. A few had been built prior to 1793, but no more were constructed during the war and in 1808 there were only seven in service, all of these being very old or captured.

However, the Navy also had large numbers of 22s and in 1805 a newly-designed Sixth Rate of 22 guns was developed, again carrying 9-pounders, but now strengthened by a further eight 24-pounder carronades on the quarterdeck. Six of these ships were constructed and, along with older vessels and captures, there were no less than fifty-two of these ships in the Navy in 1813. These ships typically displaced about 500 tons and were manned with crews of between 150 and 240.

These Sixth Rates were designed as a first command for a post captain (today simply referred to as a captain), who was posted in the *London Gazette* as having achieved a command of a rated ship. As a post captain with experience, he could then progress on to command frigates and even 74s in time.

The reconstruction of HMS *Surprise* of 28 guns.

87

32

The Reconstructed Brig HMS Pickle *at Sea*

The final class of ship in the Royal Navy were those under 20 guns, which were officially listed as 'Unrated' of which there were a number of different types. These vessels were generally seen as too small for a post captain and were therefore officially commanded by commanders.

The larger vessels in this class were the sloops, which were two or three-masted, although there was also a brig sloop and a brig which were of

Sloop of war *Queensboro*.

similar size and can easily be confused. The naval distinction was that a brig was commanded by a lieutenant rather than a commander. They were popular for use in the role of escorting convoys and for carrying important communications at speed, but were not used so much in shoreline blockade duties, where they were very vulnerable to enemy frigates. The number of sloops grew dramatically during the war, with the Navy listing only 53 in 1793 but having over 200 by 1801. This rapid rise in numbers clearly indicates the ease with which they could be built in even small dockyards very quickly and was helped by the development of the carronade, allowing sloops to be armed quite respectably despite their size. The *Conway* class built after 1807 sported no less than eighteen 32-pounder carronades on the upper deck, a fearsome arsenal for such a small vessel. A smaller brig carrying fourteen 24-pounder carronades was also built in numbers.

The American schooner rig was not well established in Britain but a large number were constructed after 1803 as despatch boats, the most famous of which, HMS *Pickle*, brought home the news of the Battle of Trafalgar and the death of Nelson.

In 1813 the Navy boasted no less than 77 sloops, 181 brig sloops, over 50 smaller brigs and 39 schooners. Some of the other specialist ships, such as the fireship, bomb vessel and gunboats will be dealt with separately.

A contemporary drawing of a 74 and a brig, showing their relative size.

33
Model of a British Gunboat circa 1800

Gunboats were the smallest vessels used by the Royal Navy, but they varied considerably in size from no larger than a ship's boat to a small brig. The only essential attribute to allow it to be classed as a gunboat was that it carried at least one large cannon. Gunboats were particularly useful in very shallow coastal waters and some of the larger gun brigs had retractable keels for this purpose. They also had the advantage of being able to be propelled by sails or by oars, depending on the wind conditions. In periods of light winds or calms, gunboats therefore had a significant advantage over conventional warships and if they attacked en mass, they could overwhelm much larger opposition. The British were to discover this when facing Danish gunboat squadrons in the Baltic and a number of warships were lost or at least badly mauled in the frequent calms that occurred there. However, the success of these gunboats has been greatly overstated, even entering Danish national mythology as a true story of David against Goliath. In reality British losses were minimal and vast numbers of merchant ships were successfully convoyed through the Baltic, but these rare victories were good for propaganda.

The British had recognised their worth, both in supporting an assault on an enemy shore, but could also prove very useful in disrupting any attempt by Napoleon to invade Britain, which was likely to occur in light winds. A number were deployed in the Baltic to help counteract the Danish gunboats.

In 1794, the Royal Navy was building large brig gunboats, rowed by eighteen oars and heavily armed with two 24-pounders in the bow, but also armed with ten 18-pounders. Thirty-one of this type were constructed up to about 1799. The construction of large gunboats continued up until 1805, with ten of the *Bloodhound* class being constructed with a similar armament and no less than fifty-eight of the slightly larger *Archer* class which carried a fearsome armament of two 32-pounder bow guns and a broadside of ten 18-pounder carronades. Eventually all of these gunboats were reclassified as brigs.

Smaller gunboats had been constructed in fewer numbers since 1796, some of which closely resembled a ship's launch but with a 12-pounder in the bows. In 1805 however, with the urgent need for coastal defence craft, Commissioner Hamilton designed a gunboat of only 40 tons and armed with two 18-pounders on slides in the bow and a further 18-pounder on a swivel, allowing it to be deployed through 360 degrees. The first six were sent to protect Gibraltar, and a further eighty-five were built for coastal defence in Britain, some of which operated in the Baltic.

Model of a ship's boat fitted with a cannon.

34

Painting of the Battle of Basque Roads 1809

Fire was the greatest danger to a wooden sailing vessel and therefore the use of fireships to cause panic and confusion in the enemy's fleet had been common practice since ancient times. There was a resurgence of their use during the Napoleonic Wars, particularly by the British, in an attempt to drive enemy fleets out of safe, well-defended anchorages into the open sea, where they could attack them. Purpose-built fireships were a rarity, but a number (around fifteen) were constructed in the late eighteenth and early nineteenth century, including the *Prometheus* (which took Arthur Wellesley – the future Duke of Wellington – to Copenhagen and back in 1807). Most ships used for this role, however, were old worn out warships or merchant ships bought for the purpose. It made more sense to use these vessels than pay large amounts of money to have purpose-built ships constructed. Forty-seven merchant ships were also purchased for the role but very few of them were ever utilised as such. Another twenty-one merchant ships were purchased and all used in the attack on Basque Roads in 1809. Twelve old warships were also converted to be fire ships in 1778–9.

Fireships were modified so that the gunports were hinged at the bottom rather than the top so that they would fall open when the holding ropes burnt through and help to feed oxygen to the flames. The ships were filled with every available combustible material, such as rum-soaked hay, to help the fire catch hold and the barrels of tar or pitch were broached to spread the flames, just as they went into action. Old cannon were sometimes left on board, fully charged and triple loaded so that they would fire as the flames reached them, to deter the enemy from attempting to extinguish the fires by boarding. Later, large numbers of rockets were left facing out from the ports and strapped to the masts and yards, where they would ignite and cause further confusion in the enemy fleet.

When being deployed, usually at night, the ships would be sailed in close by a skeleton crew, who would then ignite the combustible materials and having set the sails, took the ship close to the enemy fleet, the crew retiring to the ship's boats at the last moment and departing. The plan was hopefully to approach the enemy fleet without causing alarm until too late to stop them, the enemy fleet would have to scatter to avoid their own ships catching fire and would be forced to manoeuvre out to sea, where they could be attacked piecemeal, or they ran aground, where they were vulnerable to being destroyed without being able to offer any defence, as happened at the Basque Roads. Fourteen French warships ran aground in the ensuing panic and had Admiral Gambier sent his ships in to finish them off, they would almost all have been destroyed. However, most of the French ships were eventually re-floated but the French did burn five ships that they could not save and many others required extensive repairs. The use of fireships had been vindicated on this occasion, although they were rarely, if ever, used again.

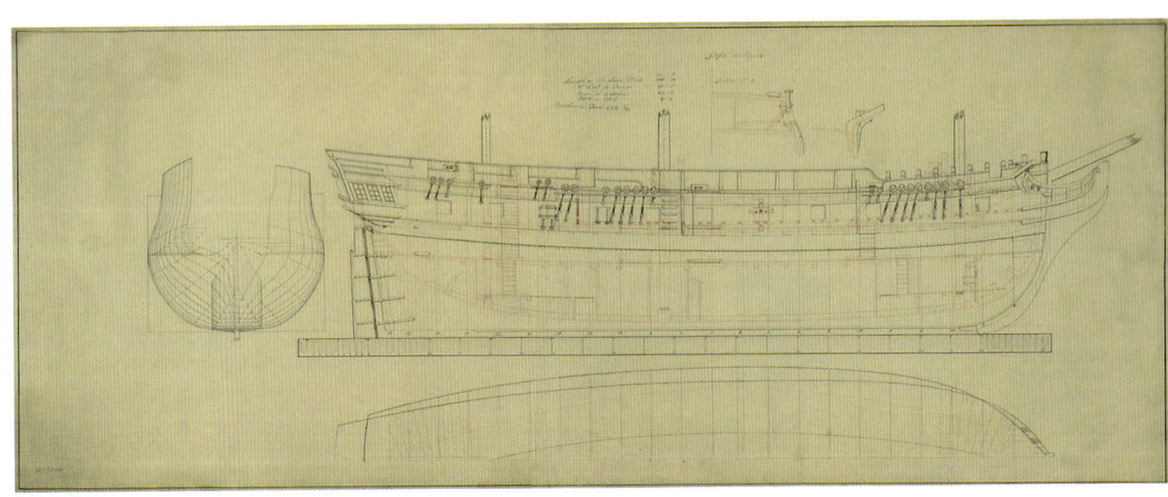

Plans of HMS *Spitfire*, fireship.

35
A 12-pounder Naval Mortar

The bomb vessel was produced for only one role and carried only a few conventional cannon for self-defence. It was designed purely for bombarding enemy harbours and fortresses, using angled mortars to throw shells at a high trajectory over defensive walls into the target area, where conventional artillery could not reach. Because of this, it was also the only vessel to carry explosive shells at sea, which were very dangerous and the hulls were specially designed to store them safely and to avoid a catastrophic detonation. The hulls were also greatly strengthened to cope with the extreme stresses from the firing of the heavy mortars. They were also designed with a shallow draught of only 12ft (3.66m) fully loaded to allow them to approach close inshore to engage their targets. When firing, square wooden screens were hoisted over the mortar to stop any flash catching the sails and rigging and wetted tarpaulins sealed the hatchways to the magazines.

Developed in the 1680s by the French, the British were not slow to copy the idea, early versions being ketch-rigged, meaning that the mast did not get in the way when firing, but led the ship to be quite unstable as a firing platform. By 1790 bomb vessels were using traditional ship rigs and firing past the foremast. Most bomb vessels were originally built in merchant dockyards but were then converted when purchased by the Navy, but a number were later built to specific naval designs. They were generally of about 400 tons displacement and had crews of between sixty-seven and ninety-six including Marines from the Royal Marine Artillery to man the mortars. Most bomb vessels were named after volcanoes or had names which suggested hell and fire. In 1793 there were only two bomb vessels in the Navy, but this rose to fourteen in 1799 and nineteen in 1805, although this shrank to only thirteen in 1812. Royal Navy bomb vessels usually carried one 13in mortar and one 10in mortar and eight 6-pounder cannon for protection, but a few bomb vessels built in 1810 had two 10in mortars instead and four 68-pounder carronades. However, this was not popular with crews and later vessels received one 13in mortar again.

Bomb vessels played a significant part in the bombardment of Copenhagen in 1807, Flushing in 1809 and Fort McHenry in 1814. A number of these vessels were used after the war for polar exploration as their strong hulls could withstand the pressure of ice on the ship for longer.

Bomb vessels *Fury* and *Hecla*.

A 'Leaguer' Water Barrel used to Transport Nelson's Body Home

The most precious item on a ship at sea is fresh water. Warships at sea for long periods relied on casks stored low down in the hold for their water supply. Vast amounts of water were needed for the large crew of a warship and the weight of all this water was a major problem for ship designers to accommodate.

Water butts were of a standard design to accommodate 108 gallons (491 litres) of water weighing half a ton when filled, but larger ships also carried bigger barrels known as 'leaguers' which carried 159 gallons (602 litres) of water weighing 0.7 of a ton of water when filled. The barrels were typically filled to 95 per cent capacity when sailing from a dockyard to allow for expansion.

Admiral Bridport, the commander of the Channel Fleet, in a letter to the Admiralty dated 31 July 1798 advised that using the entire supply of water, down to the very bottom barrels, would allow a 74-gun ship to remain on station without replenishment for nine weeks. However, he put great emphasis on stating that the process of refilling these lower-level casks was actually very difficult and very time consuming and that it should only be done as a last resort. HMS *Victory* carried some 300 tons of fresh water when sailing from a dockyard, which equated to 675,000 gallons (just over 3 million litres)

Water was a constant worry for ships' captains and although a water barrel was routinely left on deck for anyone to use at will to quench their thirst, it was specifically placed where the officer of the watch on deck could constantly keep an eye on it to avoid overuse. Indeed, when water became short and it had to be rationed, it was normal to place a Royal Marine sentry over it. Ships were regularly forced to run to harbour to replenish their water supply and when in more remote locations, it was normal for the ship's boats to be used to transport empty barrels ashore to be filled from streams etc and to return with full barrels. This of course would be a very long and labour-intensive process. Water was also routinely transferred from ship to ship at sea. Water kept in barrels for long periods did become rank and eventually became unfit to drink, hence the constant need to replenish with fresh water. It is also why beer was far more popular to drink.

When Nelson was killed at the Battle of Trafalgar near Gibraltar, it was determined that his body would be preserved so that he could be buried in St Paul's Cathedral. The largest cask on board *Victory* was a 'leaguer', therefore his body was placed into an empty one and the cask filled with brandy and spirit of wine, the best preserver they had. A Royal Marine guard was placed over the barrel to ensure that none of the sailors syphoned off any of the spirit. Rumours that it was found to be empty of brandy when the ship arrived in London is a myth.

The hold of HMS *Victory* with water barrels. In the foreground can be seen the iron ingots used as ballast.

37

Sea Service Pistol

The armourer was another appointment made by the Navy Board by warrant. He was the expert on board for all ironworking and was often used to repair damage to any ironwork on the hull or the rigging. He and his armourer's mates were also responsible for the maintenance and repair of the ship's small arms. The equipment he had on board included a mobile forge and tools for servicing muskets and pistols.

The Sea Service Brown Bess musket was shorter than the Land Pattern used by the Army until they started using the shorter India Pattern, for ease of handling around the tight confines of a ship. Muskets were issued to the Royal Marines on board, but also to sailors on the upper deck or when sending parties ashore. At sea these were generally used to fire volleys onto the enemy's deck. It was rare for the Royal Navy to employ sharpshooters from the tops as the French did, as the muskets were not particularly accurate and, added to the ship's movement, aimed fire was generally useless. The death of Nelson from the fire of such a marksman was certainly a very lucky shot indeed.

Sea service pistols were often issued in pairs because of the difficulties of loading during an action, or singly along with a bladed weapon. This was the usual issue for boarding parties or those organised to repel enemy boarders. Pistols were, however, notorious for being very inaccurate and it was recommended that it was only fired at distances of less than 4 yards (3.65m) as the last resort to save their own life. Once fired, pistols were simply discarded, to be collected after the action.

The cutlass was the standard weapon for the sailors. Officers encouraged their men to favour the point in combat as swinging it like a sword was likely to cause it to become entangled in the rigging.

Another weapon carried by boarding parties was the naval axe, sometimes called a 'tomahawk'

Sea Service Brown Bess musket.

An 1804 Pattern Royal Navy cutlass with the distinctive 'figure of eight' handguard.

A naval pike.

A boarding axe.

A case of Brown Bess muskets as delivered.

because of its similarity to the Native American version. The axe had a short handle to allow it to be swung in tight spaces and had an axe blade and a point on its head. Not only was the axe useful for close combat, but it could also be used for cutting through rigging.

One other weapon available was a pike, which was purely used for fighting off enemy boarders because it was too unwieldy for any other use. The naval pike, with its 9ft (2.7m) shaft, was deployed in squads to deter boarders, by presenting a hedge of points towards the enemy, at a distance beyond the range of their own edged weapons.

It was a throwback to previous centuries and utterly impossible to manoeuvre between all of the masts and rigging, so it was more of a deterrent before the enemy boarded. Once the enemy were at close quarters, it would be abandoned and recourse made to pistols, cutlasses or axes.

38

HMS Victory *Firing a Broadside in Drydock in Portsmouth*

The initial moment when the ship would open fire was under the control of the captain, but once the order to fire was given, control of the gun decks fell to the officers commanding them, with little opportunity for communication with the captain on the upper deck, except by occasional runner. Once within 150m of an enemy ship the order was usually sent down to 'fire as you bear' which effectively meant fire at will, as targets presented themselves. Although some shots may have been fired at ranges of up to 600m, most naval actions took place at extremely short ranges of 10 to 50m.

A full broadside, when every gun on one side of the ship would fire was a massive amount of firepower, with ships such as *Victory* having fifty-two guns and carronades per side. The effect of all of these guns being fired simultaneously would, however, cause the ship to heel over from the force of all the guns, which would make reloading extremely difficult and might expose part of the hull normally under water to enemy fire, with the risk of receiving a number of shot holes below the waterline. To avoid this, the guns would engage in a rolling broadside, with the guns firing in sequence rather than all at once.

The part of the enemy ship aimed at varied depending on the deck level they were firing from and also what they hoped to achieve. The lighter cannon and carronades situated on the upper deck were almost invariably used as anti-personnel or anti-rigging weapons and fired grapeshot or bar shot. Gun captains here were trained to fire as the enemy's deck rolled towards

HMS *VICTORY* FIRING A BROADSIDE IN DRYDOCK IN PORTSMOUTH

them, exposing more of the enemy crew and rigging in an attempt to maximise the damage caused.

As for the lower-deck guns, these could be used against the enemy ship's hull or the masts. The destruction of rigging and bringing down masts with a lucky shot would severely hamper the enemy's movement, leaving them unable to manoeuvre and very vulnerable to attack from the bow or stern where they were themselves at their weakest. This was a tactic strongly favoured by the French and Spanish navies.

The Royal Navy and the Americans preferred to fire at the hull of a vessel, the cannonballs penetrating the hulls at such short ranges and causing carnage amongst the enemy gun crews, particularly from the cloud of huge razor-sharp splinters sent flying through the air in all directions, slicing through flesh like butter. The cannonballs would also hopefully damage the enemy cannon or their gun carriages putting them out of action. Some cannonballs would still have the power at such short ranges to punch through the other side of the hull, or would embed themselves in the stout frame of the ship.

The most dangerous, however, were those that rebounded from the opposite hull and bounced around the deck, destroying everything in their path. Even when coming to the end of its travels, a cannonball rolling along the deck still retained the power to tear a foot off.

Another tactic was to fire at the enemy ship's roll, at or just below the waterline, causing the ship to take on water and become less manoeuvrable, and large numbers of the crew would be forced to leave their guns to man the pumps. This was, however, very difficult to do with any accuracy as the ships rolled in the swell.

The Royal Navy generally recommended firing on the up roll rather than the down roll of the ship. Their reasoning for this, was that when firing on the down roll, with any delay in the gun firing, the cannon would have dipped too far and would fire harmlessly into the ocean. If on the other hand, the cannon was fired on the up roll, just as it pointed at the waterline, any delay in the gun firing would see the shot strike higher up in the hull or it might cause damage to the masts and rigging, with less chance of it missing completely.

The Battle of Copenhagen, illustrating the amount of smoke generated.

39

The Red Ensign from 1800

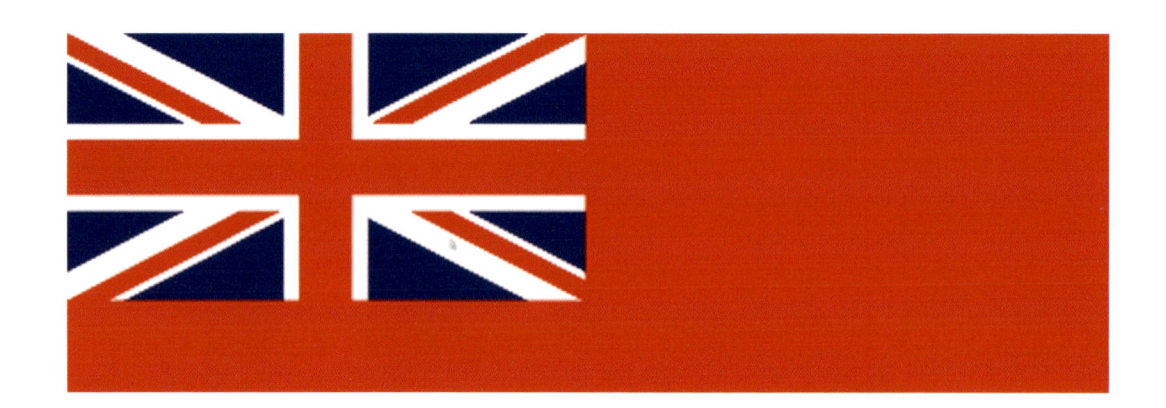

Queen Elizabeth I had felt that as the Royal Navy was growing larger, the fleet should be subdivided into three squadrons, each commanded by an admiral. This had continued since then, the three squadrons being named in order of seniority Red, White and Blue, being the colours of the Union Flag. As there were also three levels of admiral, this meant that there were nine ranks within the hierarchy.

1. Admiral of the Fleet, also Admiral of the Red
2. Admiral of the White
3. Admiral of the Blue
4. Vice Admiral of the Red
5. Vice Admiral of the White
6. Vice Admiral of the Blue
7. Rear Admiral of the Red
8. Rear Admiral of the White
9. Rear Admiral of the Blue

Until 1805 there was only one Admiral of the Red and he was the most senior of all admirals and known as Admiral of the Fleet, which was an appointment for life. Following Trafalgar in 1805, the rank of Admiral of the Fleet was made a separate, more senior rank and a number of Admirals of the Red were appointed.

The admiral's ship also flew a flag at the top of the main mast, Admirals of the Red using a plain red flag, Admirals of the Blue using a plain blue flag whilst Admirals of the White used the flag of St George from 1702, as the plain white flag could be mistaken for a sign of surrender. The Admiral indicated his rank by the number of white balls on the flag. The list below shows the sequence of flags from 1805.

Admiral of the Fleet, Union Jack
Admiral of the Red, Plain Red flag
Vice Admiral of the Red, Red flag with one white ball
Rear Admiral of the Red, Red flag with two white balls
Admiral of the White, Plain St George's flag
Vice Admiral of the White, St George's flag with one blue ball
Rear Admiral of the White, St George's flag with two blue balls
Admiral of the Blue, Plain Blue flag

THE RED ENSIGN FROM 1800

Flag of the Admiral of the Blue.

The White Ensign.

Vice Admiral of the Blue, Blue flag with one white ball
Rear Admiral of the Blue, Blue flag with two white balls

With the increase in the size of the Royal Navy, the number of admirals in service grew dramatically. In 1769 there were only 29 admirals, but by 1816 there were 190 in service, although there were really too many and a number were left on the 'half pay' list.

The coloured squadrons were abolished in 1864, with the Royal Navy adopting the White Ensign on all of its ships. The Red Ensign, affectionately known as the 'Red Duster', now became the official flag of the British Merchant Navy and the Blue Ensign was appropriated by the Naval Reserve.

40

Admiralty Commission for the Captain of HMS Ramillies

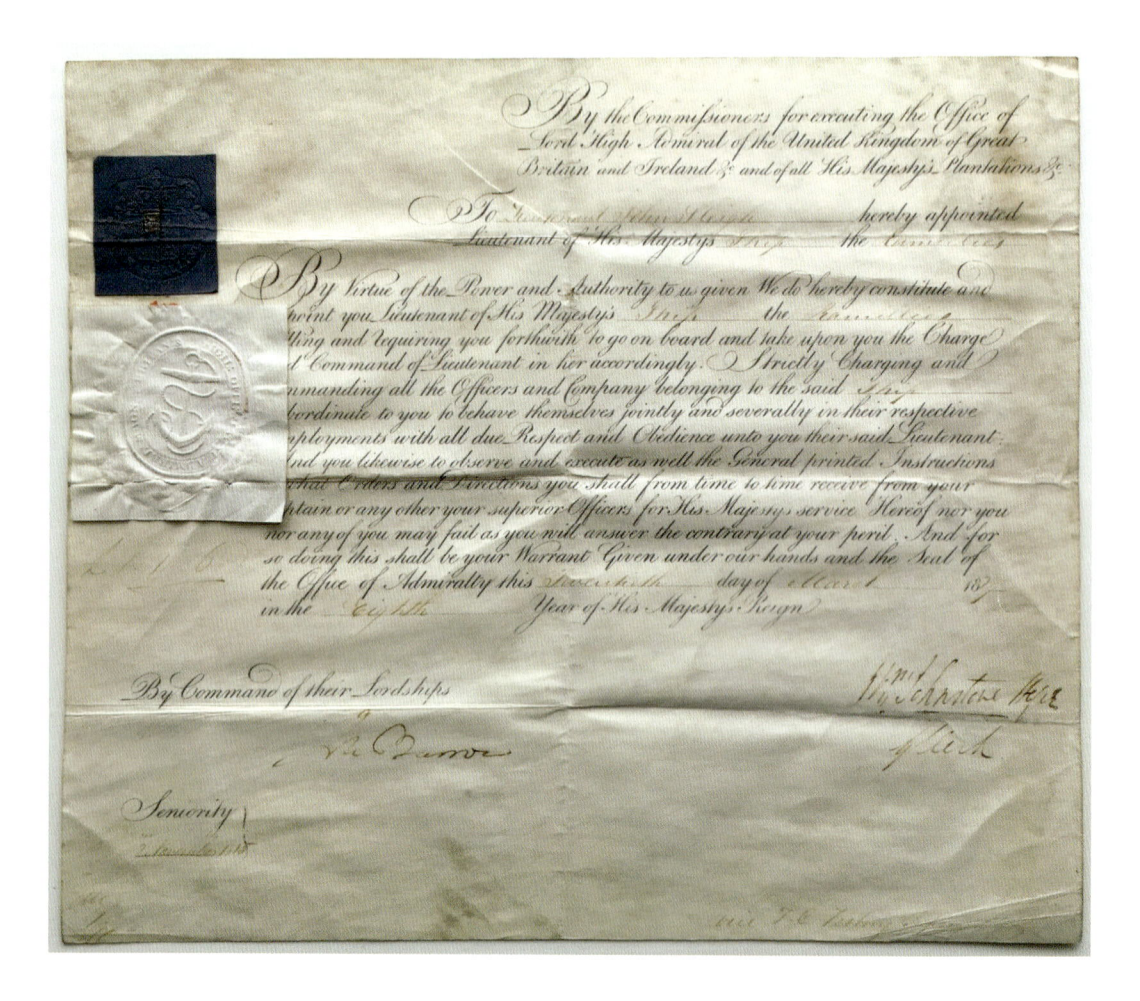

aptain was the rank which denoted command of a warship, but confusingly it could be either a courtesy title or a specific rank.

Sixth Rates or above were commanded by a captain and to denote this seniority they were known as 'post captains' which was deemed equal to a full lieutenant colonel, the uniform denoted their rank by the wearing of only one eppaulette, on the right shoulder. After three years as a post captain they were considered as equal to a full colonel in the Army and were denoted by wearing two eppaulettes. The pay of post captains was governed purely by the size of ship they commanded: a captain of a First Rate in 1808 earned £32 and 4 shillings per month

A post captain of over three years' service (two eppaulettes).

whereas the captain of a Sixth Rate would only earn £16 and 16 shillings. This was the only rank in which the pay scale differed by size of the ship they were on and this was because post captains would progress slowly up the ladder from the command of a Sixth Rate to a First Rate over many years. Senior captains commanding squadrons were given the temporary rank of 'commodore' to make their position clear to all.

Captains of lesser warships were given the title 'captain' as a courtesy, but to denote the difference, they held a different official rank. The very smallest sloops and brigs of under 10 guns could be captained by a 'lieutenant in command', who remained a lieutenant in rank, but those between 10 and 20 guns (Sixth Rates began at 20 guns) were commanded by an intermediate rank, initially known as 'master and commander', as the ships were too small to carry both officers and their role was combined in the one officer, but by 1794, the role had been renamed simply as 'commander'. By the 1750s the rank of commander had become officially recognised as a step in rank between lieutenant and post captain and all officers had to become a commander before they could become a post captain.

In 1812 there were no less than 586 commanders on the Navy List, but only 186 sloops and brigs available for them to command, causing a huge bottleneck. Indeed, many commanders found themselves trapped, unable to get a ship and languishing at home on half pay for the rest of their lives. The problem was only solved in 1827 when larger warships had a commander appointed to them acting as second-in-command.

Officers who tired of sea service could still continue in active service ashore, either with the Impress service or manning one of the many coastal signal stations that had been established during the invasion scare. Many were employed commanding the local Sea Fencibles, which were effectively a seaborne militia. Post captains could also take jobs overseeing the Tranport Department or the naval dockyards, or working in the naval administration.

Captains of ships were provided with a larger cabin, which also generally served as his office and many had a secretary to help maintain their files of correspondence. These cabins were invariably under the quarterdeck for ease of access in emergencies and with an array of windows looking over the quarters and the stern making it very light and airy in comparison with much of the rest of the ship. The room was partitioned into a bedroom, dining room and 'day room' or study, but all the partitions were easily removed during action and a number of guns were deployed within the space. Captains furnished their own cabins to their personal taste. They could also live in solitary splendour or hire a number of servants and dine frequently with the other officers, all at their own expense of course: most chose the latter course.

The captain's day cabin set up for dining on HMS *Trincomalee*.

41
Original Lieutenant's Jacket circa 1805

When not in possession of a commission sea officers received 'half pay' which acted as a retainer, therefore maintaining a ready pool of experienced officers who could take up another career without resigning. Sea officers were also known as 'fighting officers', who received almost all of the plaudits for naval successes.

All commissioned officers were sea officers, fully trained in seamanship, ship handling, navigation, signals and gunnery and having successfully passed an examination. They were not, however, the experts in most of these fields, other warrant officers being responsible for many of these aspects, such as the masters for navigation and the gunners for the weaponry. Certainly there was no specialisation of navigating or signals officers at this period. Commissioned officers were also referred to as the 'military branch of the service'.

Naval officers considered themselves to be much better trained and more highly skilled than army officers, nevertheless the army officers of an equivalent rank tended to receive higher pay than naval officers. Lieutenants could be of all ages, depending on patronage to step up to command of a vessel, which some lacked. In 1812 there were 3,327 lieutenants on the list of which 223 were deemed totally unfit to be employed. Eight lieutenants were appointed to a First Rate and three to a frigate. Lieutenants could be given command of smaller sloops, but most served as subordinate officers, usually commanding a watch as 'Officer of the Watch'.

Lieutenant was the lowest rank of the commissioned sea officers who could rise all the way to admiral. The commissions were issued by the Admiralty and were specifically for a particular ship in a particular position i.e. Second Lieutenant. If transferred to a new ship, or a new position, a new commission was required and if the ship was decommissioned or put into dock for a long period, the commission would end. The Navy was therefore usually awash with officers, particularly in peacetime, not appointed to a ship, who were desperately lobbying for a commission from the Admiralty.

The officer of the watch was fully responsible for the safety of the ship and ensured that all functions of the ship were carried out fully throughout his watch. He had clear instructions when to call the captain, but until the captain was on deck and formally relieved him he remained fully responsible. All lieutenants had subsidiary roles, such as looking after the welfare of a section of the crew and administering the wardroom or the signal books.

In an extreme shortage of officers, master's mates, who were usually senior midshipmen, could be created acting lieutenants and command a watch.

Promotion from lieutenant to captain was perhaps the most tricky to navigate in the Navy. Promotion of midshipmen was automatic on passing the examination and from captain promotion was purely by seniority, but a lieutenant relied on the goodwill of his captain, patronage or by bringing himself to the attention of senior officers by his daring actions. There was no official system of appraising officers, therefore sons of the peerage and those with friends in high places would often seek to smooth their path by corresponding with influential family members or friends. On distant stations senior officers were allowed to appoint officers to vacant positions (from disease or war) until the Admiralty could make a decision. Admirals and commodores therefore possessed great influence on these stations, the Admiralty often simply accepting the temporary appointments they made. Otherwise, a lieutenant could distinguish himself in battle, but it needed to be dramatic, therefore naval officers vied with each other to be the most courageous, and to gain the approval of senior officers in reports that were sent to the Admiralty. Such was the competition for promotion that often a number of such reports were necessary to achieve their goal.

A lieutenant as portrayed by Rowlandson.

42

Contemporary Painting of a Warrant Officer

Warrant officers were appointed by the Navy Board rather than being commissioned by the Board of Admiralty. However, the term warrant officer did not then indicate their seniority as there were actually four levels, from master to lowly sailmakers and caulkers.

The highest level, which included the master, purser, chaplain and surgeon (the latter three known as 'Civilian Officers', as their jobs were similar to those ashore) were highly skilled individuals and as such were allowed to be members of the wardroom and were virtually equal to commissioned officers, being allowed to also walk the quarterdeck. In the next bracket were their deputies, such as the master's mate and surgeon's mate who were of gunroom status and messed with the midshipmen on the lower deck.

The third tier consisted of the 'Standing Officers' who were largely associated with the maintenance of the vessel, who generally remained with the same ship throughout even when it was taken out of commission or in dock for long refits. These included the gunner, the boatswain and the carpenter, who had the status of a senior non-commissioned officer.

The lowest rate of warrant officer consisted of the cook, the sailmaker and master at arms, who were specifically denoted as petty officers according to naval regulations and messed with the other petty officers.

All warrant officers were required to be literate and capable of simple arithmetic, but beyond this few were required to attain any formal qualifications, but simply to prove that they had the knowledge and expertise to carry out their functions correctly. For this reason many warrant officers came up through the ranks from the lower deck.

Uniform of a gunner, boatswain and carpenter.

43

Ship's Speaking Trumpet 1801

The most senior warrant officer of all was the master or sailing master, who was effectively the navigating officer of the ship, although junior to all the lieutenants in the wardroom. He was appointed by the Navy Board rather than the Admiralty and was responsible for navigating the ship as directed by the ship's captain. He was there purely as an expert on navigating and handling the ship and would have come up through the ranks from a master's mate or transferred in from the merchant navy: he left the fighting of the ship to the commissioned officers. He was, however, the best-paid officer on the ship after the captain and had the best cabin after the First Lieutenant. Line-of-battle ships were allocated a second master, who was a master's mate who had passed all of his examinations and was awaiting appointment as master when a vacancy occurred.

On commissioning, the master was responsible for ensuring that the ship was fully fitted out and that all sailing supplies required had been loaded. He was also responsible for overseeing the stowing of all supplies in the hold, to ensure that the weight was evenly distributed and that loading limits were not exceeded. He also oversaw the operations of anchoring and docking the ship and was expected to carry out daily inspections of the anchors, sails and rigging and bringing issues to the captain's attention.

The main duty of the master was to take the ship's position at least daily using a sextant and setting the required course and sails for the conditions. He was in charge of entering the

Ship's log HM Brig *Foxhound*, 1807.

SHIP'S SPEAKING TRUMPET 1801

weather and the ship's position in the official ship's log throughout each day and the safe pilotage of the ship in restricted waters. The master also supervised the instruction of the midshipmen in the use of the sextant and navigational principles. He was stationed next to the captain on the quarterdeck whilst in action, but was there purely to handle the ship as ordered by the captain. The master supplied his own navigational instruments, charts and nautical books. He was also responsible for overseeing the issue of all alcohol on board. Their authority on navigational issues was virtually unquestioned. Nelson himself complained that he could not get his masters to sail closer to the Danish ships at the Battle of Copenhagen because they feared running the ships aground.

At this time the right of the ship was known as to 'starboard' and to the left as 'larboard' rather than the modern 'port'. It is thought that these terms originated in Anglo-Saxon times as 'steorbord' indicating the side with the rudder on (central rudders came much later) and 'laddebord' or side to load on (protecting the rudder from damage). Port was only introduced to replace larboard in 1844 to avoid any confusion with starboard.

If ever captured, their rank often caused confusion and often they were not treated the same as commissioned officers. It was not until 1843 that wardroom warrant officers became commissioned and in 1869, the position of master was replaced by the navigating lieutenant.

A master in 1812.

44

A Purser's Button

Pursers were one of the highest levels of warrant officer and was able to mess in the wardroom. To become a purser you had to have served a minimum of one year as a captain's clerk or 18 months in the office of a secretary of a flag officer.

Pursers were required to put up a bond when they took up the role as they were responsible for such large amounts of stock. The bond was sizeable, being as much as £600 (about £28,000 today) in a Sixth Rate ship, up to a huge £1,200 (about £55,000 today) in a First Rate. They also had to provide the names of two people willing to put up sureties. Their official pay was the same as for a boatswain and gunner and therefore much less than the other officers in the wardroom. Pursers usually did not sleep with the other officers, but often near their valuable stores in the hold to ensure that there was no pilfering.

However, the government paid for the goods he had supplied to the ship at a standard rate, so if he managed to purchase them cheaper, or did not need to issue all that was allocated to the ship each day, he could make a handsome profit. In theory, the government was ensuring value for money, but the system was obviously open to abuse, with rogue pursers providing substandard provisions and failing to issue the full allowances to the sailors. They were, however, responsible for losses of foodstuffs unless they could get the captain to sign a certificate to confirm that the stock had gone off or had been destroyed or made unfit for consumption for some reason, so they could claim this loss against their account. Pursers were not thought highly of by the crew for these reasons. Indeed, goods were issued with official sanction by the 'purser's pound', which meant that each sailor only received ⅞th of his official allowance each day, to cover the purser for shrinkage or evaporation. A manual published in 1761 had stated clearly that pursers issued 7 pints to the gallon and 14 ounces to the pound of cheese and butter. However, after the mutinies in 1797 the 'purser's pound' was abolished and pursers needed to be more creative in their false accounting.

Balancing the books was always fraught and a number of pursers did go bankrupt, but the continuous stream of applicants to become a purser would indicate that if well organised, the job was very lucrative indeed. Pursers also traded in non-official goods, supplying tobacco, candles and extra groceries at a price. He could also act as a banker to the men and officers, adding interest charges to their loan accounts. In larger ships the purser was helped in his role by a steward and a cooper, who were both paid by the purser himself.

A Rowlandson cartoon of a purser.

45
A 'Bosun's Start' – Rather a Fine Example Made out of Snake Skin

The boatswain, or bosun, was one of the warrant officers on each ship and was a 'standing officer', meaning that he remained with the same ship throughout, even when the ship was out of commission.

The boatswain was always a very experienced sailor and almost always had risen from the ranks, as the regulations stipulated that he had served at least one full year as a petty officer. The boatswain was required to be literate but there were no other specific qualifications for the role. He was responsible for the state of the sails and the rigging of the ship, supervising all of the cutting and ropework for rigging out the entire ship on first commission. Once complete, he was responsible for carrying out a full survey of the rigging daily and ordering repairs wherever necessary. He was also responsible for checking that the anchors, booms and ship's boats were all secured properly. Under his command, he had a sailmaker and a ropemaker, who carried out the repairs that the boatswain deemed necessary.

From this description, it is clear that the role required him to be on deck for many hours a day and he and his more junior 'mates' ensured that the men performed their duties with speed and efficiency and without noise. Boatswains were well paid, but given their lowly background,

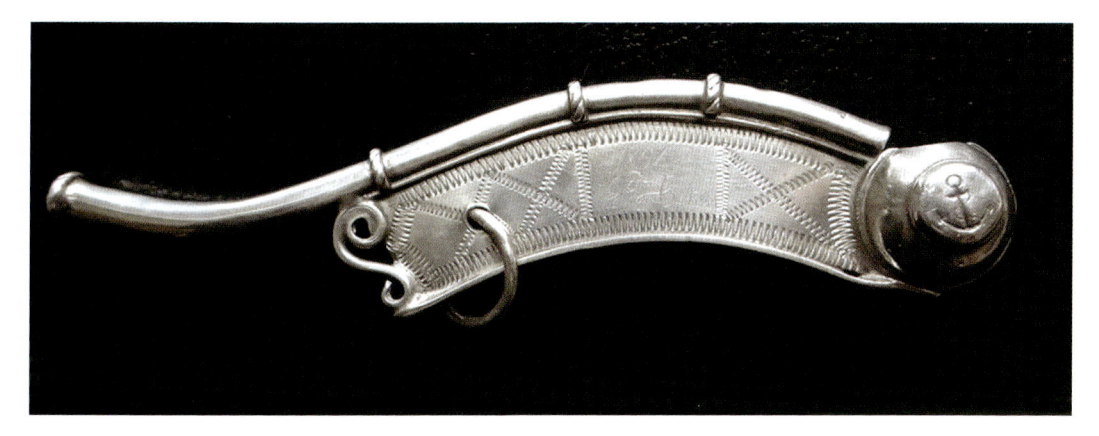

A 'BOSUN'S START' – RATHER A FINE EXAMPLE MADE OUT OF SNAKE SKIN

A Georgian bosun's call.

records do show that they were twice as likely to be court-martialled as other warrant officers.

For speed and efficiency, the bosun's mates were issued with calls (whistles), whose harsh shrill warbling was easier to hear and identify by the crew when high up in the yards than trying to understand shouted instruction. There were a number of set 'calls' for different operations and every man on deck was expected to know exactly what each call meant instantly and act upon it.

When Napoleon Bonaparte was on board HMS *Bellerophon* in 1815, he particularly admired the way in which orders were given and how efficiently and silently the crew worked, in comparison apparently to the cacophony of voices to be heard on French warships. The bosun's call is still used today by the Royal Navy for ceremonial occasions, such as piping the captain when coming on board or going ashore.

To ensure the crew reacted promptly to their orders, the boatswain's mates carried either a short length of knotted rope end, or a short wooden cosh or even a metal cosh, with which they could rap a man across the back if they deemed him to be slacking or too slow to respond. These were referred to as Bosun's 'Starts' or sometimes ironically called 'persuaders'.

Another piece of ship's equipment named after the boatswain was the bosun's chair, which consisted of a rope with a plank of wood at one end, which formed a makeshift seat. This was used in harbour mostly for work over the ship's side or when aloft.

Boatwain's mates also administered floggings when sailors were sentenced to receive a number of lashes for serious misdemeanours.

Sketch of a boatswain's mate in 1812 carrying a rope 'start'.

46
Carpenter's Workshop HMS Victory

The carpenter was one of the few warrant officers who was expected to have learnt his trade ashore before gaining his position. He had to prove that he had completed an apprenticeship to a shipwright and had served a minimum of six months at sea as a carpenter's mate before he could apply for the position. He was also required to produce certificates to prove his good conduct. A number of carpenters therefore came from the Royal Dockyards, whilst others had previously been carpenter's mates on merchant ships before they joined. Shipwrights were also in danger of being pressed into the Navy, as they were not exempt if it could be proven that they had ever served at sea previously.

The carpenter had a number of men assigned to him to carry out the never-ending work of repairs on a wooden ship; large ships like the *Victory* would have teams of up to ten men. In smaller ships carpenters received the same pay as the boatswain and gunner, but if serving on a line-of-battle ship, he earnt a pound a month more, indicating the heavy workload he had to undertake.

In basic terms, the carpenter and his team was responsible for maintaining the watertight integrity of the ship and keeping her afloat. In peacetime the role was still strenuous with a constant need to maintain and repair, but in combat the role of his team was vital. He maintained a large store of spare wood and nails, as well as a full range of carpentry tools to effect running repairs at any time. A caulker, who repaired the caulking between the wooden planks, and a cooper, who repaired or constructed new barrels for storage, were under the carpenter's control.

A cannonball striking the hull on or below the waterline was very dangerous, as water could enter at an alarming rate, causing the ship to sink lower in the water, become unresponsive to the helm and prone to excessive rolling as the water flowed freely through the decks. Modern ships would attempt to counteract this problem by having internal bulkheads to restrict the water, but warships of this time had no concept of this. A very small 2in (5cm) hole below the waterline allows water in at the rate of 78 gallons (295 litres) per minute and larger holes allow exponentially greater volumes in. It is therefore not long at all before the hold is flooded, making repairs to stop the water coming in, very arduous work indeed.

Because the holds were full of stores which would get in the way when trying to stem a major leak in the hull, all of the storerooms had a bulkhead built into them to stop goods being piled right up against the ship's side. This gap, usually less than a yard wide, ran the entire length of the ship below the waterline. It was known as the carpenter's walk, allowing the carpenters easy access to the hull to stop up the holes as quickly as possible. This was where the carpenters were stationed during a battle, ready to attend to any leak as quickly as possible. At the same time that the carpenters worked to stop the ingress of water, teams of men would be required to constantly work the bilge pumps, in an effort to reduce the water level and to prevent the ship from sinking.

The carpenter's walk on HMS *Victory*.

47
Painting of Divine Service On Board a Frigate

The chaplain was also a warrant officer who was allowed to attend the wardroom. His primary task according to the Naval Regulations of 1806 were to ensure that 'the morality of his conduct and the decency, sobriety and regularity of his manners be such as become the sacred office to which he is appointed, and such as may inspire the ship's company with reverence for it and respect to him'.

In earlier times, naval chaplains had not deserved much respect. Indeed they had usually been viewed as the absolute dregs of the ecclesiastical barrel. For many years their access to the wardroom had been hotly debated, as was the restriction requiring them to use the ship's heads with the crew, rather than use the officers' privy. The sailors had a healthy disrespect of religion and the few evangelical officers, such as Admiral Gambier, were sometimes accused of being less bold in their actions against the enemy, turning the other cheek so to speak. However, as Nonconformism grew in wider society in the early years of the nineteenth century, it began to appear within the Navy and a few began Bible-reading classes and informal prayer meetings.

Basic pay was lower even than an ordinary seaman, but this was bolstered by four pence per month for each crew member on board. Even with these perks, he could still only hope to earn about £25 per year on a 74-gun Third Rate, which was no more than many petty officers and it is no wonder that the profession did not attract the best and the brightest. Rather belatedly, in 1812 a commission reviewed the position and pay of the chaplain and his pay was increased dramatically to £150 per annum, he was ensured an officer's cabin and after eight years' service he was also allowed to receive half pay when not employed.

Every warship of the size of a Fifth Rate upwards was supposed to have a chaplain on board, but there were not enough to go around and even Third Rates and above could not actually be sure of getting one. In fact, despite the improvements in pay and conditions, there were only seventy-nine chaplains in the Navy in 1814, of which fifty-one were serving on ships. Chaplains were of course all Anglicans at this time, other religions were not represented at all. Quite often the Chaplain was also required to take on the role of schoolmaster, to educate the men in reading and arithmetic, which also gave him access to another £24 per annum.

Life on board a warship could be very tedious for a chaplain and a number found solace in the bottle, but there was a slow and subtle improvement in the spirituality of crews throughout the wars and by 1812 the Society for Promoting Christian Knowledge (SPCK) had supplied Bibles to some 375 ships and prayer meetings (attendees were known as 'Psalm Singers') were regular features on at least eighty warships.

Contemporary print by Charles Williams of Admiral Gambier (a very religious officer) holding a service with a minister while Lord Cochrane and a sailor try to attract his attention to the Battle of Basque Roads outside.

48
Admiral's Barge HMS Victory

Being of deep draught, ships often require the use of boats for numerous tasks, particularly when close to the coastline. Boats were required to land or take up men from the shore, to transfer men or stores between ships at sea, for bringing water and stores from shore, helping to manoeuvre the ship in still conditions and to assist the ship to anchor or moor at a buoy and more.

Therefore all warships were supplied with at least two boats to enable them to carry out these necessary functions, while ships of the line were issued with six boats, with different functions. The traditional longboat had been superseded by this time, being replaced by the launch which was shorter and broader in the beam, allowing it to carry a great deal more weight of stores. A barge was also carried for the use of the captain or admiral of the ship. Being narrower, it was ideal for rowing him between ships or to shore.

Ships of the line would generally carry a pinnace, two cutters and a jolly boat in addition.

Ship's pinnace.

The pinnace was usually the largest boat and could be powered by either oars or sail. They were often used for exploring inlets, carrying out watering duties ashore or for landing parties. Pinnaces were also occasionally armed with small carronades. The cutter was a smaller boat which was usually powered by sail although it could take oars and was generally designed for speed rather than its capacity. The jolly boat, probably from the Dutch term '*jolle*' meaning

"GOOD-BYE, MY LADS!"

Admiral Nelson in his barge.

'small boat', was designed to transport only a few men by oars between ships or to and from shore.

The larger boats sat in cradles on the upper deck and it took some time to launch them, therefore the two cutters were generally positioned on davits on the ship's quarters and the jolly boat usually hung over the stern. All of these could be launched quickly if needed, such as in the case of a man overboard.

Before a battle, if there was time, the boats were all launched and towed along well astern of the ship in the hope that they would not be destroyed by a cannonball as they almost certainly would if kept on deck. Often the livestock kept aboard for fresh milk and eggs and such, were put onto the boats where they hopefully remained safe during the fighting.

49

Ship's Wheel with Binnacle for a Light and Two Compasses, HMS Victory

The large double wheel was standard for all sailing ships of the period, which housed a drum between the two wheels, allowing a continuous cable to be turned around the drum a number of times and the two ends passed through the deck below to either side of the wheel. The rope ends were attached to the tiller a number of decks below via a number of pulleys and as the wheel was turned, the tiller would be pulled to port or starboard and thereby move the ship's rudder and alter the heading of the ship. To physically move the rudder took quite an effort and a team of two or four men would usually be required to turn the wheel. In stormy weather even this number was often insufficient.

To help identify when the wheel was central, there would be six turns of the rope on the drum either side of a brass marker fixed in the centre of the drum which held the centre of the rope in position. When pointing directly upwards, the brass-capped spoke indicated when the wheel was exactly in the centre. To aid the helmsmen, larger ships were supplied with a gauge which helped to indicate the position of the tiller.

Being on the upper deck, just forward of the raised quarterdeck, the wheel and the men working it were very vulnerable to enemy fire and it was not a particularly rare occurrence for the wheel to be struck by a cannonball and rendered unusable. In such cases an emergency system could be rigged up at the tiller, but this would require orders to be relayed from the upper deck down to the bowels of the ship by a series of messengers posted at each ladder, a cumbersome process.

Even on the upper deck, the view for the wheelmen was very poor and they were therefore never ordered to steer at an objective, but rather to steer a heading via the points of a compass, two of which were housed in the binnacle immediately in front of the wheel, in case one became unserviceable. A lantern was housed between them to allow the compass headings to be seen at night with a chimney to draw off any smoke from the oil used.

Ship's wheel of HMS *Trincomalee*, clearly showing the ropes attached to the tiller below.

50

Model of the Murray Shutter Semaphore System

The establishment of a mechanical telegraph system in Britain was in direct response to the introduction of such a scheme in France using shutters, implemented by Claude Chappe in 1794. The idea of a British system was put forward to the Admiralty in 1795 by Lord George Murray, Archdeacon on the Isle of Man. Murray's system followed Chappe's, utilising a rectangular frame with six octagonal shutters which could be rotated to show a flat front or side edge, a combination of all six in positions making a letter. This gave sixty-three combinations of positions which allowed for the twenty-six letters, ten numbers and the others could be used for preselected messages, such as 'Enemy Invasion Fleet at Sea'.

In September 1795, Murray's system was accepted by the Admiralty and the first chain of fifteen repeating stations was soon established between Deal and London, later being extended to Sheerness. Further chains were set up between Portsmouth and London the following year, and extended to Plymouth by 1806, the line to Yarmouth was completed in 1808. The towers in each chain were placed in high buildings (such as church towers) or on hills because the stations had to be in direct line of sight with the next. They were usually set about 10 miles (16km) apart and never more than 14 miles (22.5km). Bad weather could potentially prevent the system from working, although great efforts were made to establish the system high above the local fog banks.

Simple test messages could be sent from London to Deal or Portsmouth in two minutes and to Plymouth in three, which sounds very impressive. In reality, however, messages took on average about 15 minutes to reach Portsmouth from London: this was still a huge improvement over the many hours required for a despatch rider to make the same journey. It facilitated rapid transfer of orders and news between the fleets and the Admiralty, allowing virtually real-time decision making.

The system's shortcomings were highlighted in 1805, however, when the ship carrying news of the victory at Trafalgar landed at Falmouth and the message had to be carried by coach to London which took more than 38 hours, as the telegraph did not extend there. The Home Popham arm telegraph system did not replace the Murray system until 1820.

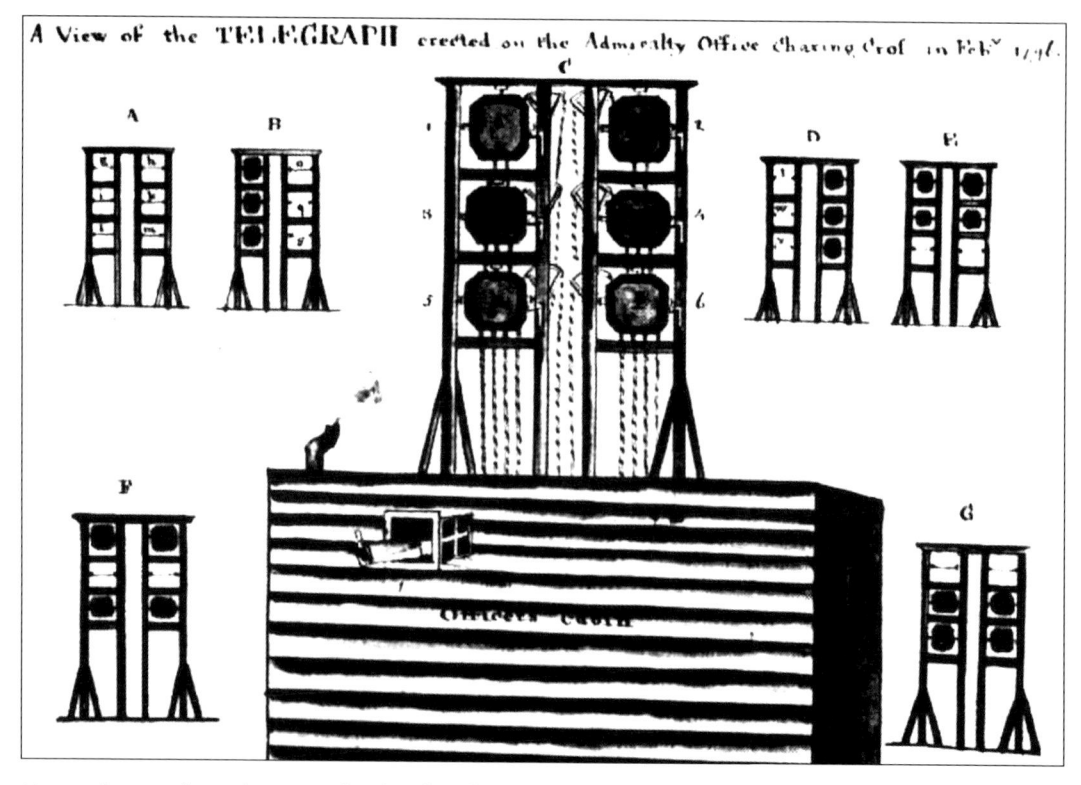

Murray shutter telegraph system, showing the officer's cabin with a telescope and chimney, with a few of the positions for individual letters.

MODEL OF THE MURRAY SHUTTER SEMAPHORE SYSTEM

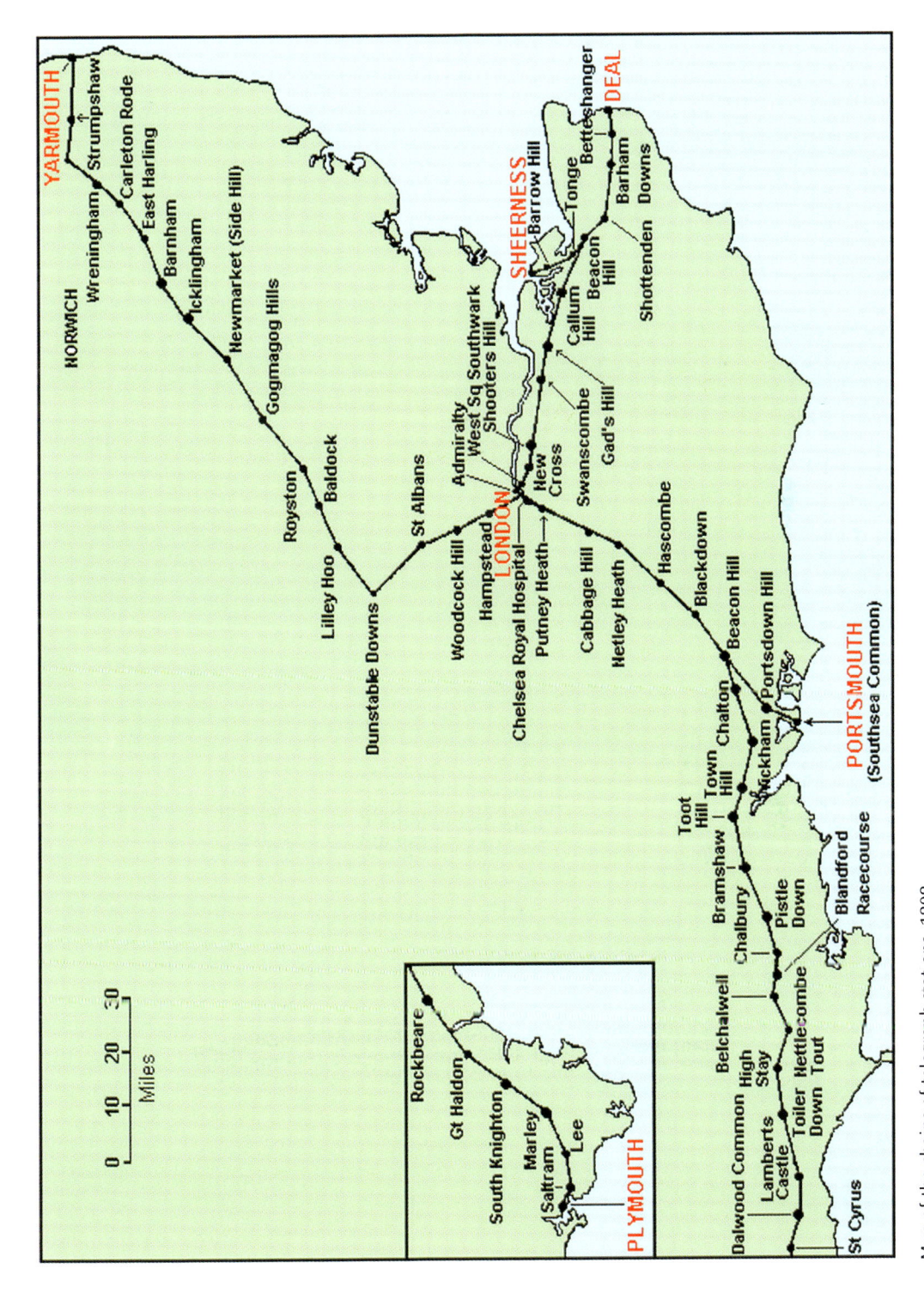

Map of the chains of telegraph stations, 1808.

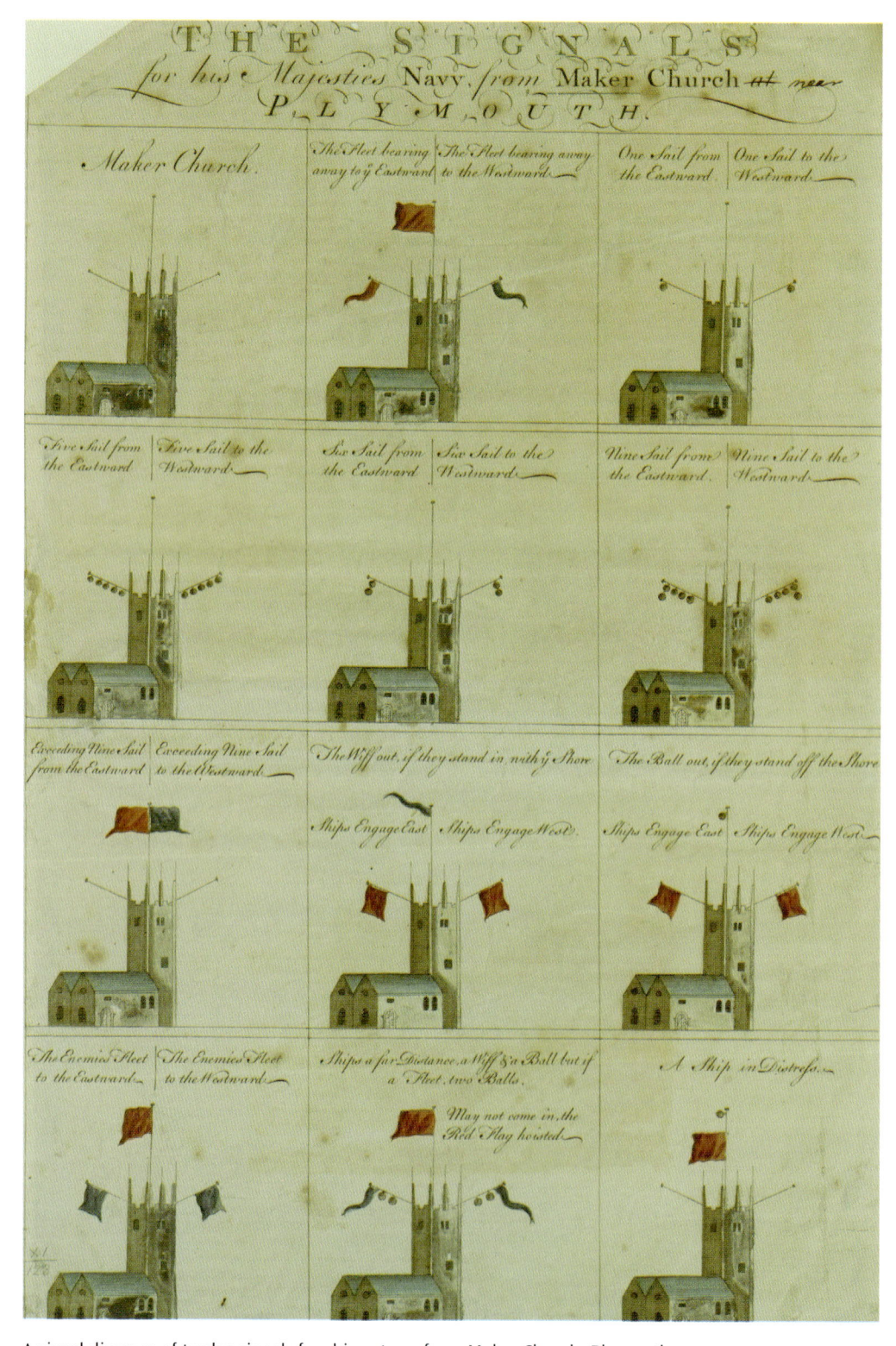

A visual diagram of twelve signals for ships at sea from Maker Church, Plymouth.

Contemporary Chart of Halifax, Nova Scotia

Until the late eighteenth century, the production of charts (maps of the sea are called charts) was largely done by commercial companies. The Navy had commissioned a survey of the coasts of Britain in 1681 and these charts had been first published in 1693, but they were notoriously inaccurate and new surveys were conducted by Murdoch Mackenzie in the 1780s and updated by Graeme Spence in the 1800s. However, maps of foreign shores were not available from official sources, so masters of ships were required to purchase their own (often French) for far-flung destinations.

It became increasingly evident that the Navy needed its own accurate charts of coastlines throughout the world and in 1795 the Hydrographic Department was formally set up under Alexander Dalrymple. In 1799, his department included an assistant, two draughtsmen, three engravers and a copperplate printer. They were to commission new surveys and compile charts from the mass of existing surveys and drawings sent in from ships at sea, which filled the Admiralty attic rooms. Their work was aided by the fact that Dalrymple brought with him a mass of charts of India and the surrounding waters, from his time working for the Honourable East India Company. By 1808 they were issuing boxes of charts for specific destinations. For example, a ship patrolling the North Sea would receive a set of twenty-eight charts of the sea and its adjoining coastlines and

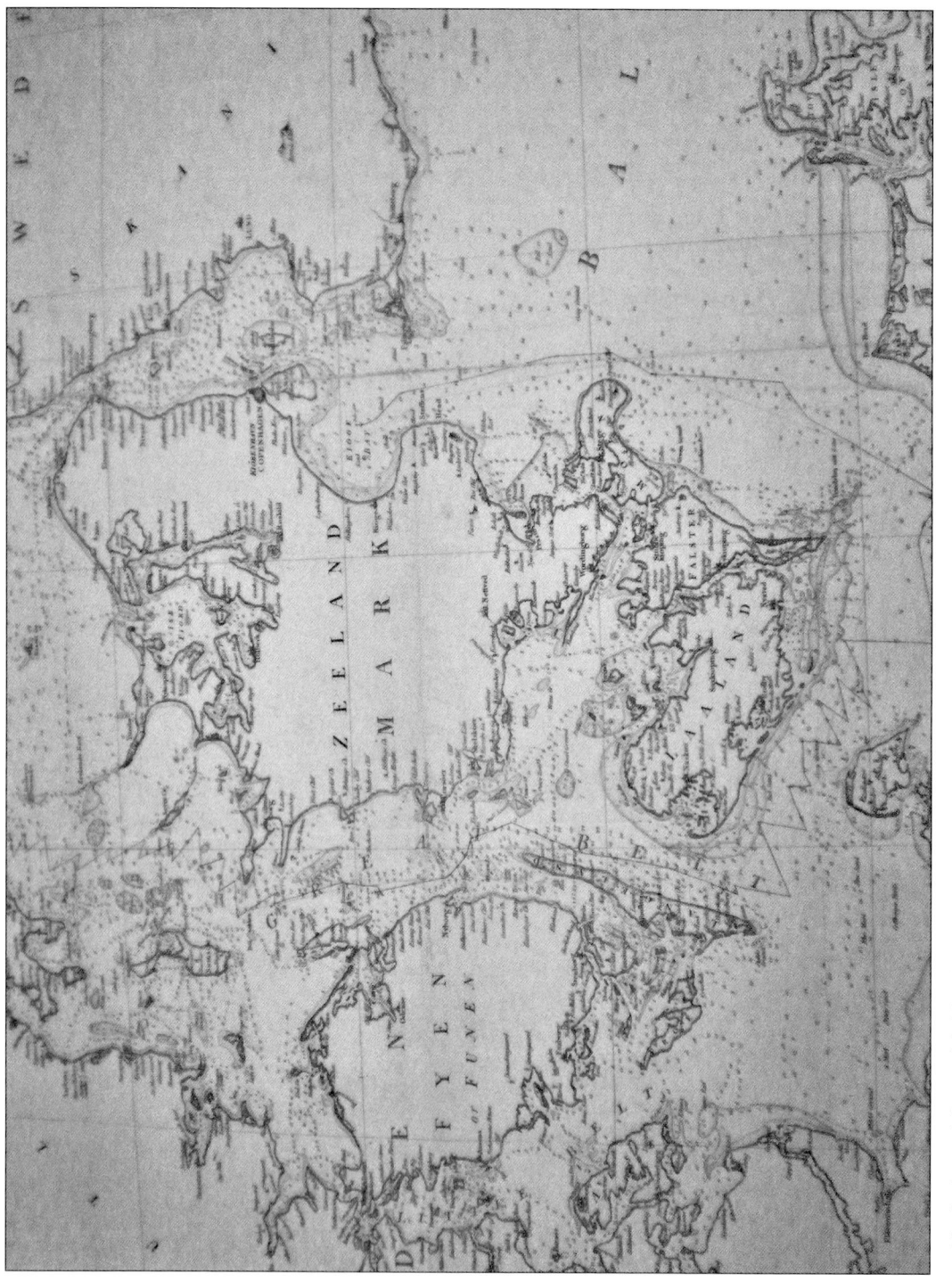

Fadden's chart of the Danish islands, 1807.

View of Brest.

A view of Brest harbour entrance.

four more of the Baltic, just in case. Charts were standardly produced to Mercator's Projection which makes the lines of longitude to run parallel to each other, as they are generally to this day. Little detail appeared on the charts beyond the shape of the coastline and depths marked in fathoms, often accompanied by a view of the coastline from the sea.

Instruments for plotting on charts were few and far between, with usually little more than a straight ruler and a pair of dividers. Apart from bearings of particular landmarks or celestial observations by sextant further out to sea, dead reckoning was practised, calculating the speed of the ship and the strength and direction of the currents by tables or local knowledge.

The master's cabin was also his office, which he used as the chartroom, and it was fitted with a plotting table and chart stowage. He also completed the ship's log with bearings, weather information, soundings and ship's positions.

As well as utilising their present stock of images, marine artists like John Serres were commissioned to go to sea to prepare accurate drawings of the coastlines, including identifying features to aid navigation. These were either issued on the charts as a visual aide, or were put into books of views of specific coastlines which were printed and issued to ships on that station.

Within a few decades Admiralty charts had become renowned worldwide for their excellence and accuracy, a reputation they retain to this day.

52
Turner's Painting of the Wreck of HMS Minotaur, 1793

In the age of sail, shipwreck was probably the most feared occurrence at sea, other than a fire, but in fact disease and accidents accounted for six times as many deaths in the wars of 1793–1815. However, the toll in ships for the Navy was high, with at least 101 rated ships being lost to shipwreck during this period, including 28 line-of-battle ships.

In an age of few accurate charts, grounding was a professional hazard which occurred on a relatively regular basis. Running aground in calm weather on a mud or sandbank was little more than inconvenient, as long as the ship's hull was not damaged and it could usually be safely refloated after a lot of hard work, involving boats and anchors. However, grounding in such circumstances in bad weather could easily lead to significant damage to masts or the hull and the subsequent loss of the ship. Running onto submerged outcrops of jagged rocks or being driven ashore was a great deal more serious in any weather, often leading to the ship being broken up with great loss of life.

In an effort to prevent such disasters, a number of improvements were begun, but had

Smeaton's lighthouse, Plymouth Hoe.

unfortunately not been completed until well after 1815. Charts were produced in even greater quantities, with visual aids to help correctly identify the land in sight and there was a drive to add a great deal more depth information on the charts, but more was necessary.

Lighthouses had been used to help warn ships off dangerous coastlines or away from isolated outcrops since ancient times, but most of these had disappeared over the years. The first lighthouse of the modern era was Eddystone, built on a very dangerous outcrop of rocks in the English Channel in 1698, although it disappeared completely in a storm five years later. A wooden replacement was built in 1709, but this was lost to fire in 1755. A more durable stone structure was constructed by John Smeaton in 1759 and this remained in place until 1877, when it was replaced and moved to Plymouth Hoe, where it remains today.

The first of the Scottish dynasty of lighthouse builders, Robert Stevenson, constructed Bell Rock lighthouse off the coast of Angus in 1810, but little else was built in Britain until after 1815. These lighthouses were highly profitable commercial ventures, collecting revenue from passing ships until the Lighthouse Act of 1836, when Trinity House was given over £1 million to purchase the lighthouses and effectively bring them into public ownership.

The use of buoys to mark safe passages of water was in its infancy and the few buoys then placed in British harbours were merely to denote particular hazards such as rocks or shipwrecks, which could damage the hulls of passing ships. Indeed a description of the entrance to Portsmouth Harbour in 1805 described there being 'not near so many buoys as the safety of men of war required, nor did the few that were there lie in the most proper situation . . .'.

Because of the lack of buoys and lights, ships entering or leaving harbour routinely relied on local pilots, who were fully conversant with the local tides, currents and hazards. In the River Thames the Navy Board supplied pilots who were licensed by Trinity House and in the Downs, by the Society of Pilots at Dover. Masters were however discouraged from using pilots if they knew the harbour well, as all pilot fees were taken out of the master's wages.

Bell Rock lighthouse.

53
Midshipman's Fighting Sword circa 1805

The net was cast wide across a range of social backgrounds for the young midshipmen who would ultimately be the future admirals of the Navy. A number of second or third sons of the aristocracy and landed gentry were sent to the Navy, but the great majority were the sons of professional people such as clergymen, lawyers, doctors and of course naval officers themselves, the Navy often running traditionally through many generations of a family. Less than one in ten came from commercial backgrounds and very few indeed from the lower orders of society, indeed without influence few of these every achieved a commission.

The number of midshipmen to each class of ship was set down in regulations, with a First Rate carrying twenty-four and a 74 having twenty, down to a sloop of war with two. Influence and patronage filled most of these posts, the ship's captain enjoying a very high status in society in this regard. Boys were usually taken to sea as midshipmen around the age of 15, meaning that after six years' service and having passed their examination for lieutenant most ceased being a midshipman around the age of 21 to 22. However, a number of midshipmen were much older, as they were precluded from gaining a higher rank until they passed the lieutenant's examination. One renowned case was Billy Culmer, who finally became a lieutenant aged 57, having served as a midshipman for 35 years.

Midshipmen were a bit of an anomaly, being a trainee officer and thus having rank over non-commissioned officers, but were themselves not a commissioned officer until they passed for

Cartoon of a young midshipman off to sea for the first time.

A young gentleman shocked at his first introduction to the midshipmen's berth.

lieutenant. In the Royal Navy today, this still stands, but after two years a midshipman, having passed his naval training, automatically becomes a sub-lieutenant which is a commissioned rank and the monarch's signed commission is dated from this day.

Midshipmen were expected to furnish their own uniforms, bedding, books and equipment, which required substantial financial backing from their parents. Their rank was, as it still is, denoted by a white square at the collar.

As midshipmen were not commissioned officers, they were not generally allowed into the wardroom but were allocated their own midshipman's berth on the lower decks. Here their youthful raucous behaviour, petty pranks and bullying went on largely unchecked. It was a tough environment for a young gentleman, but it had to be endured and survived to get on. Even the future King William IV was a midshipman on a number of ships during his six-year apprenticeship, but he undoubtedly received rather better treatment as nobody wanted to receive the veangeful wrath of a future king.

Midshipmen or 'mids' took an active part in the ship's watches and was often given command of boat duties, signals and might even be given command of a prize ship. During battle they often served as a deputy to the lieutenant commanding a deck, supervising a section of guns for him. They also received formal training at casting the lead, practising on the yards furling sails, firing small arms, learning knots and exercising the great guns; they were expected to become experts in every aspect of the ship. They also practised navigation and took noon and sunset readings with the sextant to calculate their position, regularly handing in their journals to be checked.

Midshipmen were not above being publicly punished as they were not commissioned officers, a regular punishment being mastheading, when they were forced to sit at the top crosstrees of the main mast for a period of hours in whatever weather. Midhipmen could not be flogged, but they could be forced to 'kiss the gunner's daughter', when they were put over the barrel of a cannon and beaten on the backside.

Midshipmen were served the same food as the crew, but they were allowed two or three servants in their berths to serve them and clear up afterwards. They could also purchase extras if they had money and occasionally were favoured with the leftovers of the wardroom's fare.

Senior midshipmen in their last year or so before examination often served in the role of master's mate as deputy to the lieutenant on each watch and the most senior on board was head of the midshipman's berth.

Passing for lieutenant was and still is one of the greatest trials a naval officer ever undergoes. Candidates were summoned individually before a board of three captains who asked questions on seamanship and navigation and checked that all necessary journals and certificates had been produced. Its importance was the significant fact that once passed, they were fit to command a ship's watch at sea, a very responsible position.

A midshipman in full dress.

54
The Royal Naval Academy, Portsmouth

As early as 1733, an Academy had been set up in Portsmouth Dockyard in an effort to provide an alternative means of joining the Royal Navy as an officer and to provide a model for the training and education of young men. It was renamed the Royal Naval College in 1806.

The Academy could only take forty students at a time (seventy after 1806) but it provided both theoretical and practical experience of the Navy. To become a lieutenant it was required to serve at least six years as a midshipman, but attending the course at the Academy counted as three years' service and a graduate could sit his exams after only three further years' service at sea.

However, the traditional method of entering the Navy remained the primary one, where influence and favour was used to gain a place on board a ship under the patronage of the captain. Learning at sea from the very beginning was viewed by many as the best, if not the only, way of becoming an excellent seaman. The future King William IV had served in the Navy himself and was recorded as saying that 'there was no place superior to the quarterdeck of a British man of war for the education of a gentleman'. Indeed the nobility chose largely to ignore the Academy and it was only half full, until in 1773 it was opened up to the sons of serving officers. Boys could join as young as 11 but did not leave to go to sea until aged 17 no matter how many terms they had studied there. Lord St Vincent, who was often against change, regarded the Academy as 'a sink of vice and abomination', which ought to be abolished. There was also a privately-run naval academy set up in Gosport to take eighty boys a year, but little else is known about it.

The graduating cadet from the Academy was promoted to midshipman at sea, however to denote that he had limited sea time, he was denoted a 'midshipman by order', meaning that he was viewed very much as a second-class midshipman and he received lower pay than those who had served on board for all six years.

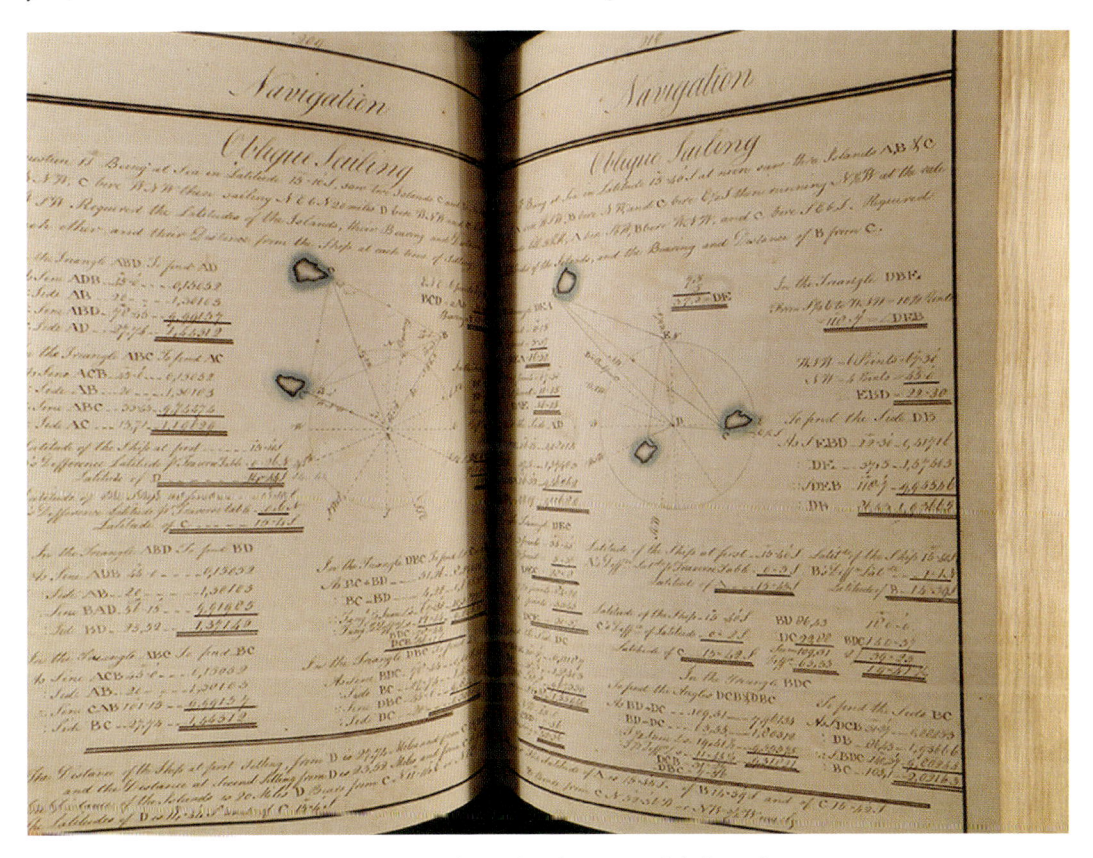

Book produced by a student at the Naval Academy showing some of their work.

55
Marine Compass

Safe navigation of a ship has always been of prime importance and it was an essential skill for every officer. The equipment for navigation had improved markedly during the eighteenth century, including the ability to work out the longitude of the vessel, but it was still rudimentary by modern standards. It required a good level of literacy and a high level of mathematical ability to be able to navigate well.

The compass was of vital importance, the helmsman being set a compass course to steer. The main compasses (at least two in case one malfunctioned) were held in a case in front of the wheel known as a binnacle, which had glass panels, through which the men on the wheel could see the compass heading and was supplied with oil lamps for night. Compasses were marked through 32 points and these could be divided into quarters, therefore as an example a helmsman might be ordered to steer north, north-east, ¼ north.

The fact that there was a difference between magnetic and true north was understood to some extent, but deviation, caused by the influence of

MARINE COMPASS

Pocket sundial owned by Nelson.

metal objects in close proximity to the compass, was not. The bearings of landmarks could also be recorded, three such bearings giving an accurate position in coastal waters. The effects of currents were also understood and logged and the effect of tidal flows caused by the moon had been studied and tide tables were produced for the English Channel and a few other key waterways around Britain.

Out of sight of land, navigation was estimated from the bearing travelled and the speed of the ship, so it was therefore essential that the ship's timepieces were kept correct by use of sundials and no respectable naval officer would be without a pocket sundial.

The ship's position could be pretty accurately established by taking observations of the stars. As stars are fixed points in the sky, the precise measurement of the angle between the horizon and the star gave an altitude, from this a calculation can be made and a line produced on a chart, the ship would be somewhere on this line. Three such calculations produced a small triangle, within which the ship was. Latitude could also be measured by the height of the sun at noon. Longitude could be calculated by sextant from the 1760s by measuring the angle between the moon and a fixed star and using a quite complicated series of calculations of spherical trigonometry. The invention in 1774 by John Harrison of the ship's chronometer, a highly accurate clock which compensated for the variations of temperature, movement and damp by internal mechanisms, made the ability to know the ship's longitude relatively straightforward. Not all ships were equipped with chronometers as

A sextant.

they were very expensive, but all ships deployed on a long passage could apply for one.

Originally these measurements were made by a quadrant, which had been invented in 1731, but by the end of the century this had been refined into the much more accurate sextant, which is still used today. However, the sextant was a much more expensive instrument and quadrants were still in use with some officers well into the nineteenth century.

Recruiting Poster for the Royal Navy circa 1793

VOLUNTEERS.

G. R. III.

God Save the King.

LET us, who are Englishmen, protect and defend our good KING and COUNTRY against the Attempts of all *Republicans* and *Levellers*, and against the Designs of our NATURAL ENEMIES, who intend in this Year to invade OLD ENGLAND, *our happy Country*, to murder our gracious KING as they have done *their own*; to make WHORES of our *Wives* and *Daughters*; to rob us of our Property, and teach us nothing but the *damn'd Art of murdering one another.*

ROYAL TARS
Of OLD ENGLAND,

If you love your COUNTRY, and your LIBERTY, now is the Time to shew your Love.

REPAIR.

All who have good Hearts, who love their KING, their COUNTRY, and RELIGION, who hate the FRENCH, and damn the POPE,

TO

Lieut. W. J. Stephens,

At his Rendezvous, SHOREHAM,

Where they will be allowed to Enter for any SHIP of WAR,

AND THE FOLLOWING

BOUNTIES will be given by his MAJESTY, in Addition to Two Months Advance.

To Able Seamen,	*Five Pounds.*
To Ordinary Seamen,	*Two Pounds Ten Shillings.*
To Landmen,	*Thirty Shillings.*

Conduct-Money paid to go by Land, and their Chests and Bedding sent Carriage free.
Those Men who have served as PETTY-OFFICERS, and those who are otherwise qualified, will be recommended accordingly.

LEWES: PRINTED BY W. AND A. LEE.

Such a huge organisation as the Navy, with some 120,000 sailors and 30,000 Marines, saw constant losses from disease or age and occasionally war, which meant that there was always a need to recruit men. The popular misconception is that this was wholly filled by the indiscriminate sweeps of the 'press gangs' but this is far from the truth.

The great majority of those recruited into the Navy in peacetime came from other methods and in wartime they still accounted for at least half of recruitment. By far the great majority came as 'volunteers' who were attracted by bounties as shown on the recruitment poster. In 1793 the bounty for an experienced sailor volunteering was £5 (about £400 today) but within a few years, as the situation became more desperate, bounties are said to have risen to as much as £70 (around £3,250 today), which was a huge amount of money. Those officers on recruitment service often made great claims regarding the prize money men could earn, as well as appealing to their patriotism. It is unclear, however, how successful this effort was, as many cornered by the press gangs may well have bowed to the inevitable and thought it better to take the bounty.

Recruiting men who were completely new to the sea was avoided unless absolutely necessary, as it took about seven years to fully train a seaman. These raw recruits were termed 'landsmen' and they received a much lower bounty and wages, indeed some captains thought that it was impossible to turn a landsman into an excellent seaman, simply because they were too firmly inured into the ways of the land to fully change. Other captains saw their long-term potential, but a crew was rarely thought to be efficient with more than a quarter of the crew being landsmen. The charitable association, The Marine Society, helped with the recruitment of landsmen, by taking in orphans and giving them a basic education in seamanship, feeding and clothing them until they were taken into the Navy. In the years 1793–1815, the Society provided nearly 23,000 adult landsmen with sea clothes before they entered the Navy. This is in addition to the 500–600 orphans who they prepared to enter the Navy every year throughout the wars.

Despite this, recruitment remained far below the levels needed and other avenues had to be explored. Although it has been claimed that the dregs of the prison system were forced into the Navy, the Admiralty were actually quite cautious over the numbers of ex-prisoners it took on, as the Navy had no desire to see difficult characters fomenting trouble, even mutinies.

Sailors who had been convicted of minor charges were often persuaded to join the Navy in preference to remaining in prison, and debtors could volunteer, the bounty paying off their debts. Another type of prisoner allowed to be recruited were the 'Lord Mayor's Men' in London. They were defined as those who wished to relieve themselves of public disgrace for a 'street frolic or night charge', but covered all noisy drunks. This soon became notorious as a catch-all for any recruit the Navy wanted to take up.

The unemployed were also a useful source of men, and an Act of Parliament of 1795 formalised the process by which local authorities could drastically reduce its unemployment problem by sending 'any able bodied and idle persons' into the Navy. The term 'idle persons' covered 'rogues, vagabonds, smugglers and embezzlers of Naval stores'. This was thought to be an issue with some of the mutinies in 1797, after which the Admiralty were less keen on taking these individuals and by 1811 positive orders to refuse to accept them were issued.

Foreign sailors were also a regular source of men, with many crews having between 5 and 10 per cent of their crew being 'foreign'. Many of these were recruited from the prison hulks moored in most estuaries during the wars, as a more attractive

RECRUITING POSTER FOR THE ROYAL NAVY CIRCA 1793

ALL YOUNG MEN,

ANIMATED by the Love and Glory of their Country, rouſed by the Spirit of the Britiſh Lion, to ſupport the Honour and Dignity of her inſulted Flag, and whoſe Hearts burn to ſcourge and chaſtiſe her Natural Enemies for their daring Perfidy and infamous Treachery, have now an Opportunity of immortalizing their Valour, as well as of enriching themſelves to their Hearts deſire, by voluntarily entering into the ROYAL NAVY of the beſt of KINGS, the Glorious Bulwark of theſe Kingdoms; for which Purpoſe they are entreated to repair to

Captain JOHN FORTH,

At Malden, in the County of Eſſex;

Who, as an Encouragement to every ſprightly and willing Perſon, will give him,

	£.	s.	d.
To every able Seaman	5	0	0
To every ordinary Seaman	2	10	0
To every able-bodied Landman	1	10	0

To Honour we call you, not Regiſter'd Slaves,
But freely and boldly, ye Sons of the Waves.

GOD bleſs the KING,
AND
The Royal Britiſh Navy.

---

option while being paid and fed, than spending many years in such terrible conditions.

There was a general distaste for the press gang, even in naval circles, at the turn of the new century and alternative methods of recruiting were experimented with. In 1795, the Quota Acts were passed by which each British county was required to provide a set number of recruits each year, for example Berkshire was to provide 108 and Buckinghamshire 117. They were to raise them from the poor of the parishes or provided by a bounty, paid by the local taxpayers. A second Act required every port in the country to provide a certain number of sailors, with Arundel providing 33, Aberystwyth 69 and London 5,704. Ports could embargo any ship leaving from 18 February until whatever day the quota was complete, forcing the merchant ships to comply. The success of the Acts was loudly proclaimed by the government with the Navy growing from 87,331 men in 1794 to 114,365 two years later, but what the quality of these

GREAT ENCOURAGEMENT.
AMERICAN WAR.

What a Brilliant Prospect does this Event hold out to every Lad of Spirit, who is inclined to try his Fortune in that highly renowned Corps,

The Royal Marines,

When every Thing that swims the Seas must be a

PRIZE!

Thousands are at this moment endeavouring to get on Board Privateers, where they serve without Pay or Reward of any kind whatsoever; so certain does their Chance appear of enriching themselves by PRIZE MONEY! What an enviable Station then must the ROYAL MARINE hold,—who with far superior Advantages to these, has the additional benefit of liberal Pay, and plenty of the best provisions, with a good and well appointed Ship under him, the pride and Glory of Old England; surely every Man of Spirit muſt bluſh to remain at Home in Inactivity and Indolence, when his Country and the beſt of Kings needs his Assistance.

Where then can he have ſuch a fair opportunity of Reaping Glory and Riches, as in the Royal Marines, a Corps daily acquiring new Honours, and there, when once embarked in the BRITISH FLEET, he finds himself in the midſt of Honour and Glory, furrounded by a ſet of fine Fellows, Strangers to Fear, and who ſtrike Terror through the Hearts of their Enemies wherever they go!

He has likewise the inſpiring Idea to know, that while he ſcours the Ocean to protect the Liberty of OLD ENGLAND, that the Hearts and good Wiſhes of the whole BRITISH NATION, attend him; pray for his Succeſs, and participate in his Glory!! Loſe no Time then, my Fine Fellows, in embracing the glorious Opportunity that awaits you; YOU WILL RECEIVE

Sixteen Guineas Bounty,

And on your Arrival at *Head Quarters*, be comfortably and genteely CLOTHED.—And ſpirited Young BOYS of a promiſing Appearance, who are Five Feet high, WILL RECEIVE TWELVE POUNDS ONE SHILLING AND SIXPENCE BOUNTY and equal Advantages of *PROVISIONS* and *CLOATHING* with the Men. And thoſe who wish only to enlist for a limited Service, ſhall receive a Bounty of ELEVEN GUINEAS, and Boys EIGHT. In Fact, the Advantages which the ROYAL MARINE poſſeſſes, are too numerous to mention here, but among the many, it may not be amiſs to state,—That if he has a WIFE, or aged PARENT, he can make them an Allotment of half his PAY; which will be regularly paid without any Trouble to them, or to whomsoever he may direct: that being well Clothed and Fed on Board Ship, the Remainder of his PAY and PRIZE MONEY will be clear in Reserve for the Relief of his Family or his own private Purposes. The Single Young Man on his return to Port, finds himſelf enabled to cut a Daſh on Shore with his *GIRL* and his *GLASS*, that might be envied by a Nobleman.—Take Courage then, seize the Fortune that awaits you, repair to the ROYAL MARINE RENDEZVOUS, where in a FLOWING BOWL of PUNCH, in Three Times Three, you shall drink

Long live the King, and Success to his Royal Marines

The Daily Allowance of a Marine when embarked, is—One Pound of BEEF or PORK.—One Pound of BREAD—Flour, Raisins, Butter, Cheese, Oatmeal, Molasses, Tea, Sugar, &c. &c. And a Pint of the beſt WINE, or Half a Pint of the best RUM or BRANDY; together with a Pint of LEMONADE. They have likewise in warm Countries, a plentiful Allowance of the choicest FRUIT. And what can be more handsome than the Royal Marine's Proportion of PRIZE MONEY, when a Sergeant shares equal with the First Class of Petty Officers, such as Midshipmen, Assistant Surgeons, &c. which is Five Shares each; a Corporal with the Second Class, which is Three Shares each; and the Private, with the Able Seamen, One Share and a Half each.

☞ *For further Particulars, and a more full Account of the many advantages of this invaluable Corps, apply to Sergeant Fulcher, at the Eight Bells, where the Bringer of a Recruit will receive* THREE GUINEAS.

S. AND J. RIDGE, PRINTERS, MARKED PLACE, NEWARK.

Royal Marine recruiting poster for 1812.

sailors was is much harder to define. Overall, however, the system of naval recruitment was seen by all as brutal and was very unpopular even with those whose duty it was to implement it.

The Royal Marines ran a system of recruitment more akin to that of the Army and had to offer large bounties to entice volunteers, but seem to have been quite successful in maintaining numbers.

57

A Press Gang Cudgel

Immediately on the declaration of war, warrants were traditionally issued for the crews including Marines of the guard boats in the various ports to form press gangs and to go ashore to begin the work of rounding up men for the Navy. To aid their work, there was usually an embargo on all merchant ship sailings until adequate numbers had been collected. Learning from experience, the large-scale press authorised on the renewal of the war in 1803 was more than usually effective, as the government sent out secret orders before the declaration of war was announced.

Press gangs took two basic forms, those arranged to man particular ships when first launched or after a major refit, and those run by the permanent Impress Service. In both cases, the head of the press gang was awarded £1 for every seaman pressed. The Impress Service was set up in the various ports to control the previously unregulated press gangs of all of the ships then looking for men, by 1795 there were eighty-five such gangs in the UK employing close on a thousand naval personnel. A captain ran a district with anywhere from two to seven gangs, each commanded by an aged, passed-over lieutenant. The gangs usually set up a 'rendezvous' at a local public house, which was equipped with a room in which the pressed men could be held securely. The gangs were led by a midshipman or a non-commissioned officer and had up to ten men in total. The press were specifically instructed to round up experienced seamen, but they had to find evidence to prove they were seamen, tar ingrained in the hands often being a sure sign.

Each day the pressed men were marched to a tender which took them out to a receiving ship, where they were kept securely in the hold by a guard of Marines until they could be processed. Some men were provided with a 'protection' against being pressed, established in law. Crews of vessels hired by the Ordnance, Transport or Navy Boards were exempt. Apprentices, boys under the age of 18 and landsmen who had not served two or more years at sea were also not allowed to be taken up. Some fishermen were also exempt, to ensure food supplies were maintained. Outbound merchant ships were also officially exempt as were the master and chief mate, but if a merchant ship was excessively crewed, the supernumeraries could be taken. The protections were generally observed although unsurprisingly there was a huge black market in forged documents and the lieutenants were tasked in checking them thoroughly. In times of emergency the government could sanction a 'press from protections', sometimes referred to as a 'hot press', when no protection saved you from being taken up.

When the press was out, seamen would use every artifice available to avoid being taken, many concealing themselves away, dressing in civilian clothes, some even dressing as women, but the impress men were experienced campaigners who knew every trick in the book, it was a real game of cat and mouse. Foreigners were also exempt from being pressed, but Americans particularly had a problem in proving their nationality beyond doubt.

Impressment was recognised as a necessary evil to ensure the fleet, Britain's greatest line of defence, was able to function, but it was hated by many and images of press gangs attempting to drag away the father of a young family also with elderly dependents, was a regular image of the period. The problem was that nobody had yet come up with a completely successful alternative, as in wartime it still brought in half of the men recruited for the Navy each year.

A press gang dragging away a father.

58

A Swatch of Cloth for the Royal Marine Uniform and the Lining Material sent by a Supplier to the Admiralty in October 1806

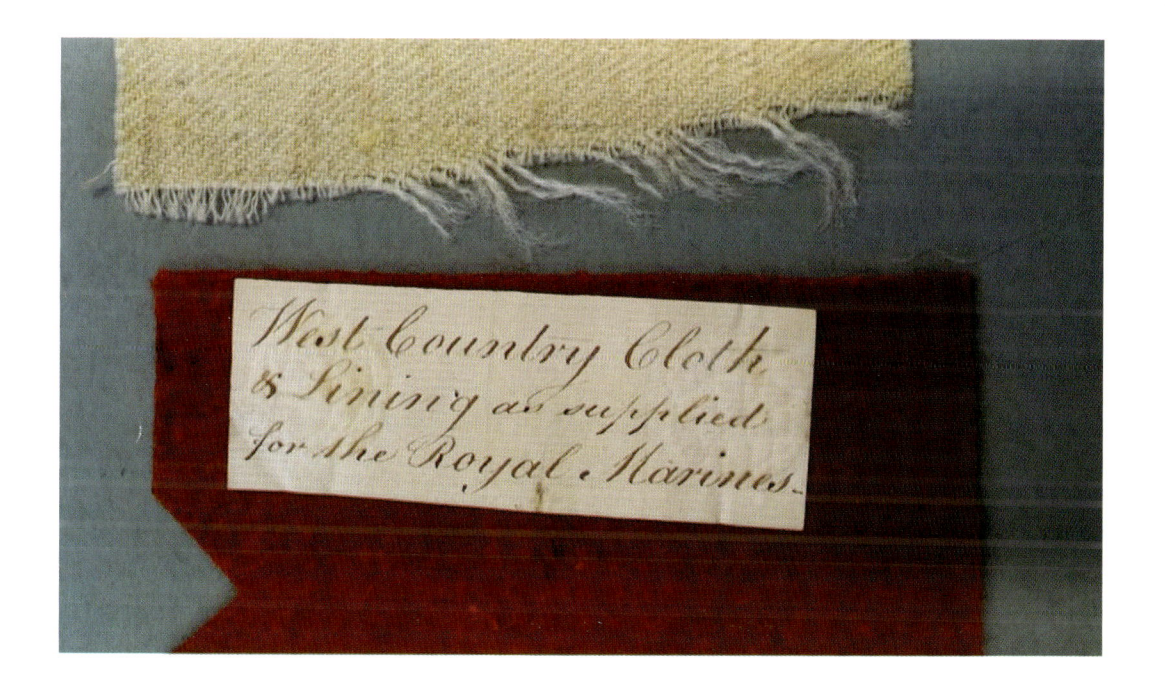

Marines acting as soldiers at sea, originated in 1664 with the raising of the Duke of York and Albany's Maritime Regiment of Foot, but that meant that they were under Army control and orders. It was only in 1755 that the Marines came under Admiralty control and they became a 'Royal' regiment in 1802, which entitled them to bear blue facings on their uniform.

Every warship of twelve guns or more had a Royal Marine detachment allocated to it although in small warships this would often be commanded by an NCO. The Marines retained Army ranks and a red uniform to readily distinguish them from the sailors in blue, although the Marine Artillery branch, formed in 1804 to man bomb vessels, did wear a blue artillery uniform. Marines were to be separate whilst on ship: they were specifically not to be forced to work aloft by regulation but could volunteer to do so to gain extra pay. They were required for tasks which required all hands, however, such as hauling in the anchor.

The Marine corps grew dramatically in size throughout the war from 5,000 in 1793 to 31,000 of all ranks in 1805, divided into four divisions, each attached to one of the main naval dockyards, 1. Chatham, 2. Portsmouth, 3. Plymouth and 4. Woolwich. Each division was normally commanded by a major general and consisted of anywhere between forty-one and forty-eight companies, each officially consisting of a captain, two first lieutenants, two second lieutenants, eight sergeants, eight corporals, five drummers and 130 privates totalling 156 all ranks, although the companies rarely if ever served as a single unit together, but were broken up into detachments as necessary. Like Army battalions, Marine battalions initially had an elite grenadier company and a light company, but these were abolished in 1804. The number of Marines on each ship was surprisingly high, amounting to one-sixth of the crew or more.

The Marines were viewed as better disciplined than the average sailor and they were tasked, amongst other things, with the guarding of stores, including the spirit room and the magazines and the captain and officers from mutinous sailors. When on guard for a two-hour watch, the Marines always wore full uniform and carried a loaded musket with bayonet fixed for immediate use, although guards on the upper deck traditionally sheathed their bayonets while the sailors were aloft. Despite this position of high trust and responsibility Royal Marine pay was the same as Army pay but in reality was actually very poor, with their pay at sea being reduced with charges for food, so that even a newly-pressed 'landsman' received higher pay at sea. Even so, they were seen as very reliable and trustworthy by the officers, and incorruptible by the men. Indeed they were not encouraged to socialise with the men. However, during the mutinies of 1797, the Marines failed to protect the officers and some even joined the mutineers, but their reputation seems to have remained intact overall. Marine officers usually required patronage to gain a commission and they had no 'purchase system' like the Army, meaning that promotion was strictly by seniority and very slow.

The Marines were fully trained in the use of small arms and were practised regularly, but they were also expected to be fully trained in firing the great guns as well so that they could bolster the ship's company when needed. When the ship was ordered to 'beat to quarters', it was signalled by a drum roll played by the Marine drummers. In action, Marines fired on the enemy crew from the forecastle or quarterdeck or from the fighting tops on occasion. They were rarely used to form part of boarding parties as they were not as agile in clambering onto enemy ships, but were to defend their own deck from enemy boarders and to reinforce gun crews when they had suffered casualties. However, Marines did not fire in ranks, but individually picked their own spots and were encouraged to move about so as to form a moving target, taking cover when reloading and firing at will. Marines could, of course, also be landed ashore, where they could form up and fight like regular infantry. When not at sea, the Royal Marines were housed in purpose-built barracks near the naval dockyards and would provide guards for the yards and man the defences.

Marines were armed with the 'Sea Service' Brown Bess musket which was slightly shorter than the Army version at around 37in (0.91m) long to make it easier to handle in confined spaces and had a slightly wider bore presumably because of deterioration of the barrel in sea air. Sergeants carried halberds.

Recruitment followed Army regulations with recruiting parties being sent out offering bounties for joining, this rose from 8 guineas in 1794 to £30 in 1808. Army recruits were even offered a further £5 bounty to transfer to the Marines.

A SWATCH OF CLOTH FOR THE ROYAL MARINE UNIFORM

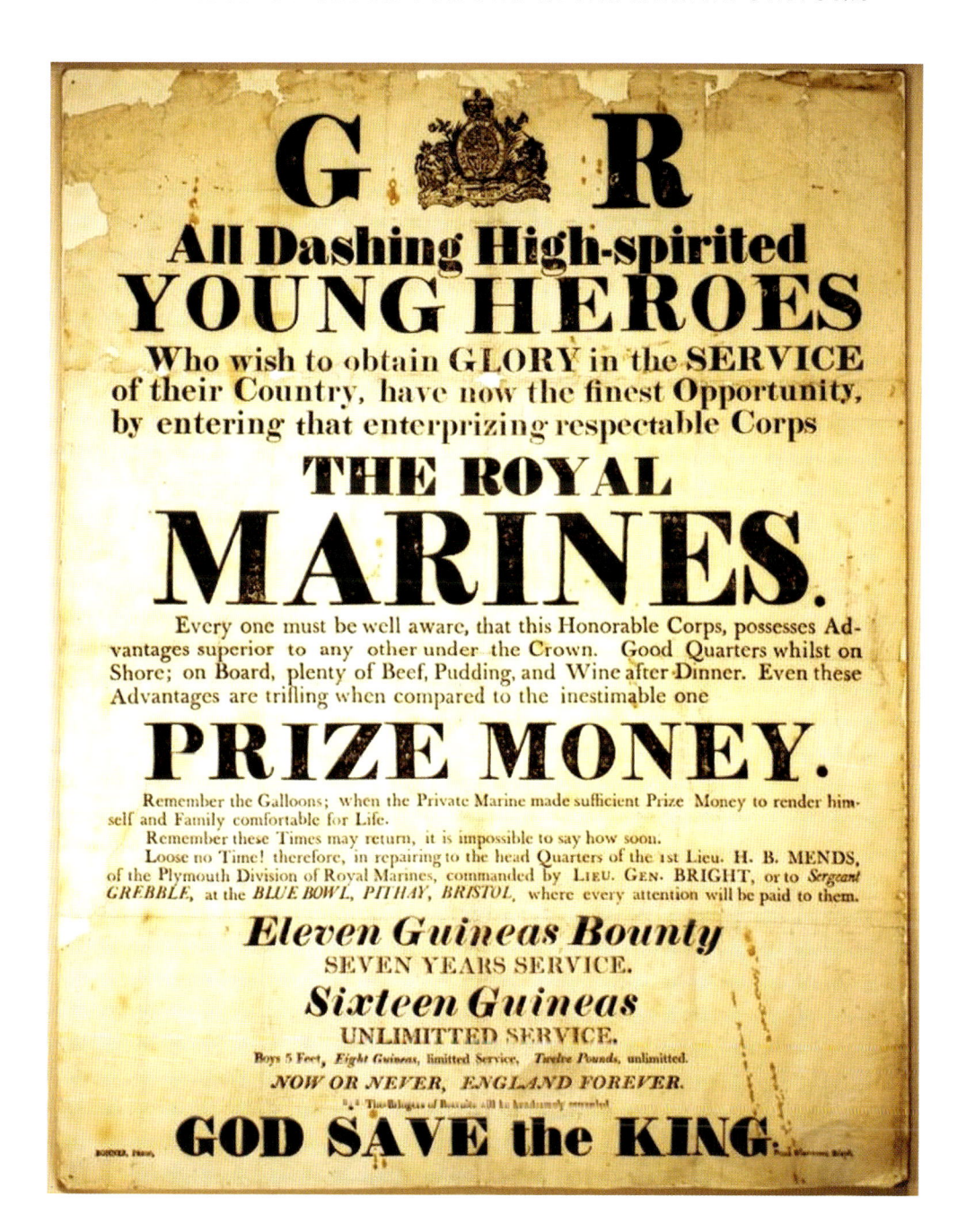

G R

All Dashing High-spirited
YOUNG HEROES

Who wish to obtain **GLORY** in the **SERVICE** of their Country, have now the finest Opportunity, by entering that enterprizing respectable Corps

THE ROYAL
MARINES.

Every one must be well aware, that this Honorable Corps, possesses Advantages superior to any other under the Crown. Good Quarters whilst on Shore; on Board, plenty of Beef, Pudding, and Wine after Dinner. Even these Advantages are trifling when compared to the inestimable one

PRIZE MONEY.

Remember the Galloons; when the Private Marine made sufficient Prize Money to render himself and Family comfortable for Life.

Remember these Times may return, it is impossible to say how soon.

Loose no Time! therefore, in repairing to the head Quarters of the 1st Lieu. H. B. MENDS, of the Plymouth Division of Royal Marines, commanded by LIEU. GEN. BRIGHT, or to *Sergeant GREBBLE*, at the *BLUE BOWL, PITHAY, BRISTOL*, where every attention will be paid to them.

Eleven Guineas Bounty
SEVEN YEARS SERVICE.
Sixteen Guineas
UNLIMITTED SERVICE.
Boys 5 Feet, *Eight Guineas*, limitted Service, *Twelve Pounds*, unlimitted.
NOW OR NEVER, ENGLAND FOREVER.

GOD SAVE the KING.

Sea Service Brown Bess musket.

As in the Army, a proportion of Marines were allowed to take their wives with them and this led to a number of women being present at the major naval battles, where they were usually assigned to help the surgeon. In 1804 boys of 15 were allowed to join the Marines and height restrictions were lowered to 5ft 2in (1.57m), but it is believed that most boys were retained in barracks training until they became of age. A number of foreigners including prisoners of war were also enlisted and although this was stopped in 1810, a number of these Marines went on to have long careers.

Particularly in the early years of the war, when the number of Marines was often inadequate for the Navy's needs, Army battalions were drafted on board to do the role. At the Battle of Copenhagen in 1801, the 49th Regiment of Foot were on board Nelson's ships, a role the regiment still proudly commemorates.

Private Grenadier Coy. 1790   Officer Grenadier Coy. 1799   Privates 1802—1810 Battn. Cos.   Officer 1807

UNIFORMS. ROYAL MARINES.

59
Ship's Bell, HMS Victory

Everything on board a Royal Navy vessel was run on a watch system as it is today and time was indicated throughout the ship by the striking of the bell. The bell was rung every half an hour through the four-hour watch, one strike of the bell indicating half an hour into the watch, two bells an hour etc up to eight bells, when the watch ends and it start at one bell again. Some ships were also supplied with a four-hour sand glass which could be hung up to keep a check on the times.

Each watch ran for a four-hour period and the six watches were traditionally named as the First, Middle, Morning, Forenoon, Afternoon and the Dog Watches, although the Dog Watches are split into two two-hour watches, called the First and Second Dog Watches. Each team of men or 'watch' carried out the duties of the ship on deck during their allocated four hours, but to avoid the watch having to do the same watches every day (the Middle Watch being the most exhausting), the Dog Watches were split so that it changes the sequence of watches each day, to make it fairer. During the two two-hour Dog Watches, the bell system continued across the two with the same one to eight bell system.

Traditionally the Navy had run a two-watch system as shown below in the first table, meaning that fully half of the ship's crew were available on deck at any one time for any duties required, but this was beginning to be recognised to be too punishing a schedule by some naval officers.

The Older Two-Watch System

	Time	Day 1	Day 2	Day 3	Day 4
First Watch	2000–0000	A	B	A	B
Middle Watch	0000–0400	B	A	B	A
Morning Watch	0400–0800	A	B	A	B
Forenoon Watch	0800–1200	B	A	B	A
Afternoon Watch	1200–1600	A	B	A	B
First Dog Watch	1600–1800	B	A	B	A
Second Dog Watch	1800–2000	A	B	A	B

By 1800, a number of officers were beginning to realise that once the ship's crew was fully trained, it was often not necessary to have so many men on deck to carry out the necessary operations and a three-watch system began to be introduced by some captains, this three-watch system eventually became standard practice and it still continues to this day. Here the sequence of four-hour watches remained, but the crew was divided into thirds and these three watches continue the same pattern but are now one watch on and two off.

The Newer Three-Watch System

	Time	Day 1	Day 2	Day 3	Day 4
First Watch	2000–0000	A	B	C	A
Middle Watch	0000–0400	B	C	A	B
Morning Watch	0400–0800	C	A	B	C

SHIP'S BELL, HMS *VICTORY*

	Time	Day 1	Day 2	Day 3	Day 4
Forenoon Watch	0800–1200	A	B	C	A
Afternoon Watch	1200–1600	B	C	A	B
First Dog Watch	1600–1800	C	A	B	C
Second Dog Watch	1800–2000	A	B	C	A

A few men on the ship in specialist roles, such as the gunner, carpenter and purser, were exempt from the watch system as their work required them to be available during daylight hours and they normally worked from 0800 to 1800 daily and also required to attend if needed at any other time beyond this that was deemed necessary. These were traditionally called 'idlers' and are still to this day.

A ship's four-hour sand glass.

60

A Seaman's Jacket

There was no official naval uniform until 1857, although medical officers had been advocating one for a long time. Some captains supported this and introduced their own. The captain of HMS *Mars* ordered that his crew should 'be discouraged from purchasing any other clothes than blue outside jackets, red white or blue waistcoats, long white trousers and hats'. Meanwhile, on the frigate HMS *Tribune* the captain paid for the uniform to ensure that: 'Every man wears a smart round japan hat . . . a gold lace band, with the name of the ship painted in front in capital letters; black silk neckerchief, with a white flannel waistcoat bound with blue, and over it a blue jacket with three rows of gold buttons very close together and blue trousers.'

Other captains only uniformed their boat's crew whilst a few others bought blue jackets for their crews to 'man the yards' on special occasions. It was also specified that all sailors attending Nelson's funeral should wear a blue jacket and white trousers. It is clear therefore that the Navy was moving slowly towards uniformity.

The short blue jacket was the most universal item, to avoid the long tails of civilian dress becoming entangled in the rigging. Check-patterned shirts were becoming very popular and they also generally wore loose-fitting trousers in white or striped as in the illustration, which were easily rolled up when working. Shoes were rarely used on board ship at sea, as it was found easier to work in the rigging in bare feet unless the weather was freezing.

It was easy for captains to influence the sailors' dress through his purser. The purser was responsible for selling clothes to the men, which were purchased with their wages. As the clothes were bought in bulk to improve the price and increase the purser's profit, this tended to bring standardisation on board ship, but there was not much commonality between ships beyond the almost obligatory blue jacket. Traditionally the clothing was and still is known as 'slops' in the Navy.

Landsmen, who had just arrived on board usually, had to make do with their civilian clothing, but often their restrictive jackets and trousers and long tails were soon found to be an inconvenience and they would often purchase slops with an advance from their wages. It also had the benefit of hiding their differences and of being looked down upon as a 'landsman'.

Seaman's trousers.

61

An Officer's Trunk

Almost all of an officer's worldly goods were meant to travel around with him in his trunk, which was transported from ship to ship with each commission and kept in his cabin, often serving as his wardrobe and drawer for clothes and, being lockable, the only secure place to keep his few valuables.

Officers' cabins usually measured no more than 8ft (2.4m) square, and many also accommodated a cannon, over which the officer's bed was slung. The cabins were set against the hull of the ship and were originally divided simply by hanging a canvas sheet. Few cabins were lucky enough to have natural daylight except by opening the gun port in good weather.

In time, the partitions became more sturdy, being made of either canvas stretched over a frame or even of light wood, making them appear more permanent. However, the frames were constructed to be easily dismantled when the ship cleared for action, while all of the officers' possessions and bedding were bundled into their trunks, which were then taken to relative safety in the hold during action.

Officers usually provided their own beds and any furniture that they wished to have in their cabin, although it needed to be portable to be easily removed when necessary. They also supplied their own silver knife, fork and plate

AN OFFICER'S TRUNK

and fine glassware, otherwise they would use the issue pewter implements and mugs.

Most officers actually used a cot, a rectangular canvas-framed hammock, which was a little more spacious being 3ft 3in (1m) wide and therefore more comfortable than the sailor's hammock, but could still be removed quickly when needed. Fixed bunks were a later introduction.

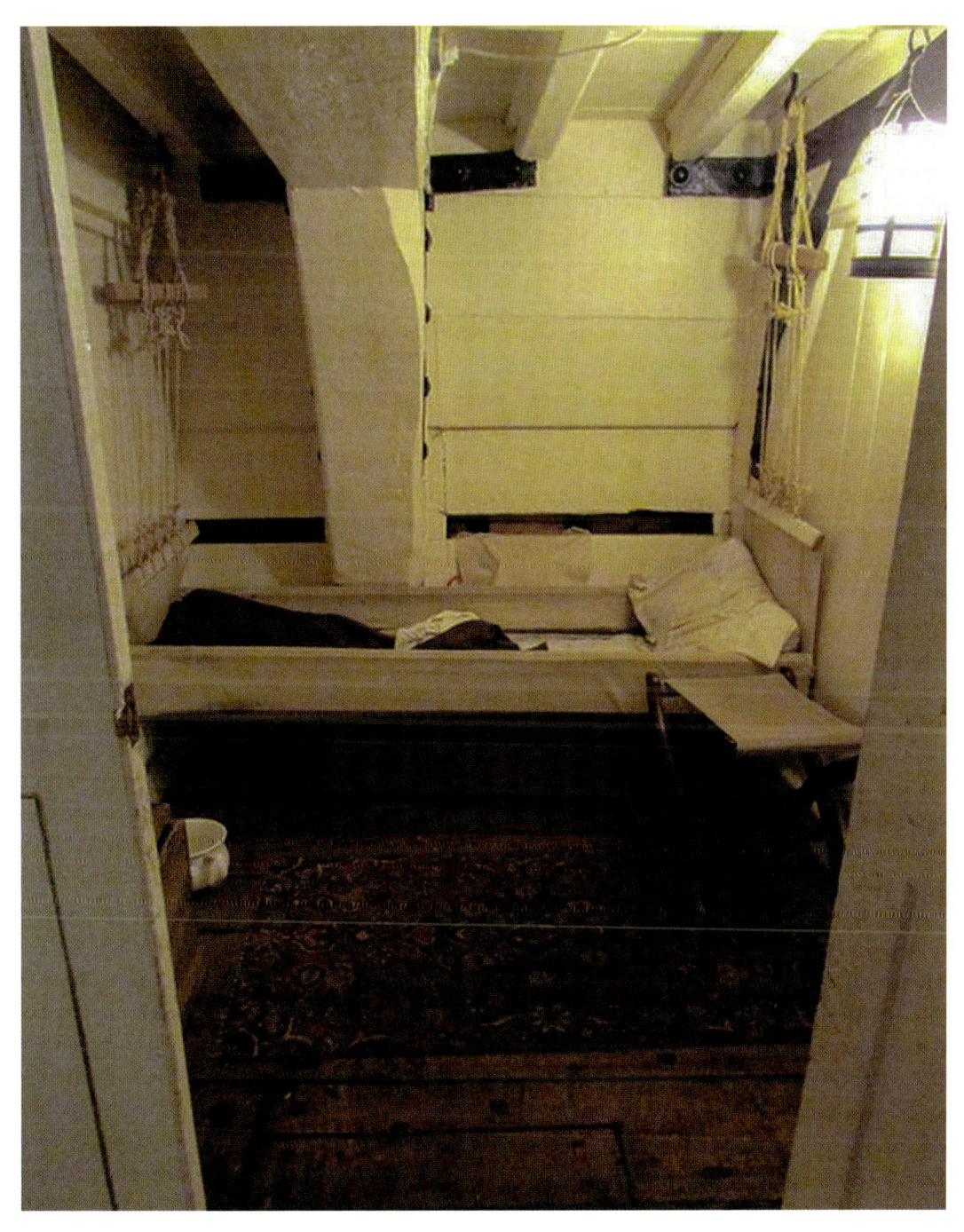

Officer's cabin with cot, HMS *Trincomalee*.

62

Sailors' Hammocks

Every sailor was issued with a hammock, although after 1800 they were more often issued with two, so that they could occasionally be cleaned and dried. The hammock consisted of a length of hemp cloth 6ft (1.83m) long and 3ft (0.91m) wide, gathered at each end by a clew and slung horizontally from the deck above. The hammocks were issued on loan: they remained government property and stayed with the ship.

The hammock was merely a receptacle for the actual mattress they slept on, which could be replaced by the sailor at his own expense and he carried the mattress with him from ship to ship. The mattress was usually filled with flock or wool, but sometimes old rags were used and soon these apparently emitted a terrible smell. They were also issued with a blanket and a bolster or pillow.

Although not every man would sleep at the same time, because of duties on deck, the ship had to provide enough positions for every hammock to be strung up, not an easy task in a warship with 500 men or more. Every man was allocated a specific place by the First Lieutenant, men with duties in the same part of the ship being placed together, but the men of each watch were placed alternately so that there was a little more space between each sleeping man. Only 14in (36cm) was allowed

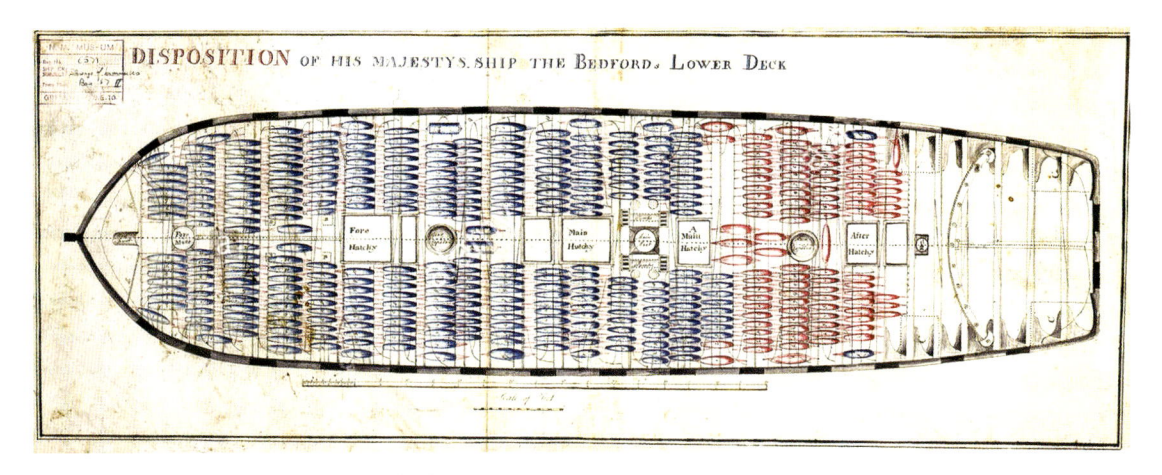

Disposition of hammocks, HMS *Bedford*, 74.

between each hammock, but this was effectively doubled when the ships were on watches at sea. Petty officers were placed nearer the ship's side, where they enjoyed fresher air and the space between hammocks was increased to 28in (72cm). Large iron hooks were placed along the underside of the wooden deck for the hammocks to be hung.

In the daytime, the hammocks were rolled up with the bedding into a tight ball and lashed up. The hammocks were then placed in netting along the sides of the ship where they had some benefit as protection from enemy fire. In stormy weather the hammocks were stowed below decks to keep dry.

More luxurious hammocks for the senior non-commissioned officers.

63

A Chocolate Pot from HMS Triton

Commissioned officers, some senior warrant officers, such as the master, purser, chaplain and surgeon, and the Marine officers lived in the wardroom which was always situated aft on the deck below the captain's cabin. On a 74-gun ship it had around twelve members. The wardroom was placed centrally towards the stern with the officers' cabins running alongside of it and consisted primarily of a long table and chairs for meals and was usually well lit from the stern windows. Vessels of the size of a frigate and smaller had a gunroom instead, which was placed lower in the ship and had little natural light. The First Lieutenant was president of the wardroom and neither the captain, admiral or midshipmen could dine in it unless invited, a convention that remains to this day.

The officers were entitled to the same food as the men, but they usually provided themselves with better fare at their own expense via a

Wardroom silverware on HMS *Victory*.

A Georgian wine glass from HMS *Victory*.

subscription paid by all wardroom members. One of the lieutenants was usually appointed treasurer of the fund and caterer, laying in stocks whenever possible to keep the other officers content, including good quality wine.

The charges levied on members varied depending on the level of entertainment they planned, but one estimate puts the cost to each member of the mess on a 74 as £60 per annum (around £3,000 today), although others claim this as too low and may have reached £80 (£4,000 today) or more. The wardroom and sometimes the midshipmen's berth also had a stake in the live animals kept on board for eggs, milk and meat along with the captain.

At sea officers generally still drank alcohol, up to half a pint of wine per day, with greater relaxation apparently on Sundays, but it was socially unacceptable and dangerous for an officer to be on duty at sea while under the influence and he would be severely punished by the captain. In harbour, the restrictions were generally lifted and at a wardroom dinner even with the captain in attendance it could be very raucous indeed.

The wardroom was also used as an area for recreation during the day, as the officers; personal cabins were very small, only useful for sleeping and quiet contemplation, with no natural daylight to read by. Therefore, officers would use the cleared table as a desk to write letters home sitting near the stern windows where the natural light was usually bright enough to read by. It was not by all accounts a particularly peaceful place, with officers often practising their singing or playing on a violin or flute, not always harmoniously. Others might practise their fencing at one end of the room or play backgammon, chess or cards. It was rarely a place for peace and tranquillity.

Officers often had a servant from the crew or paid for their own and a trained chef was a luxury that many felt necessary, when the ship's cook was really barely able to do much beyond boiling water.

A weekly set of toasts had been established and were comprehensively used throughout the Navy, these, including that to the monarch, traditionally being drunk sitting down as wardrooms rarely had enough headroom for people to stand up.

Sunday 'Absent friends'
Monday 'Our ships at sea'
Tuesday 'Our men'
Wednesday 'Ourselves' (usually followed by the informal reply 'for nobody else will concern themselves with our well-being!')
Thursday 'A bloody war or a sickly season'
Friday 'A willing foe and sea-room'
Saturday 'Our wives and sweethearts' (usually accompanied by the reply 'May they never meet!')

A very drunken wardroom dinner.

64
Thomas Rowlandson Cartoon of a Ship's Cook

The Brodie Stove, HMS *Victory*.

The ship's cook in the time of Nelson's navy was undoubtedly the most misused title, as he had very little to do with what we would regard as cooking today. Cooks had no qualifications to pass, nor had to sit before a selection panel to prove their culinary prowess. Indeed, the only qualification necessary for ship's cook was to be an ex-sailor who had lost a limb in combat.

The duties of a cook were really little more than to ensure that the fires in the galley were kept going and safely contained and that there was plenty of hot water for the oatmeal or salt meat to be boiled. Indeed, the cook was to oversee these operations, as he had a cook's mate and the aid of the mess cooks to prepare the food. His main duty was to then apportion the food fairly and he was responsible for any shortfall. The mess cooks brought their rations in a cloth bag and the cook saw them put into the cauldrons to cook and he marked their return to the mess cook later.

Ships were supplied with a Brodie Stove, which incorporated greater safety measures for avoiding a fire on board, and also had a number of clever functions. Apart from heating the water vats, it also contained a grill, a mechanical spit turned by a fan in the oven, and even had a small copper still which converted seawater into fresh in small quantities, usually reserved for the sick bay.

A Mess Table on HMS Victory

The 'mess' was the centre of every sailor's universe onboard a Navy warship, as it was where they ate, socialised and spent most of their recreational time. The core of the mess was the table which was firmly attached to the ship's side and hinged down when in use, the other end suspended by ropes from the deckhead above. The tables on two and three-deckers were situated between each pair of cannon, whereas on frigates where the lower deck was not armed, they had more space. Benches were also supplied or the sailors used wooden trunks as seats.

Sailors were initially allocated to a mess on joining, but they were free to move and join another mess if they preferred the company there. However, seamen and Marines were not encouraged to mix and they rarely joined each other's messes. Changing mess was a right of every man, but it could only be effected at a given time every few weeks, to stop continuous hopping about as they had to inform the First Lieutenant of the change so that their victuals could be allocated correctly. Some ships' captains put a physical limit on numbers, usually at about eight men, and did not allow messes to reduce below four.

The messes stored and took care of their own basins, jugs, plates, knives and spoons, forks rarely being used at this time. Earthenware cups and plates or even pewter were not unknown, but were liable to damage in stormy weather and it appears that messes usually carried a wooden set in case of breakages. The square wooden plates are the origin of the phrase 'a square meal'.

Each day one of the men in turn was appointed mess cook who collected the day's victuals for the entire mess from the steward each morning and took the linen bag marked with the mess number, to the ship's cook to be placed in the huge kettles of water to boil. At mealtimes the cook would hand each mess cook his linen bag of cooked food to ensure that there were no mistakes.

The messes between decks were not heated, as hundreds of men in such close confinement with little ventilation when the gunports were closed meant that the combined body heat kept the place warm, if not stiflingly hot.

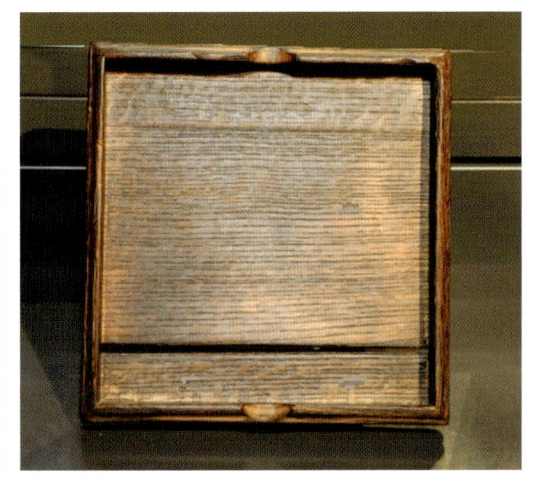

A square plate.

A messmate tells a tall tale.

The men received their 'grog' in their messes and particularly in the evening after dinner, until 'lights out' sent them to their hammocks, they often regaled each other with tall tales or of battles past. Many smoked a pipe, which was issued after 1798 at the rate of 2lbs (0.9kg) of tobacco per month for those that wanted it and it is very likely that many non-smokers drew their ration to sell at a profit, tobacco being widely believed to be a cure for all fevers. However, smoking was not permitted below decks because of the threat of fire.

Others turned to, making good and mending their clothes, whilst others practised their skills at painting, hat-making or cobbling, whilst a relative few sought to find enough light to read by, write a letter or learn their signals.

When in harbour, the opportunities of fishing to supplement the rations or breaking out the fiddle for impromptu singing or dancing was occasionally allowed by the captain to boost morale. Singing and dancing were a particular favourite apparently, as it helped the sailors forget the hardships and drudgery of their lives for a brief period at least.

Fishing off a cannon.

66

Skull Clearly Showing the Effects of Scurvy

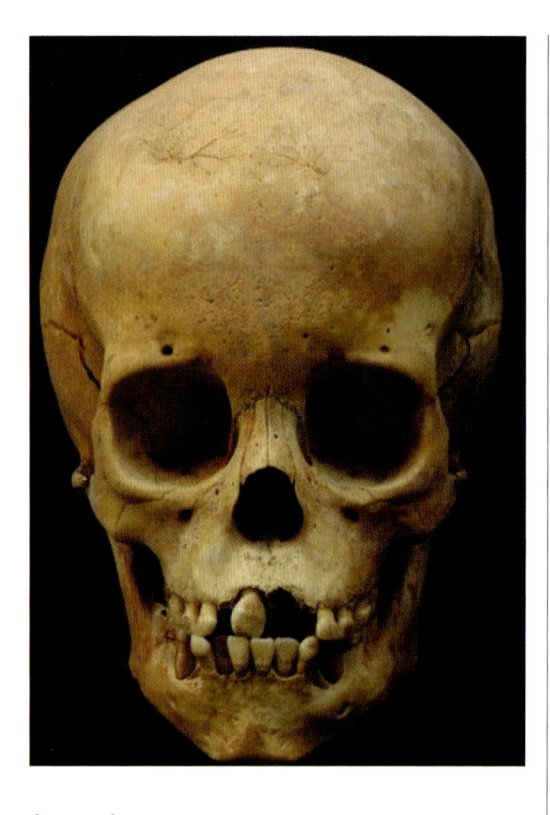

The Navy had recognised that the health of sailors suffered markedly on long voyages, with Admiral Anson's expedition to raid Spanish possessions in the Pacific in the 1740s losing no less than 1,300 men of the crews out of a total complement of 2,000. Anson described the symptoms of the men as 'a luxuriancy of fungous flesh . . . putrid gums and . . . the most dreadful terrors'.

The cause of the problem, Vitamin C deficiency, was not understood and various solutions were recommended. Some of the more bizarre included Captain Cook's recommendation of the use of malt and sauerkraut, bloodletting and the insertion of a piece of turf into the patient's mouth to counter the 'bad qualities of sea air'. However, without knowledge of the different vitamins, the search for a remedy was very hit and miss.

Some success was derived strangely from eating the ship's rats, as the animal naturally synthesizes its own Vitamin C, but others were soon noticing the beneficial effects of eating fresh fruit and vegetables, especially citrus fruits.

As early as 1601 Captain James Lancaster had carried out an experiment on the long voyage to India. He issued lemon juice daily to the crew of one ship but did not issue it to the other three accompanying ships. By the half-way point of the voyage the three ships without lemons had lost 110 men out of a total of 278, while the men with lemons all remained healthy. The results were outstanding and in 1622, Sir Richard Hawkins had also recommended the use of 'sower lemons and oranges' but it was to be well over a century before this theory was properly investigated by scientists.

Surgeon's Mate James Lind observed the effects of scurvy on the men under his care aboard HMS *Salisbury* in 1747. Taking twelve serious cases from amongst his crew, he gave each pair a different proposed remedy in order to evaluate which, if any, of them actually helped. The remedies tried were: a quarter of a pint of cider per day; 25 drops of elixir of vitriol (a

SKULL CLEARLY SHOWING THE EFFECTS OF SCURVY

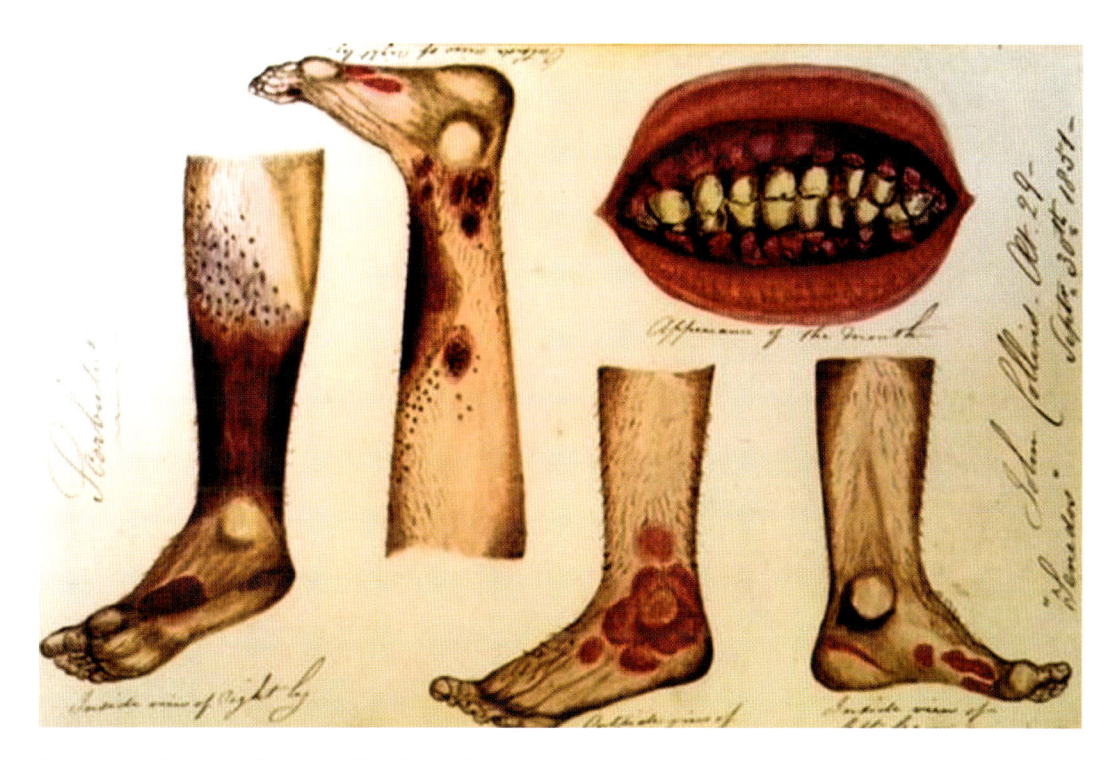

An early medical record showing the effects of scurvy.

mixture of sulphuric acid, aromatics and alcohol) three times a day; half a pint of seawater daily; a concoction of garlic, mustard seed, horseradish, balsam of Peru and gum resin three times a day; two spoonfuls of vinegar three times a day; and two oranges and one lemon per day. Within a week those on the citrus diet were well enough to help tend the others. Lind published his findings in a 'Treaties of the Scurvy' in 1753 but it was not until 1795 that the Navy took this up and began issuing lime or lemon juice, which was added to the rum ration. Unbelievably it was not until 1865 that the British Board of Trade adopted a similar policy for the merchant fleet.

Initially lemon juice from Europe was used, but limes grown in the British colonies later replaced them, although unfortunately limes naturally contain only half the Vitamin C per 100 grams in comparison to lemons. The American term 'Limey' would seem to have originated around 1850 from the original term 'lime juicer', a derogatory term used for sailors of the Royal Navy because of their use of limes to combat scurvy. The name then spread by 1880 to incorporate all British people and was heavily used during the two World Wars.

Limes.

67

Early Photograph of a Sailing Whaling Ship

The Royal Navy had a confusing attitude towards the seagoing merchant fleet, disdaining them, yet totally reliant on them for their supplies of both equipment and rations. Despite this attitude, warships spent much of the war protecting the vast British merchant fleet from the actions of both privateers and enemy warships. The British merchant fleet was the largest in the world at this time, numbering just over 16,000 vessels in 1793, employing close on 120,000 men. It was, however, serious competition for the limited supply of experienced sailors and Navy captains often saw them as an easy target when requiring more hands. The fleet grew throughout the war and in 1807 there were nearly 23,000 ships listed, but this also required proportionately more crewmen, putting further strain on the Navy recruiting system.

However, this was not a time of free trade, a series of Acts of Parliament having been passed to protect trade, requiring only British ships to trade with British overseas possessions and insisting that crews were three-quarters British. Certain goods imported into Britain were also banned from any source other than a British possession, ensuring a virtuous circle of profitable trade and slowly destroying the merchant business of many European competitors, particularly the Dutch. The government also licensed trade with certain parts of the world, such as the Mediterranean, for a hefty fee or the trade was restricted by law, for example allowing the East India Company a complete monopoly with that part of the world.

The most heavily used trade routes were to India and the Far East, with £6.5 million worth of tea being imported in 1784 alone (around £700 million today). The other was the West Indies triangle, in which ships sailed from Britain to West Africa to collect slaves (until the trade was banned in 1807), which they transported to the West Indies for sale and then sailed to Britain with a full cargo of cane sugar.

The Baltic and Mediterranean were both important for oils and certain naval supplies, such as hemp and masts, but these seas saw a much lower volume of trade and were less dominated by British merchants.

The coastal trade was also very important, although serious losses to enemy privateers during the war stimulated the expansion of the canal system, allowing materials to travel across

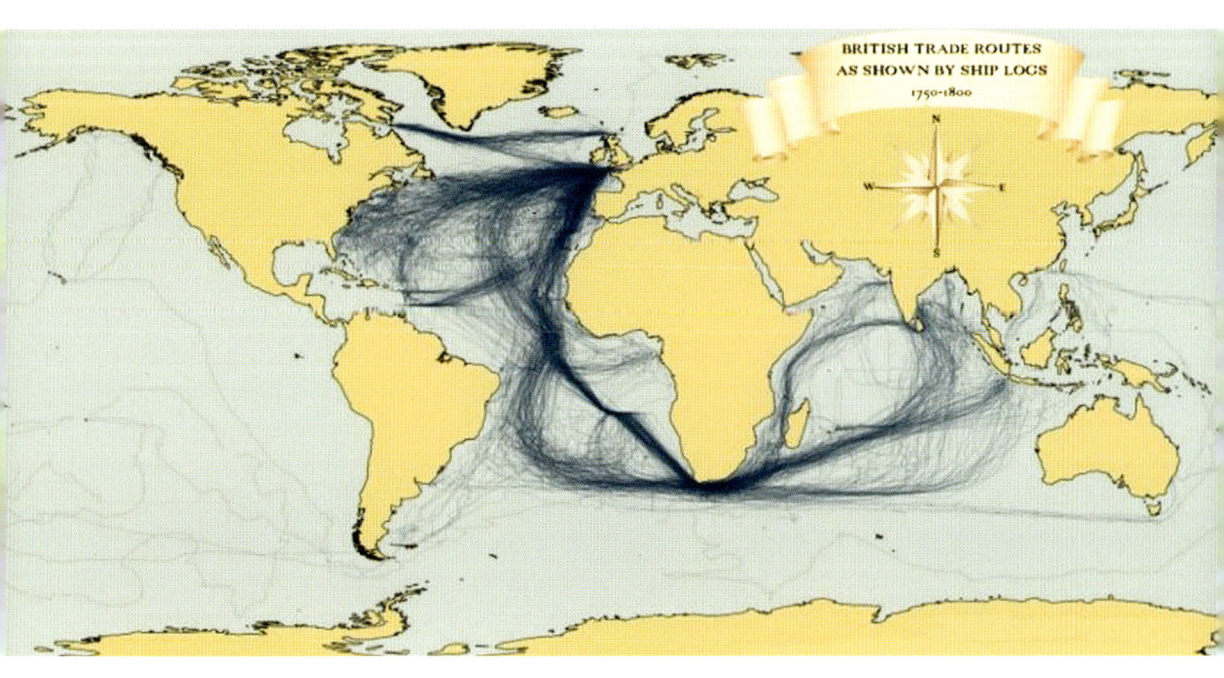

British trade routes 1750–1800.

Merchant vessel at sea.

the country in safety. In the 1790s no fewer than forty-eight new canal acts were passed and the Caledonian Ship Canal was begun in 1803 to avoid the dangerous passage around the very top of Scotland. A large trade of coal from Newcastle to London, however, continued throughout, with no viable alternative.

Fishing and whaling boats were also very numerous and highly lucrative ventures, herring being caught in huge quantities in Scotland and salted, then exported worldwide. The Newfoundland Banks were also important fishing grounds and vast numbers of boats would travel across the Atlantic to fish there until privateers made it too risky. The waters around Greenland were particularly favoured for whaling, the oil produced being used to fuel lamps and to make soap, and over 250 ships were involved in this lucrative trade.

Merchant ships still tended to be quite small in comparison to warships and more boxy in shape to improve the capacity for goods, but still square-rigged like warships. Very few merchant ships exceeded 150 tons however, except for the East Indiamen, owned and manned by the East India Company which were up to 1,200 tons and resembled Navy 64s in size. These ships were specifically designed to carry very large cargoes on these long passages and were heavily armed to protect themselves against enemy ships. It was quite normal for most merchant vessels to carry a few guns or carronades as self-protection against small privateers, but they rarely prevailed against heavily-armed warships.

EARLY PHOTOGRAPH OF A SAILING WHALING SHIP

Whalers at work.

As the depredations of enemy warships and privateers grew worse and the number of merchant losses mounted, Parliament (heavily influenced by its merchant members) demanded better protection and naval escorts were set up to see ships safely through a particularly vulnerable channel, whilst huge convoys with armed escorts were formed to safely see the merchant fleets safely across the Bay of Biscay and through the Mediterranean and the Baltic. This work was vital, but very tedious, with few moments of excitement and were generally hated by naval officers, their being little opportunity to gain prize money.

68

A Barrel of Salt Pork

Because of the irregular availability of fresh vegetables, and the total lack of refrigeration or modern preservatives, feeding a crew of hundreds of men at sea for weeks at a time was a major challenge, but one that the Victualling Board seem to have risen to pretty well. Specific rations were to be provided per day per man by regulations and when away from British coastal waters, it was permitted to offer substitutes available locally. The ration per week for each man was set at:

7lbs (3.2kg) of ships' biscuit
4lbs (1.8kg) of beef
2lbs (907g) of pork
3/8 of a 24in cod
2 pints of pease [peas]
3 pints of oatmeal
6oz (180g) of butter
12oz (360g) of cheese
A gallon of beer per day

Breakfast invariably consisted of an oatmeal porridge, the oats having been left to soak overnight only requiring heating in the morning. Breakfast was served promptly at 8 am and lasted 45 minutes (those going on watch at 8 getting

A plate of traditional 'Lobscouse' or beef stew.

theirs earlier). If available, the porridge could be sweetened with molasses, sugar or honey.

Once breakfast was cleared away, preparations began immediately for the meal at 12 noon, usually called 'dinner'. This often consisted of salted meat, 1lb (450g) of pork on Sundays and Thursdays and 2lbs (900g) of beef every Tuesday and Saturday, and on the other three days they had salted fish and cheese. This sounds like a lot of meat, but the entire carcass was cut up and the meat was left on the bone, which was counted in the weight. Part of the head was a favoured delicacy. Because salt meat cannot be used in its immediate state, the meat was often soaked for many hours prior to use in empty barrels filled with fresh water, which had to be changed frequently. This was a real drain on the ship's water supply, but was essential. The meat was then boiled and often any fresh vegetables available were added to make a stew, called 'Lobscouse'. The pease (*sic* – peas) were always cooked and served with the pork meals. The food was served with 1lb (450g) of ship's biscuit. These ¼lb round biscuits of flour and water with no yeast or salt were baked at least three times to ensure all moisture was eradicated to make them last longer in storage. They were not called 'hard tack', that is a name used much later. The biscuits were too hard and dry to enjoy alone and they were normally broken up into the stew or laid down in the watery juices that were served with the meat. They were also allowed half of their daily beer allowance with this meal. The men were allowed 1½ hours to enjoy their meal.

Supper was served at 4 pm and lasted 90 minutes, usually consisting of cheese, butter and more ship's biscuits. It was topped off by the other half of the beer allowance.

At times, one of the beef meals per week was replaced by a pudding, made of flour, suet

Figgy duff in a cloth bag.

and butter, with raisins added if they had any. The puddings were rolled into large balls and placed into a linen bag and then lowered into boiling water to cook. This was a simple and sweet meal

The food at sea was wholesome and nourishing, but very monotonous indeed. It has been calculated that Royal Navy sailors received around 5,000 calories a day, which sounds very high, but their work was very demanding and physical and there was no chance of sailors becoming obese. The gallon of beer per day may sound excessive, but it must be understood that they were issued 'small beer' with a maximum alcohol content of 2 to 3 per cent, a third of most modern lagers.

As an indication of the huge amount of stores required for a ship going to sea, this is the list of stores ordered for HMS *Victory* in 1796:

Bread, 76,054lbs (34,498kg); vinegar 135 gallons (614 litres); beef 16,808 1lb pieces (7,623kg); fresh beef 308lbs (140kg); pork 1,921½ 4lb pieces (3,486kg); peas 279 ⅜ bushels (10,161kg); oatmeal 1,672 gallons (7,601 litres); flour 12,315lbs (5,586kg); malt 351lbs (159kg); oil 171 gallons (777 litres); biscuit bags (100lbs each) 163 (7,400kg).

69

A Rum Cask

Rum was originally served to sailors in the West Indies as it was wrongly believed to help prevent scurvy. It replaced the daily beer issue (1 gallon or 4.5 litres), but the half pint (0.28 litres) of neat rum issued daily was soon found to be too strong and caused problems with drunkenness and an increase in the number of accidents whilst working aloft. In other parts of the world the issue was sometimes made with a half-pint of arrack (an East Indian spirit) or a pint of wine.

Georgian 1 gill rum measure.

In 1740 Admiral Vernon, commander-in-chief in the West Indies, decided that the rum was to be diluted. The men would still receive their half pint but now watered down with a quart (1.14 litres) of water and it was to be issued in two halves. The first half was issued between 10 and 12 in the morning, the second between 4 and 6 in the afternoon. This order was eventually to become general throughout the Royal Navy, although the issue of beer in its stead remained the norm outside of the West Indies. This watered-down rum was to become known forever as 'grog' from the 'grogam' coat Admiral Vernon wore, causing his nickname to be 'Old Grog'. Non-commissioned officers retained the right to receive their rum ration straight without dilution. In 1795 lime or lemon juice was added to the 'grog' to help fight scurvy.

The watering of the rum was done in plain sight on the main deck and was overseen by the officer of the watch, who took particular care to ensure that the men clearly saw that they were not being defrauded of their correct allowance. Men were not forced to drink the rum: those who chose not to were marked with a 'T' for temperance and received 3 pence a day extra wages in lieu, this could be the origin of the phrase 'Teetotal'. Sailors were not issued rum until their 20th birthday and were marked in the books as 'UA' for Under Age.

Apart from the daily ration, rum was also served to 'splice the mainbrace' when a special allowance of one-eighth of a pint was issued to every man over the age of 20 for a special occasion as deemed by the current monarch, such as a christening of a prince or the investiture of a monarch.

Because of the continued problems with drunkenness, the rum ration was halved in 1823 and halved again in 1850, when it became the standard ration which continued until its eventual abolition in 1970.

70

Congreve Rocket

British troops serving in India had faced Mysorean forces who deployed massed rockets against them and William Congreve was soon experimenting with the technology using his own money. Congreve was able to demonstrate that he could produce rockets which could travel more than 1,500 yards/metres and he was given permission to develop them further at the Royal Arsenal at Woolwich. By early 1806, Congreve had developed an 32-pounder rocket which travelled up to 3,000 yards and by 1813 he had versions up to 300lbs, but these were too cumbersome for general use. With the fervent support of the Prince Regent, the rocket was brought into service. The Army formed two rocket troops and they were deployed at the Battles of Leipzig and Waterloo. However, the Navy were much quicker to take up the technology and to experiment with many options for their use, indeed the Navy were by far the greater proponents of the weapon during the wars.

In 1805, Commodore Sir William Sidney Smith undertook a bombardment of Napoleon's invasion fleet in the harbour of Boulogne, but high winds meant that the attack was unsuccessful. Smith also used them more successfully against the fortress of Gaeta in southern Italy the following year.

In October 1806, Commodore Owen attacked Boulogne again. In a night attack, twenty-four naval cutters fitted with firing frames fired around 2,000 32-pounder rockets into the town in just 30 minutes. A number of fires were reported, but little significant damage was caused. The Navy also took rockets to Copenhagen, which

A 32-pounder Congreve rocket.

was bombarded in 1807. The Danes found the weapons terrifying and they certainly had a major effect on the morale of the defenders, despite the fact that out of a total bombardment of over 14,000 projectiles fired into the city, only 300 were rockets. However, the Royal Navy personnel were not so impressed, Congreve, who was present, earning the nickname of 'Commodore Squib'.

Lord Cochrane utilised rockets in the attack on Basque Roads in 1809, but it is unclear how effective they were, the French fleet being much more frightened of the fireships. A merchant vessel was purchased and adapted by the Navy to fire rockets arranged in troughs as her broadside, renaming her HMS *Galgo*. The ship was deployed during the Walcheren expedition of 1809 and fired rockets during the bombardment of the town of Flushing, prompting a formal complaint to Lord Chatham by the French commander.

Three detachments of Royal Marine rocket troops were eventually deployed to America in

Congreve rocket boats.

Bombardment of Fort McHenry in 1814.

the war with the United States of America. They were used at a number of engagements during this war, but by far the most famous was the unsuccessful bombardment of Fort McHenry in 1814, including the use of 32-pounder rockets by HMS *Erebus*, an ex-fireship, converted to fire salvoes of rockets. Witnessing this bombardment from a safe distance, amateur poet Francis Scott Key penned a poem, which included the line 'and the rocket's red glare'. It eventually was set to music and became the American National Anthem 'The Star Spangled Banner'. Rockets were also used at the bombardment of Algiers in 1816 to defeat the Algerian pirates.

71

HMS Victory *Flying Nelson's Signal 'England Expects That Every Man Will Do His Duty'*

Signal flags had existed in the Navy since 1337, but this simply consisted of two flag signals, one for all captains to attend the admiral and another for announcing that the enemy was in sight. It was not until 1673 when a slightly more expansive signal system was produced using fifteen different flags with each having a defined meaning.

It was only in 1790 that Admiral Lord Howe introduced a signal book based on ideas first proposed by the Frenchmen Bertrand Mahé, Comte de la Bourdonnais in 1738 and expanded on by Sebastian De Bigot in 1763. The Howe Code comprised of ten numerical flags plus seven additional flags to indicate start, finish and to change to represent actual numbers etc. The three-number codes referred to prearranged words or phrases listed in a code book. The original set of codes only used 260 of the possible 1,000 options available but in 1799 Howe increased this to 340 options.

Sir Home Popham is often mistakenly credited with producing the first signal codes, but what he did produce in 1799 under the

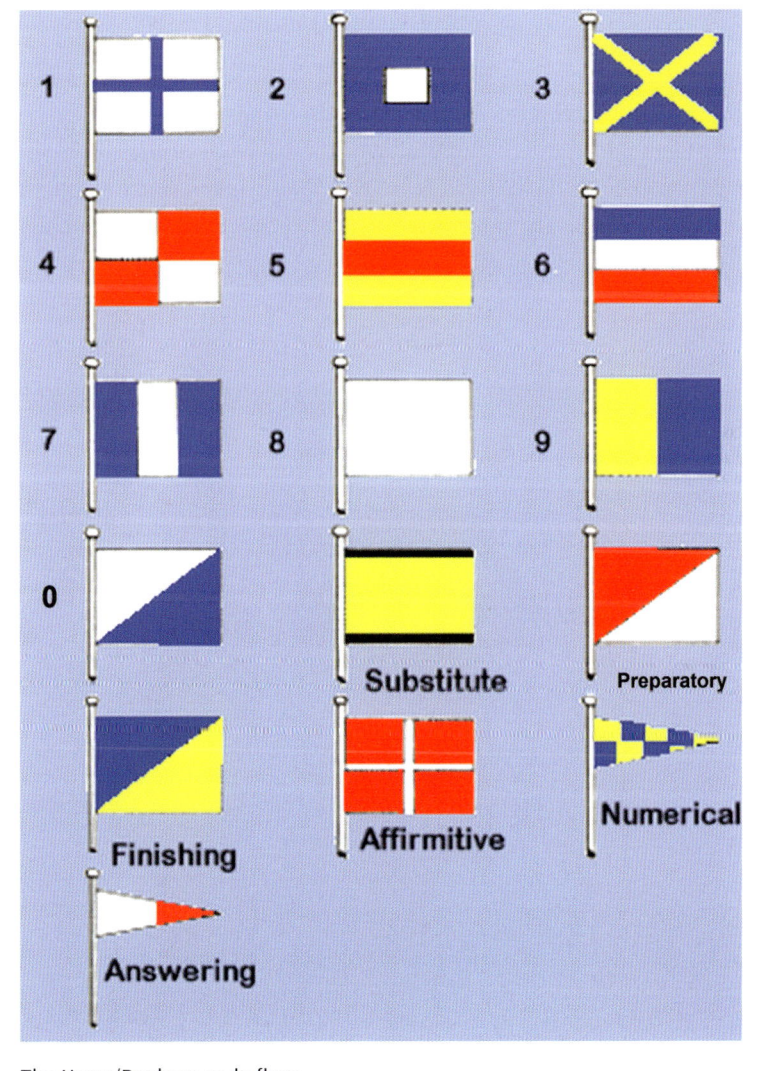

The Howe/Popham code flags.

title *Telegraphic Signals of Marine Vocabulary* was a vastly superior set of codes still based on the Howe number flags, but adding the ability to indicate letters if it was necessary to spell a word out fully. In his signal system the same ten flags could also indicate the letters A–K (I and J sharing the same flag) and the other letters were denominated by a combination of two number flags flown together up to twenty-five.

As to the list of words or phrases available, Popham massively increased the options by producing a list of no less than 3,000 words/phrases putting a different flag in front of the numbers to identify in which of the three sections the number code referred to. The code was used at Trafalgar in 1805 and proved a great success, Popham further updating the code book to 6,000 predefined sentences and phrases.

Some examples of the codes in the original 1799 version include 251 meaning 'Engage', 1381 'Hurricane', 1517 'Mutiny', 2100 'Boulogne', 2169 'Cove of Cork', 2206 'Destroy', 2258 'The enemy is anchored', 2289 'I cannot make out your third flag', 2485 'I have succeeded but with the loss of men', 2600 'The Prize is useless, shall I destroy her?', 2874 'Set fire to the town' and 2876 'She is laden with treasure'.

When Nelson wanted to set a message up to encourage his men as they sailed to attack the vast Franco-Spanish fleet at the Battle of Trafalgar, he requested that they fly 'England confides that every man will do his duty', confides indicating that 'they are sure'. Lieutenant Pasco in charge of signals requested to change the word 'confides' which was not in the signal code and would need to be spelt out, for 'expects' which was in the code as 269, Nelson agreed, so the famous signal was flown as shown below using the Popham code.

However, the signal was not received well in the fleet, according to a number of eyewitnesses, the change to 'expects' being taken as a demand that they do their duty, which they did not think they required.

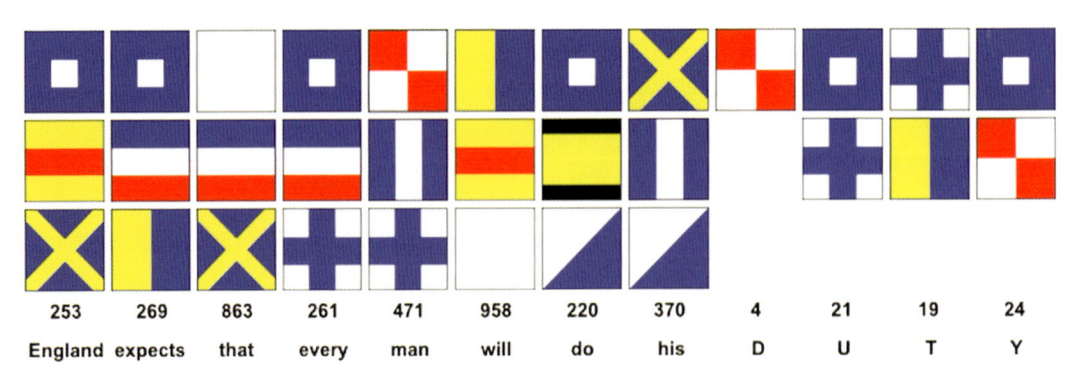

253	269	863	261	471	958	220	370	4	21	19	24
England	expects	that	every	man	will	do	his	D	U	T	Y

The flag combination using Popham's signal code.

72

Water Cask Captured from the Spanish San Josef at the Battle of Cape St Vincent, 1797

When considering the tactics employed in naval battles of this period, it is usual to refer to the vast fleet battles which were fought, although in over 20 years of almost constant warfare from 1793 until 1815, there were only six large-scale engagements of this kind. These were the battles of the Glorious First of June in 1794, St Vincent and Camperdown in 1797, the Nile in 1798, Copenhagen in 1801 and Trafalgar in 1805. There was not a single fleet battle in the final decade of the war.

Warships were fitted with very few cannon firing from their bow or stern, therefore it was of great importance that a warship could present one of its two broadsides to the enemy. Naval battles had therefore become quite formulaic actions, with each fleet forming into one long line, so as to present the greatest number of cannon towards an enemy and thus protecting the vulnerable bow and stern of the ships. Rigid adherence to this basic principle led to many naval battles during the seventeenth and early eighteenth centuries being staid exchanges of broadsides and with very inconclusive results. Any deviation from these principles was not only frowned upon, but could lead to a commanding officer being court-martialled and cashiered.

British tactics were, however, generally more aggressive, with the intention at least of achieving some form of victory over the enemy fleet, whereas the French and Spanish admirals tended to act more cautiously and defensively, taking care to preserve their fleet for future operations, rather than seeking a decisive outcome. Because of this, British commanders always sought to gain the 'weather gage' which meant that they were further to windward than the enemy ships.

The advantages of the 'weather gage' were that the smoke from the cannon dispersed more quickly, and it gave the fleet the moment of decision of when to commit the ships to battle. The 'leeward gage' was preferred by the French and Spanish navies because the ships tended to heel less, being partly covered by the ships to windward and making them more stable gun platforms. Most importantly, however, the leeward ships held the ability to pull out of the fight at any time of their choosing, the windward ships having to pass through the enemy ships before they could get away.

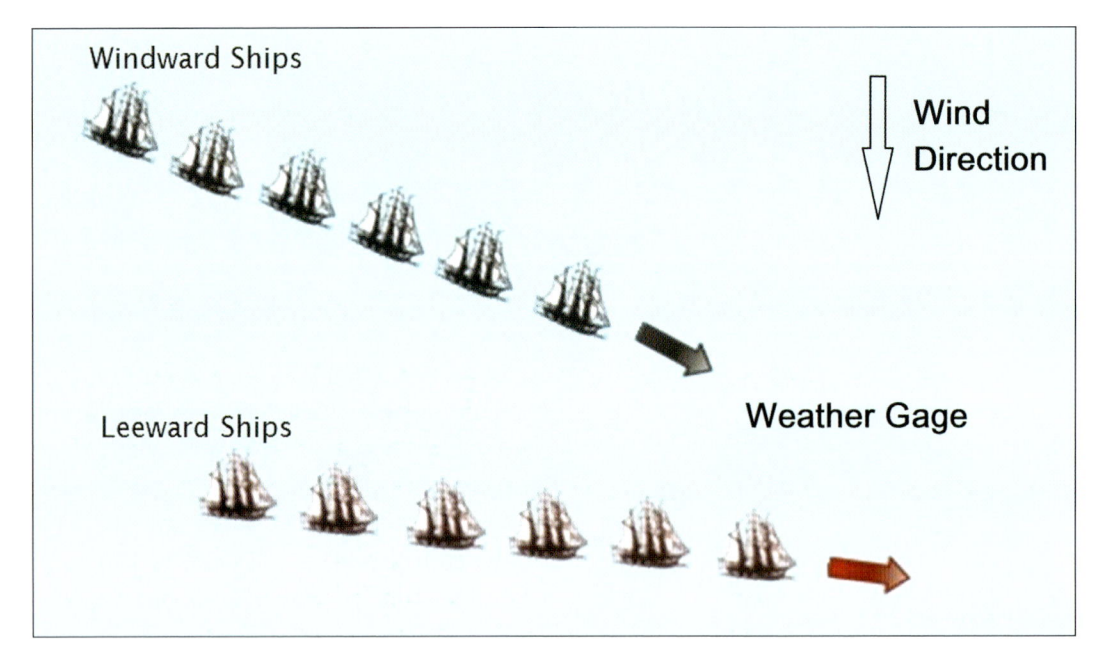

Diagram illustrating the 'weather gage'.

The linear tactics of the Battle of the Saintes, 1782.

The results of naval battles using rigid linear tactics were rarely decisive. The Battle of the Saintes in 1782 was seen as quite a decisive victory in regard to its results, but only four French ships were captured and one sunk. At the Battle of the Glorious First of June in 1794, six ships were captured and one sunk, whereas at the Battle of Cape St Vincent in 1797 four Spanish

WATER CASK CAPTURED FROM THE SPANISH

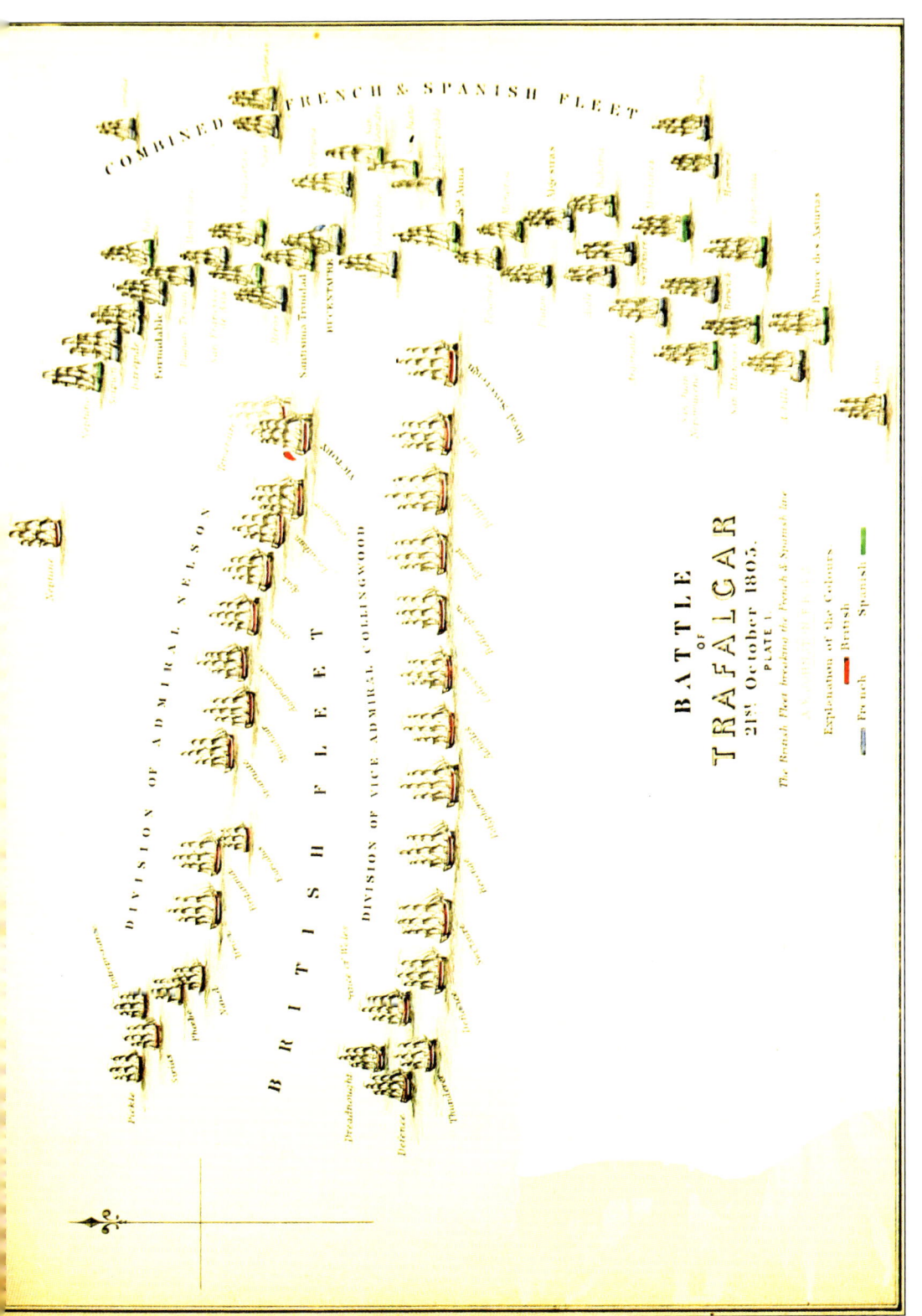

Nelson's fleet attacks in two lines at Trafalgar to overwhelm the centre and rear of the Franco-Spanish fleet.

ships were captured. The only decisive naval battle of this early period was Camperdown in the same year, where seven Dutch ships of the line were captured out of the eleven which fought there.

Admiral Lord Nelson is credited with radically altering British tactics, although the principle of sailing through the enemy line and 'breaking' it had been understood for two decades or more. But with the ships remaining in strict lines this still did not bring on a decisive outcome.

Nelson took this further, seeking not only to break the enemy line, but to concentrate his ships on the latter part of the enemy fleet, breaking up their formation and overwhelming it by concentration of firepower, before the enemy ships at the front of the line could turn back against the wind to its support. In Nelson's own words, he wanted to bring on a 'pell mell battle' in which his ships sought to come to a confused close-quarters battle, with a number of ships encircling an enemy ship so as to overwhelm it with superior gunnery and a much greater weight of broadsides. At the Nile eleven of the thirteen French ships were captured or destroyed, at Copenhagen three ships were sunk and twelve captured, almost destroying the enemy defensive line, and at Trafalgar no less than twenty-one warships were captured and one sunk, a stunning victory.

The Battle of Trafalgar – a 'pell mell' battle.

73

Powder Horn

Loading a heavy 32-pounder cannon weighing 56 cwt (2,845kg) on a wheeled gun carriage on a moving deck was very dangerous work. The potential of being crushed by a runaway cannon was an ever-present danger and a large crew, aided by a complex set of ropes and pulleys, was required to bring the cannon inboard for loading and then manoeuvring the barrel outboard again to fire in a controlled manner. This led to the term 'a loose cannon' entering the English language to describe someone who is unpredictable and liable to cause serious damage.

A 32-pounder, the largest cannon regularly used at sea during the Napoleonic Wars, was provided with a thirteen-man crew for each pair of guns (one on either side of the ship directly opposite each other), of which only numbers 1–8 had a specific role in preparing the gun for firing, the others simply supplying brawn when hauling the cannon out and to act as replacements for those killed or wounded. Gun teams for 24-pounders were usually of eleven men and 12-pounders had nine. All guns had a further man attached as the powder monkey, but he was not a part of the gun crew. The guns on both sides were run out ready to fire when in combat, but it was rare for a ship to fight both sides at the same time. One trick that helped the crews was to manoeuvre the gun in either direction 'downhill', with the roll of the ship, to preserve their energy during an extensive period of combat.

When loading a gun, the cannon was brought inward by loosening the two ropes attached to the ship's hull (side tackles) and pulling in on the rope attached to the rear of the carriage (train tackle) until the barrel was fully inboard. The port was opened outwards and the tompion removed from the muzzle of the cannon ready to load. The gun captain placed his thumb encased in a leather and horsehair stall over the vent to ensure that air could not enter and cause a premature explosion. The metal worm (like a giant corkscrew) was inserted into the barrel to scour out any residue powder and a wet sponge was then inserted to ensure that there were no still-burning embers in it. It was now ready to load.

A cartridge containing the gunpowder was inserted and pushed hard up to the end of the barrel using a rammer followed by the cannonball and then a wad to stop the cannonball rolling out with the heeling of the ship. The gun was now run out by hauling on the side tackles and easing off the train tackle, once secured everything was ready to fire. When about to fire, the gun captain pushed a metal 'pricker' down the vent hole to pierce the gunpowder cartridge. He then pushed a thin quill (the fuse) down the vent into the cartridge and filled this with gunpowder from his powder horn.

Aiming the gun and choosing the right moment in the ship's roll to fire was something only learnt from experience. When ready the gun captain lit the fuse, the cannon would fire and it would recoil backwards, which movement was checked by the side tackles and the process of cleaning out and reloading began again. Up until the middle of the seventeenth century, the gun captain still used a slow match to fire although this had long been superseded in the army by flintlocks. By the end of the century however, the navy was also using flintlocks with a lanyard attached. The gun captain pulled the lanyard, causing the flintlock to snap shut, striking a spark which lit the fuse and the cannon fired. The British navy trained to be able to fire about three times in five minutes, but such a rate of fire could not be maintained for any significant length of time before exhaustion forced the crew to slow down.

Some members of gun crews were also allocated for other duties as required, if the pumps needed to be manned, the sails trimmed, fires fought or boarders were required, then each crew would lose a proportion to these vital tasks, leaving a reduced crew to maintain the fight for as long as they could.

Some traditions have remained from these gun crews to this very day. 'Number 1' used today to denote the boss emanates from the gun captain who was always referred to as No. 1. Within the Royal Navy to this very day, the order to pull together on a rope is still 'Two – Six, Heave!' a reminder of the time when No. 2 and No. 6 in a 12-pounder gun crew hauled the gun out ready to fire.

Illustration of the ropes and pulleys required to load and fire a 32-pounder cannon and the positions taken by the thirteen-man gun crew.

74
Leather Tube for Carrying Powder Charges, HMS Ganges

In popular culture, boys on board naval ships are portrayed as 'powder monkeys' running up and down to the magazine, to transport gunpowder charges to the cannon, but this is a very distorted view of their roles.

Admiralty regulations actually specified the number of boys (referred to as Volunteers) allowed on each class of ship, with thirty-two on a First Rate, twenty-four on a 74-gun Third Rate and sixteen on large frigates. The boys were denoted as either Second Class, who were usually aged between 15 and 17 and worked on deck with the crew to learn the job, while Third Class were usually aged 11–14 and were employed as servants to the officers. The official age for boys to enlist was 13, but if their father already served on board, they were allowed to join at 11.

In action these young lads were often utilised to help deliver powder cartridges to the guns, but they were not alone, with any women on board and a number of the seamen also carrying out the role as a 'powder monkey'. However, dozens of hands running up and down the ladders between decks would cause terrible congestion and delays, while the boys were specifically banned from entering the magazines anyway.

Modern research shows that the cartridges were placed in the leather tubes as illustrated, (it contained two or three cartridges depending on the size of the gun) and were handed along a chain of 'powder monkeys' and passed up the ladders to the correct deck (the cartridges being previously prepared specifically for the size of guns on each deck). Here the 'monkeys' ran the cartridges along the gun deck, distributing a single cartridge to any powderman who was short of a cartridge in the closed wooden box behind each cannon, only being allowed to retain a maximum of two cartridges in the box for fear of explosions.

Another job was specifically carried out by the boys during hauling in the anchor cables. The huge hawsers were far too thick and heavy to be turned round a capstan, therefore a thinner, more flexible rope was tied to the hawser and as this was pulled in by the capstan, it hauled the anchor cable in with it. The short lengths of ropes tying the two cables together was called being 'nipped', as they were brought inboard these small ties were removed by the boys with a sharp knife, the boys becoming known as 'Nippers'.

The Marine Society, established in 1756, was a charitable organisation who supplied the vast majority of these boys, producing up to 600 young lads each year who were willing to embrace a life at sea, where they were fed and clothed far better than they could hope for ashore.

Another example of a powder monkey's cartridge holder.

… 75

Spanish Admiral Gravina's Personal Statement on the Battle of Cape Finisterre

By far the most important role of the Navy was the defence of the British Isles from the threat of invasion and therefore, until 1806, the Channel Fleet was the keystone of everything. However, the name of the Channel Fleet was actually a misnomer, as its area of responsibility extended from Selsey Bill near Portsmouth, out to beyond the southwestern tip of Ireland and also southward beyond the Bay of Biscay to Cape St Vincent in southern Portugal. Its importance was emphasised by the fact that even in 1812, when the invasion threat had gone, this fleet was still supervised personally by the commander-in-chief.

The Channel Fleet therefore had responsibility for watching the French naval bases of Brest, Rochefort, L'Orient, Le Havre and Cherbourg and the Spanish base at Ferrol. In 1795 it had consisted of twenty-six ships of the line including seven three-deckers and seventeen frigates, but as the invasion threat grew it increased in size, numbering some seventy-two warships in 1800, including three First Rates, eleven Second Rates, thirty-three other ships of the line, nineteen frigates and four sloops. By 1812, this fleet had reduced to fifteen ships of the line, fourteen frigates and three sloops. Because of its size and complexity, the fleet was

Blockading Brest.

commanded by a full admiral, with another as his deputy, and also included five rear admirals. This was because the fleet rarely functioned as a single unit, with squadrons blockading each of the French ports and only coming together at moments of heightened threat of invasion. It was normal to have the main fleet of around twenty ships of the line off Brest, with seven of the line off Rochefort and another seven off Ferrol, until Spain became an ally of Britain in 1808.

One reason why the Channel Fleet remained important until the very end of the Napoleonic Wars, was that ever since the defeat of the French fleet at the Glorious First of June in 1794, when six ships had been lost, the Brest fleet had remained as a very potent threat and had to be watched constantly. Up until 1800, when Lord St Vincent took command of the Navy, the blockade of Brest was carried on as an 'open blockade' whereby a few ships of the line and frigates watched the port, while the main fleet remained anchored in some sheltered spot off the English coast. St Vincent insisted on amending the policy to 'close blockade' when the fleet found itself constantly sailing along the very hazardous coast off Brest in all weathers, throughout the year. This visible threat to the French fleet did keep it pretty quiet, but at a great cost to the ships and men of the Channel Fleet, not just through wear and tear, but also

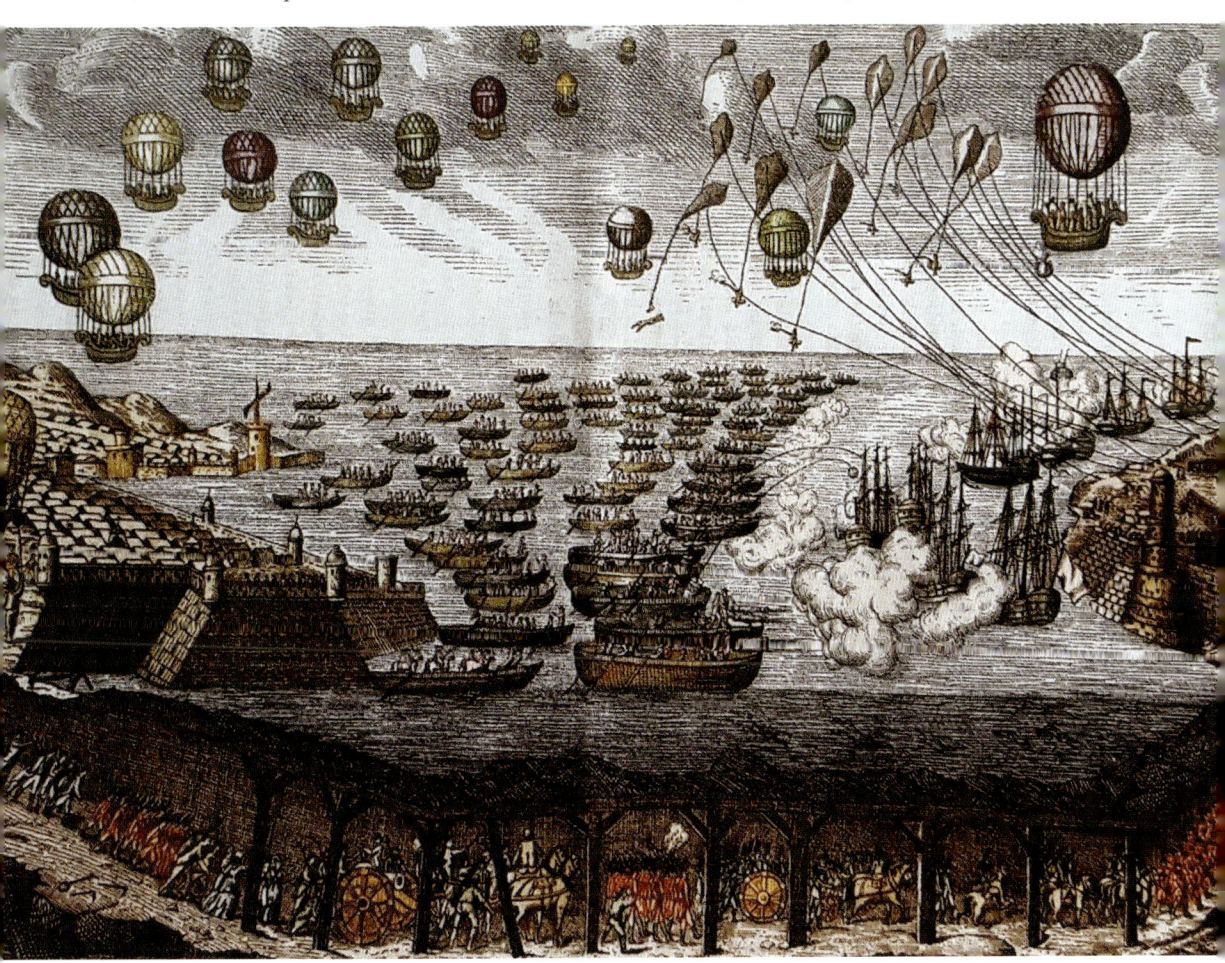

Various imagined ways in which Napoleon could invade Britain.

numerous shipwrecks which caused great loss of life. It was a very difficult and dangerous station, particularly through the autumn and winter and was dreaded and hated by crews, but it remained the policy until 1815.

Although officially separate commands, the ships protecting the Channel Islands (usually consisting of up to eleven frigates and sloops) and the Irish squadron based at Cork (fluctuating greatly throughout the war from ten to twenty-three ships, although rarely including more than one ship of the line) were effectively additional resources in the area. The Irish station was generally tasked with ensuring the safe passage of merchant shipping across the Atlantic.

The nearest this command came to a major fleet battle during the Napoleonic Wars was in 1805, when Admiral Calder encountered a Franco-Spanish squadron at Cape Finisterre, as it tried to manoeuvre towards the English Channel in July 1805. Calder's fifteen ships of the line faced a combined fleet of twenty French and Spanish ships. With poor weather and little visibility, the two squadrons fought a confused encounter battle in which two Spanish warships were captured, before Calder called off the action for the night. However, on the following day, with light winds and the threat of the Ferrol and Rochefort squadrons coming out to join the enemy squadron, Calder chose not to renew the engagement. He was subsequently court-martialled, severely reprimanded and never served again. The Franco-Spanish fleet was eventually destroyed by Nelson at Trafalgar in October 1805.

A further attempt to draw the French Brest fleet out in 1809 resulted in the Battle of the Basque Roads, when Admiral Gambier allowed Lord Cochrane to attack the fleet with fireships whilst anchored in the protected bay outside Brest. In the night attack, many of the French ships panicked and ran aground and four ships, including three ships of the line had to be destroyed, whilst most of the other French ships were damaged and required repairs in harbour. However, lack of support from Admiral Gambier saw the opportunity to destroy the French fleet in its entirety missed.

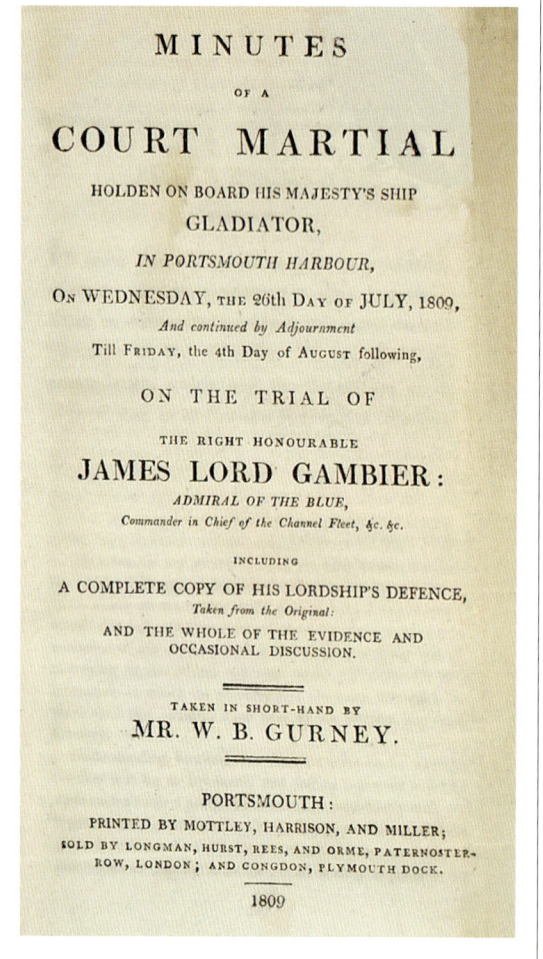

Transcript of Admiral Gambier's court martial after the action at Basque Roads – he was acquitted.

76

Identifying Flags Flown by Each Ship at the Battle of Camperdown

The North Sea Fleet was the second senior naval command and was for many years as important, if not more important at times, as the Channel Fleet in the defences to prevent invasion. Its name was again a misnomer, the command covering the English Channel east of Selsey Bill near Portsmouth and the entire North Sea, therefore the station had the primary responsibility for opposing the threatened invasion from Boulogne. The station was also required to keep watch over the Dutch fleet and their bases, which came under French control early in the wars.

A large fleet was also maintained on this station, with fifty-six ships allocated to it in 1797, including twenty ships of the line. This fleet won the stunning victory of Camperdown that year which largely eliminated the threat from this quarter for some years, although the extensive shipbuilding programme at Antwerp and other locations ensured that there was always a potent threat to Britain. The main fleet was serviced out of Deal for supplies and Chatham Dockyard for repairs, whilst the fleet generally remained at the anchorage of the

Downs. There were a small number of frigates and sloops based further north at Yarmouth and at Leith in Scotland, to provide protection for merchant shipping, particularly from privateers.

By 1805, with the increased fear of invasion, the North Sea Fleet had grown to no less than eighty warships, although many were smaller ships specifically designed to counter the French invasion craft, as it only included eleven ships of the line and twenty frigates. During the invasion threat, this fleet was divided with the main one at Dungeness to blockade the French invasion fleet at Boulogne and Etaples whilst another watched the Dutch coast in the vicinity of the Texel and the Scheldt.

The Baltic was a separate station in its own right, but it was not regularly patrolled for many years. Indeed, for decades, some Baltic countries, particularly Denmark, had successfully maintained their neutrality and with British trade flowing through the area without threat or hindrance, the Navy rarely sent its ships there. Things changed when the League of Armed Neutrality was declared, which caused Britain to react to ensure the continued free flow of vital naval stores from the region, the Navy obtaining the majority of its masts and hemp from the region.

Contemporary print of the British North Sea Fleet watching the French invasion force in 1804.

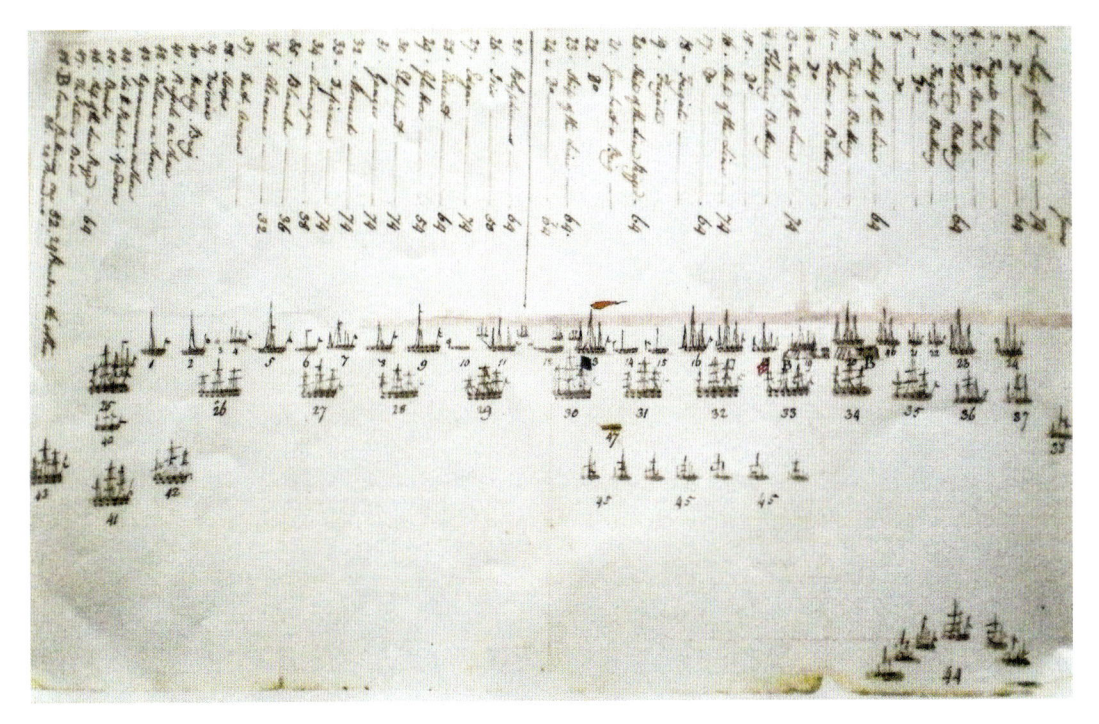

Hand-drawn plan of the Battle of Copenhagen by Captain Fremantle in 1801.

When an initial attempt was made to keep the Russian Tsar on side, by sending Captain Sir Home Popham to St Petersburg in 1799, the Navy discovered that they had no recent charts of that sea, the last known naval deployment to the Baltic having occurred in 1700. By 1801 a British fleet had sailed into the Baltic, Admiral Nelson defeating the Danish reserve fleet at the Battle of Copenhagen, before sailing on to 'persuade' Russia to abandon the league. With the murder of the Tsar at Russian hands, the crisis ended, but the tensions did not subside.

With Napoleon's control of Europe almost complete by 1807 and with Russia becoming an ally, Britain feared that the French would snap up the Danish and Portuguese fleets, despite those countries declaring themselves neutral. Pre-empting such a move, the British government sought to persuade the Danes to hand over their fleet for 'safe keeping'. Not surprisingly the Danes refused to simply hand over their ships and in 1807, a huge fleet commanded by Admiral Gambier transported a sizeable army to Denmark, which bombarded the city of Copenhagen, forcing the Danes to surrender. The Danish fleet and all naval stores were removed to Britain, although few of the ships were deemed in a suitable condition to be taken into the Royal Navy as anything more than prison hulks.

Perhaps unsurprisingly, Denmark continued a bitter naval struggle against the British until the end of the Napoleonic Wars. Unable to match the Royal Navy in ships of the line, the Danish Navy re-invented itself by building hundreds of small gunboats, armed with two or three cannon and powered by sail or oars. In the twisting, narrow waterways of the two channels allowing access from the North Sea into the Baltic, swarms of these gunboats proved themselves to be a serious hazard for British merchant ships. It was found necessary for the Navy to supply a limited number of line of battle ships and a very large

A British brig under attack from Danish gunboats.

number of frigates, brigs and sloops to counter this threat. In the absolute calms that sometimes occur in the Baltic, when the sea resembles a sheet of glass, sailing vessels were in serious trouble if attacked by these oared gunboats, which could manoeuvre into position to rake British warships. Indeed, a large number of vessels were captured, including Royal Navy sloops and brigs, some larger warships only avoiding the ignominy of defeat by a huge effort from the ships' crews and their own boats, turning the warship into a position where they could fire on the Danish gunboats. This gunboat war was acclaimed by the Danes as a huge morale-boosting victory over a Goliath of an enemy and is often still portrayed in this light. However, although the Danish gunboats did cause problems, the institution of a heavily-escorted convoy system through the Baltic successfully saw vast amounts of British merchant shipping safely through these seas and ensured that the Danish effort had little if any effect on the overall war effort, although it did tie up a significant number of warships. In 1812 for example, the Baltic command consisted of thirty-nine ships, including ten of the line, six frigates and fourteen sloops.

77
Naval Dockyard, Bermuda

As the Navy expanded across the world and maintained fleets in distant waters, there was an urgent demand for dockyard facilities in these far-flung corners of the world. Other key facilities were set up at particular ports in the world, which held significant strategic positions, giving them control of these vital shipping lanes. This allowed Britain to protect its own ships at these vital choke points and also gave her significant influence over other trading nations who were also forced to plough these same waters.

These bases were ideally situated on islands which could be easily defended or in well-established colonies where the threat was low. None of these bases had anything like the facilities of the major

British dockyards and had no manufacturing facilities but worked well as forward repair bases. Most of the skilled workforce in these overseas bases, such as shipwrights and caulkers, were supplied from Britian, but the workforce could be easily expanded using local carpenters and labourers. In the West Indies slaves were bought as boys and trained as caulkers and carpenters to work in the yards and after three years they were given a wage, although not granted their freedom.

Gibraltar was an early base, having been captured in 1704 and its possession confirmed by treaty in 1713, which gave a relatively secure anchorage for warships and allowed the Navy to control access in and out of the Mediterranean. This was too far from the French base at Toulon for the British fleet watching them and bases were set up at Corsica, Mahon in the Balearic Islands, and on Elba for short periods. Later with the capture of Malta, Britain controlled the passage throughout the Mediterranean Sea.

In the West Indies, the first base established was at Antigua, a good anchorage where ships could clean the hulls in safety, and a second base was established at Port Royal in Jamaica. In 1809 contruction began on a much bigger base with dockyard facilities on Bermuda giving Britain first class facilities in the West Indies for the first time, when it was completed in 1814.

The Cape of Good Hope was a Dutch colony, it was captured in 1795, but returned to the Dutch at the Peace of Amiens in 1802. When war broke out again the following year, it soon became a target and was successfully captured in 1806 and retained permanently this time. This gave Britain protection for her Indian convoys, but also controlled access to the Indian Ocean for other nations. The base at Cape Town was however never sizeable, forming more of a supply depot.

Gibraltar.

NAVAL DOCKYARD, BERMUDA

British vessels at Mahon.

Nelson's Dockyard, Antigua.

The Cape of Good Hope.

Bombay Harbour.

It was also important to establish bases in India and facilities were constructed at both Bombay and Madras. In 1806 Bombay had a dry dock sufficient for a 74, a ropewalk, smithy, hospital, gaol and storehouses and employed a mostly native workforce. The dockyard also started building warships in teak including the 74-gun *Cornwallis*, completed in 1813.

One other large base was established at Halifax in Nova Scotia to service the ships in Canada and other small bases were set up at Barbados, at Martinique when in British hands from 1794 till 1802 and Heligoland off the German coast when it was captured in 1807 and developed slowly.

78

Contemporary Print of the Main Deck of a Warship with Women On Board

A SCENE ON THE MAIN DECK.

Many assume that the Georgian Navy's warships were simply no-go areas for women, but that is simply wrong. It is true that the Admiralty regulations discouraged allowing women at sea, stating that '. . . no women be ever permitted to be on board but such as are really the wives of the men they come to, and the ship not too much pestered even with them'. However, in reality a number of women were on board warships for extended periods and not just the ladies of 'dubious character' who were allowed on board in harbour.

Warrant officers who were permanently attached to a specific ship for the entirety of the ship's commissioned life regularly took their wives and even their children to sea with them, who were accommodated in their small cabins.

They were not officially allowed on board and they did not receive a ration from the Navy, but it is clear from the records of court martials and other documents that women were on board routinely.

Some men also secreted their women on board and having sailed, revealed their presence when too far from Britain for them to be returned easily. These seem to have then been tolerated on board. Life for these women was not easy, however, as they had to share their man's cramped hammock and were not officially granted a ration, having to share their partner's.

Childbirth was not uncommon at sea, and in difficult births the sound of cannon fire was thought to help. Captain Glascock wrote, 'This day the surgeon informed me that a woman

211

on board had been labouring in childbirth for twelve hours, and if I could see my way to permit the firing of a broadside to leeward, nature would be assisted by the shock. I complied with the request, and she was delivered a fine male child.' It is believed that this may be the origin of the term 'son of a gun'.

As many ships' captains could not trust their crews with shore leave, especially abroad, the officers often turned a blind eye to the numerous prostitutes who came out in the 'bumboats' and were allowed on board for the sailors to enjoy their company. At such times, virtually all discipline on the lower decks was relaxed and the officers simply ensured that the inevitable arguments and fights did not get too out of hand. At Portsmouth these ladies were known as 'Portsmouth Polls' and whilst they were on board, the noise was apparently deafening, one sailor recording that 'the coarsest seamen on board were far outdone by those damsels'.

There were also a small number of women who disguised themselves as men and served officially on board ship. How they contrived to avoid being detected is difficult to explain on such crowded decks and some are undoubtedly myths, but there are a number of attested cases. One such case involved Hannah Snell from Worcester, who originally joined the Army in 1745 but deserted. She then enlisted in the Royal Marines and was badly wounded in both thighs but was apparently still not discovered. In 1750 she apparently revealed her true identity and was discharged from the Marines, having a successful career on the stage on the back of her celebrity status.

In 1815 a newspaper claimed that William Brown who had served on HMS *Queen Charlotte* for 11 years only revealing her sex on being discharged at the end of the war. She was described as being 5ft 4in (162cm), strong and burly and took her grog as well as any man. However, it has since been established that she

A bumboat carrying prostitutes out to the warships.

only joined the ship in May 1815, her identity was discovered after only a few weeks and she was discharged. Captain Beaver of HMS *Nisus* became suspicious of his boy steward in 1810 and discovered that he was actually a buxom young girl. She was sent home at the earliest opportunity.

When transporting Army units, additional women would be on board as six women per 100 men were allowed to travel with them and could bring their children as well. As an example of this, in Egypt in 1801 HMS *Charon* recorded having thirty women and twenty children of the 30th Regiment on board. During the Battle of the Nile in 1798, a sailor named John Nicol records that a lady from Leith in Scotland was severely injured whilst helping to serve the guns of HMS *Goliath* and subsequently died of her wounds.

Those women who openly stayed on board often helped out with the wounded during battles. An incident recorded on board HMS *Swallow* in 1812 records the death of another woman during battle. Louise, the wife of seaman John Phelan, and her baby were in the surgeon's cockpit during a battle with the French *Reynard*, when she received word that her husband was

Francesca Scanagalla (alias William Brown).

severely wounded. Leaving the baby with the surgeon, Louise went to her dying husband and cradled him in her arms, only to have her head taken off by a cannonball. The crew adopted the orphan child and fed it on the captain's goat's milk, but we do not know if the child survived.

79

Ship's Chronometer from Baudin's Expedition to Australia

Scientific discovery and the pursuit of greater human knowledge was seen throughout the enlightened late eighteenth and early nineteenth centuries to be a very noble cause, the pursuit of which should not be curtailed by national boundaries. In this spirit, voyages of exploration were regularly sent out by many European navies and the scientific discoveries freely shared amongst academic institutes throughout Europe. These ventures were forced to stop during wartime, which for France and Britain was most of the time, although expeditions which began in peacetime were allowed to complete their missions without interference if war broke out later.

However, in 1800 Napoleon sent an expedition with two ships, the *Naturaliste* and the *Géographe*, under the command of Captain Nicolas Baudin to Australia (or New Holland as it was then known) to continue surveys there of the coast, fauna and flora. Soon after in 1801 HMS *Investigator* was also sent to Australia under the command of Captain Matthew Flinders to establish whether it was an island or a peninsula by attempting to sail around it. Both of these expeditions were sent out accompanied by a letter granting them safe passage if they encountered enemy ships, signed by Napoleon and the British Admiralty. Both expeditions arrived in southern Australian waters and began surveying the coastline, without any coordination Baudin's ships sailed clockwise around Australia, while Flinders sailed anti-clockwise. Finally they met each other in April 1802 near modern-day Adelaide (the meeting point being named Encounter Bay to mark the occasion) and having exchanged pleasantries and some of their discoveries they again parted company to continue their work.

Baudin was able to resupply at Port Jackson (Sydney Harbour) from the British settlement there and sending the *Naturaliste* home fully laden with discoveries in 1802, the *Géographe* continued to explore before heading home herself a year later. Unfortunately, Baudin died on the voyage home, but the ship arrived safely in France in 1804. The expedition was viewed as a great success, with over 2,500 new species discovered.

Flinders successfully circumnavigated Australia in 1803 proving that it was a separate continent,

Investigator and *Géographe* meet in Encounter Bay.

A study of wildlife on the Baudin expedition of 1803.

but with his ship leaking badly, he was unable to sail *Investigator* back to Britain. Flinders took command of a tiny schooner named HMS *Cumberland* to sail home, but was forced to put in at the French Isle de France (Mauritius) for repairs. The governor, General Decaen, refused to accept his papers as they were made out for the *Investigator* and he placed Flinders under arrest, confiscating all of his papers and ship's logs. Despite orders from France to release Flinders, he was not released until 1810 in poor health. Flinders set to, publishing maps and a full account of his expedition in 1814, just before his death from kidney disease. His remains, lost due to major redevelopment of London have recently been rediscovered during the preliminary works for the lengthening of Euston Station in preparation for the HS2 project.

A Russian expedition in two ships named *Nadezhda* and *Neva* was intended to circumnavigate the world with the view of establishing links between the Russian mainland and Alaska, then a Russian possession, and to establish trade links with Japan. During their surveying of the American east coast, Baron von Langsdorff was landed to explore the interior of Alaska and a great number of specimens were shipped to St Petersburg. The expedition continued from 1803 to 1806 in the Pacific, then little frequented by British or French ships, and there is little evidence that any safe passages were arranged, although Britain was an ally during this period. The results of the expedition were published by Langsdorff in Frankfurt in 1812.

The Russian sloop *Neva* off Alaska.

80

Gravestones in the Naval Cemetery at Gibraltar

Apart from the fleet stationed in the English Channel, the Mediterranean Fleet ranked as the most important station in the world and as the Napoleonic Wars progressed it grew continuously in size. It was always given prominence with regard to the seniority of the admiral given the command, with such eminent officers as Admirals Hood, Hotham, St Vincent, Nelson, Collingwood, Cotton and Pellew commanding in succession. The Mediterranean Fleet also fought three major battles and a number of other major conflicts were centred around this sea, far more than any other station.

The Station not only covered the Mediterranean itself, but also extended out into the Atlantic towards the West Indies and northward to Cape St Vincent. This meant that the Mediterranean Fleet had the unenviable task of monitoring the main French naval base at Toulon, but also had to watch not only the Spanish naval base in the Mediterranean at Cartagena but their main naval base on the Atlantic coast at Cadiz. Therefore, it was only in the periods where Britain and Spain were allied, that the Mediterranean Fleet was not split, watching these different fleets.

Gibraltar had been the headquarters of the Mediterranean Station ever since its capture from the Spanish in 1704, its location at the entrance to that sea giving it a unique strategic position. However, the dockyard here had not been greatly developed and it could only cater for a small number of ships alongside at any one time and it had no docking facilities.

Its position on the periphery of the Mediterranean and quite some way from the French base at Toulon meant that the British constantly sought a forward base in the western Mediterranean at which the ships watching Toulon could shelter from storms and resupply.

At various periods, Mahon in the Spanish Balearic Islands, Corsica and Elba were used as forward bases, but unfortunately none of these bases proved to be long term, given the fluctuating politics and the fortunes of war in this region. Indeed, by the end of 1796 Sir John Jervis's fleet was so outnumbered by the enemy, that the Royal Navy was forced to abandon that sea in its entirety. The only permanent base remained in Gibraltar.

However, the fortunes of the Navy began to improve following the defeat of the Spanish Cadiz fleet at the Battle of Cape St Vincent in February 1797 and by the end of that year Nelson was commanding a fleet in the Mediterranean again and having destroyed the French fleet at the Battle of the Nile in 1798, Britain rapidly reasserted its dominance in this sea. The capture of the island of Malta in 1800 sealed British dominance of the western Mediterranean and effectively gave Britain the

The Blockade of Toulon.

keys to the Eastern Mediterranean, an advantage they would consequently use more and more as the war progressed, to the point where the Mediterranean effectively became a British lake. Headquarters of the Mediterranean Station soon moved to Malta which had a much larger and better protected bay than Gibraltar and a good sized naval dockyard previously set up by the Knights of St John. A prize court was also established here to deal with the huge number of coastal vessels captured. With control of Gibraltar and Malta, the Royal Navy retained its dominance in the Mediterranean for over 150 years.

With such dominance, the Navy also began to exert a significant effect on the land war in southern Europe. French forces in eastern Spain, Italy and the Adriatic were heavily dependent on coastal shipping to maintain their supply routes, the land routes being in a poor condition and very difficult. With the French fleet essentially bottled up in Toulon permanently after 1805, the Navy swamped the entire Mediterranean with frigates and sloops to destroy the coastal trade. The Adriatic and the east coast of Spain soon became very lucrative hunting grounds for these crews, with huge amounts of prize money being earnt. French attempts to disrupt this work were finally brought to an end when the frigate battle of Lissa in 1811 led to the annihilation of a superior French squadron of eleven ships by a British squadron of only four, finally giving the Navy complete and unchallenged mastery of the Adriatic.

As proof of the ever-increasing importance of the Mediterranean to the Navy, the size of the fleet that returned to that sea after the victory of Cape St Vincent in 1797 was no

View of Gibraltar.

The Naval Dockyard at Malta.

The Battle of Lissa, 1811.

less than twenty-three ships of the line, twenty-four frigates and ten sloops. At that time this was the largest single command in the entire Navy. However, with the army becoming increasingly involved in the Mediterranean on a permanent basis after 1806, the fleet continued to grow significantly in Sicily, the East Coast of Spain and the Adriatic Islands. In 1812, there were no less than ninety ships on the Station, including twenty-nine of the line, twenty-nine frigates and twenty-six sloops.

Such a continuous high level of naval personnel inevitably led to many men and their families succumbing to disease or wounds whilst on this station and they were buried in the naval cemeteries on Malta and at Gibraltar. The naval cemetery at Gibraltar has now been renamed the Trafalgar Cemetery as those who died of their wounds were buried there, those that died at the time of the battle being buried at sea as was normal.

Grave of Charlotte Bolton, wife of Thomas, of the Navy Victualling Office at Gibraltar.

81

Contemporary View of the Naval Base at Halifax, Nova Scotia, in 1804

Commissioners House, in the Naval Yard, Halifax.

A squadron was originally established in the area in 1745 in response to the French threat in the region. In 1759 a permanent naval yard had been established at Halifax, Nova Scotia and in 1767, this was designated as the North American Station, with its headquarters established there. However, it was a small squadron of only four ships, all of less than 32 guns, and another squadron at Newfoundland consisted of one 64, three frigates and five sloops.

With American independence, a further naval base was established at Bermuda, being part way between Halifax and the West Indian islands. This took some time as underwater surveys had to be completed to establish safe channels for the larger warships, but by 1794 the base established at St George's was designated as the new headquarters for the North American Station.

Land was purchased in the vicinity of Ireland Island on the western end of Bermuda to construct the Royal Naval dockyard, but construction of the base only began in 1813 and continued in a haphazard way throughout the nineteenth century.

Three 12-gun sloops were built in 1795 at Bermuda and commissioned as HMS *Dasher*, *Driver* and *Bermuda*, intended for anti-piracy operations. A large number of these Bermudian sloops were eventually constructed for the Navy

CONTEMPORARY VIEW OF THE NAVAL BASE

St George's Harbour, Bermuda.

The naval base on Ireland Island, Bermuda.

The Naval Dockyard, Bermuda.

A Bermuda sloop.

as 'Advice ships' carrying messages very rapidly across the Atlantic.

During the war against America from 1812 to 1815, Bermuda was the headquarters of the operation and the raids on Alexandria, Baltimore and Washington DC set out from here. The station grew dramatically in importance and in mid-1813, there were no less than sixty naval vessels including eleven Third Rates, sixteen Fifth Rates and twenty-five sloops. Bermudian privateers captured 298 American merchant vessels during the war.

82

Some of the Huge Treasure of Gold and Silver On Board the Nuestra Senora De Las Mercedes

The prospect of prize money was used as a major incentive to get seamen to join the Navy but it was the senior officers who gained the most in this lucrative business.

The legal capture of an enemy vessel in wartime was an ancient rite, with Admiralty prize courts being set up in stations around the world, to adjudicate on the legality of the capture, the ships with a legal claim to a share (all Royal Navy ships in view were deemed to be involved) and the value of the prize. In the case of merchant ships prize money was calculated from the value of the vessel and its cargo, whereas in the case of the capture of a warship, a fair price was agreed with the Admiralty for the value of the warship, its guns and stores plus a head count of £5 per enemy sailor captured.

The total value of the prize was then distributed in eighths

- One eighth went to the Admiral or senior officer under whose orders the ship sailed, but if the orders came direct from the Admiralty this eighth went to the captain of the ship.
- Two eighths went to the captain of the ship.
- One eighth was shared by the lieutenants, master and captain of Marines.
- One eighth was divided amongst all of the wardroom warrant officers, lieutenants of Marines and master's mates.
- One eighth was divided amongst the junior warrant officers, petty officers, clerks, mates, midshipmen and sergeants of Marines.

The last two eighths were divided amongst all of the sailors, Marines and boys, but not equally. This sum was further divided into shares, with able seamen being given two shares, ordinary seamen getting 1½, landsmen receiving a share and boys ½ a share. In a single-ship action, this could be very lucrative, but in fleet actions large numbers of ships shared the prize money and the payout was therefore often quite small. For this reason, command of a frigate in distant waters, without consorts and outside the control of an admiral, was a highly sought-after commission and many naval dynasties were founded on the huge amounts of prize money that was earned.

Private ships could also be legally fitted out with large crews and heavily armed to act as 'privateers'. Governments were allowed to issue 'Letters of Marque' to these vessels, effectively turning these ships into private warships, who sailed the seas purely with the aim of capturing enemy vessels for the prize money generated. Some of these vessels made huge profits for their owners and the crews.

It was therefore highly desirable to capture enemy ships rather than sink them, when no

The capture of the treasure fleet and the destruction of *Nuestra Senora de las Mercedes* in 1804.

Steel's Prize Pay Lists frontispiece.

prize money could be allocated. This led to many boarding operations, with fierce hand-to-hand combat, in order to capture the enemy vessel intact.

The highest amount of prize money awarded for an individual capture is believed to be the capture of the Spanish frigate *Hermione* in 1762 which was carrying bullion worth £1 million (£110 million today), when the captains of HMS *Active* and *Favourite* each received the astonishing sum of £65,000 each (nearly £7 million today) while the money for the ordinary sailors worked out at £485 per share (just over £50,000 today).

Another of the biggest prize money payouts was made to Commodore Graham Moore

> **PAYMENTS IN 1797.** 27
>
> retaken 4 and 14 July, 1797; paid, on board, at Spithead, August 16. Recall, at Mr. Maxwell's, Portsmouth. J. P. Maxwell, agent.
>
> 329. HAZARD. sp. 16, A. Ruddach....Hull and stores of Le Hardi, French brig, taken 1 April, 1797; paid, on board, on arrival at Plymouth after 12 August. Recall, at Mr. J. Drury's, Cove. E. Vidal and J. Drury, agents.
>
> 330. ST. FIORENRO, 40, Sir H. Neale, Bart; and LA NYMPHE, 36, J. Cooke....Produce of hulls, head-money, and stores of La Resistance and La Constance, French frigates, taken 9 March, 1797; paid, on board, on arrival after 12 August. Recall, at No. 7, Beaufort Buildings, London. C. Cooke, H. Darby, and S. Hemmans, agents to St. Fiorenzo; C. Cooke and S. Hemmans, to La Nymphe.
>
> 331. ARROW, sp. 18, N. Portlock....Proceeds of the French ships, La Jeune Albe, and Les Sept Freres, taken 1 June, 1797; paid, on board, at Spithead, 28 August. Recall, by Mr. J. P. Maxwell, Portsmouth, agent.
>
> 332. KANGUROO, bg. 18, Hon. C. Boyle....Hull and stores of La Sophie, French privateer, taken 9 April, 1797; paid, on board, at Plymouth, 25 Aug. Recall, last Saturdays, at the White Lion, Wych Street, London. John Druce, London, and James James, Merazion, agents.
>
> And salvage of the Macaroni, of Dartmouth, retaken, July, 1797; paid, on board, at Plymouth, 1 Sept. Recall, as above. J. Druce, agent.
>
> 333. LA POMONE, 44, Sir J. B. Warren; ARTOIS, 38, Sir E. Nagle; GALATEA, 32, R. G. Keats; and ANSON. 44, P. C. Durham...Final distribution of ordnance stores of L'Etoile and La Robuste, French corvettes, taken 20 March, and 26 April, 1796; paid, 6 Sept. Recall, every Thursday, at the Fountain Tavern, Plymouth Dock. Samuel Hemmans, agent.
>
> 334. JASON, 38, Charles Stirling....Final distribution of ordnance stores of La Robuste, above mentioned (333), with proceeds of the Pacific, taken 14 May; of the Lodoiska, taken 22 May; and of La Fantasie, French privateer, taken 25 May, 1796, in company with Sir J. B. Warren's squadron; paid, on board, at Falmouth, 1 September, or on arrival. Recall, last Saturdays, at the White Lion, Wych Street, London. Walter Stirling, agent.
>
> 335. INDEFATIGABLE, 44, Sir E. Pellew, Bart.; and AMAZON, 36, R. C. Reynolds....Proceeds of the Pacquet Sangossee, taken in January, 1797; paid, 29 August, to the Indefatigable, on board, at Falmouth; and to the Amazon, at Messrs. Poulain and Keys, London. Recall, for both, every Thursday, No. 3, Salters Hall Court, London. Agents—*Indefatigable*, Jos. Hunt, and S. Pellew; *Amazon*, S. Pellew, and J. Tippett.
>
> 336. INDEFATIGABLE, 44, Sir Edw. Pellew, Bart.; AMAZON, 36, R. C. Reynolds; REVOLUTIONAIRE, 44, F. Cole; and PHŒBE, 36, R. Barlow....Hull, stores, and head-money of La Revanche, French privateer, taken, and salvage of the Queen of Naples, retaken, 2 October, 1796, in company with the Jason, 38; paid, on board, 29 August. Recall, every Thursday, at Messrs. Poulain and Keys, London. Agents—*Indefatigable* and *Amazon* as above (335); *Revolutionaire*, J. Cole; *Phœbe*, S. Pellew.
>
> 337. RAVEN, brig, 18, W. Prowse....Proceeds of the N. S. del Caridad, Spanish ship, and of the Santa Natalia, Spanish brig, taken 3 and 5 January, 1797, in company with the Niger, 32; paid, on board, at Sheerness. 5 September. Recall, first Fridays, at Messrs. Maudes, Westminster. Thomas Maude, agent.
>
> 338. NIGER, 32, E. J. Foote....Proceeds of the N. S. del Caridad, above mentioned (337); paid, on board, 2 Sept. Recall, and agent, as to the Raven.
>
> 339. RAVEN, bg. 18, W. Prowse....Proceeds of the N. S. de la Misericordia, Spanish ship, and cargo, taken 2 Jan. 1797, in company with the Niger, 32, and several others; paid, on board, at Sheerness, 5 September. Recall, at No. 7, Beaufort Buildings, London. Chr. Cooke and R. Duncan, agents.
>
> 340. INCONSTANT, 36, T. F. Fremantle....Hull, ordnance stores, and head-money of L'Unite, French frigate, taken 26 April, 1796; paid, on board, at Woolwich, 26 August. Recall, at No. 7, Beaufort Buildings, London. C. Cooke, G. Purvis, and R. Beddek, agents.
>
> 341. STATELY, 64, B. Douglas; RATTLESNAKE, sp. 16, E. Ramage; and ECHO, sp. 16, John Turner....Hull and stores of the Carolina, Dutch ship, taken 28 May, with hull, stores, and head-money of La Milanie, French privateer, taken 7 July, 1796; paid, 15 September, at Mr. Jackson's, Union Court, Broad Street, London. Recall, first Thursdays, at same place. John Jackson and Hon. W. Elphinstone, agents.
>
> 342. UNICORN, 32, Sir T. Williams; and DRUID, 32, E. Codrington....Hull, stores, and head-money of L'Orient, French frigate, taken 7 January, with head-money of L'Eclair, French privateer, taken 11 January, 1797; paid, on board respectively, 6 September, or on arrival. Recall, first Saturdays, at Mr. Ancrum's, Chatham Place, Walworth. Agents—*Unicorn*, J. S. Ancrum and E. Vidal; *Druid*, J. S. Ancrum, E. Vidal, and J. Roche, jun.

A page from *Steel's Prize Pay Lists* for 1797.

(brother of General Sir John Moore) and the crew of his squadron in 1804. Under the terms of a secret convention Spain was required to pay France 72 million francs per annum until Spain declared war on Britain. Intelligence of the deal and knowledge that the treasure would be shipped from South America to Cadiz allowed Graham to place his four frigates in position to intercept the four Spanish vessels heavily loaded with gold and silver and capture them peacefully if at all possible. After a number of days patrolling off Cadiz, the Spanish ships were sighted on 5 October and Moore manoeuvred his ships close alongside. As Britain was not at war with Spain, Graham sent an officer on board the Spanish flagship demanding they surrender, on the premise that the treasure was on route to France, an enemy of Britain. The Spanish Admiral Bustamante refused and Moore ordered a shot to be fired across the bows of the Spanish ships. This caused the Spaniards to open fire and a major battle soon developed. Within ten minutes the Spanish frigate *Nuestra Senora de las Mercedes* blew up and sank, killing most of her crew, and the other three Spanish ships were eventually forced to surrender and were taken to Portsmouth. The four Spanish ships had been carrying nearly 4.3 million gold and silver Spanish dollars, 150,000 gold ingots plus 75 sacks of wool, 1,600 bars of tin and a large amount of copper. Even though one-quarter of this treasure went to the bottom with the *Nuestra Senora*, what remained was valued at £900,000 (around £45 million today). As Britain was not at war with Spain, prize money could not legally be issued, but an ex gratia payment was made to the crews totalling £160,000 (about £8 million today) of which Graham as commodore received £15,000 (£700,000 today). Spain promptly declared war on Britain and the Spanish treasure fleets stopped sailing for ever.

The wreck of the *Nuestra Senora de las Mercedes* was discovered in 2007 by an American Exploration company and 500,000 coins were recovered and secretly moved to the USA. However, following a protracted court case, the treasure was returned to Spain and the majority of it is now on display at the Underwater Archaeological Museum in Cartagena. Given the Admiralty valuation of £45 million in today's terms for the cargo of three ships, it is strange that the official valuation of the treasure recovered from this one ship is over £360 million!

Victorian Photograph of Three Hulks Moored at Plymouth

A major problem thrown up by the war was the vast numbers of prisoners that had to be accommodated in Britain and a number of solutions were employed, not all of which were entirely satisfactory. Until 1802, the numbers of prisoners had been kept relatively low thanks to exchanges of prisoners with the French, Spanish and Dutch governments, and then with the Peace of Amiens, all prisoners were released. But when war broke out again in 1803, the situation rapidly changed, as Napoleon refused to allow prisoner exchanges and actively encouraged his officers to break their parole and escape. Between 1803 and 1814, over 122,000 prisoners of war were brought to Britain of which some 10,000 died in captivity and another 17,000 were released or paroled on humanitarian grounds. In comparison there were only about 15,000 British prisoners of war in France during this period. The numbers of prisoners of war in Britain grew markedly after 1810 as the land war turned in their favour and with the outbreak of war against America in 1812, the numbers of prisoners rose from 43,000 in 1810 to a staggering 95,000 in 1814.

These numbers put a huge burden on the Transport Board which had been given responsibility for the detention and care of prisoners of war. Officers were allowed to live a relatively normal life within the marked boundaries of 'parole towns' having given their 'parole', by which they swore not to escape or to serve against Britain until regularly exchanged. The system continued in Britain, despite the fact that Napoleon encouraged his officers to break parole and there were a number of high-profile escapes recorded.

This was not, however, an option for the ordinary soldier or sailor and therefore a large number of prison facilities were needed and quickly. In most European countries, the hulks of old warships had been used as temporary prisons for civilian offenders in times of unrest, Britain was using hulks from 1775 onwards to relieve the pressure on the prisons, so when the huge influx of prisoners of war began to arrive, it was natural that the hulks would be looked upon as a temporary solution to an urgent problem. The hulks used were the larger vessels of over sixty guns and many captured enemy ships, too badly damaged to be made seaworthy again without huge cost were added to the numbers. At Plymouth eighteen hulks were used, at Portsmouth another twenty and at Chatham twenty-three were used to house prisoners for at least part of this period.

The French propaganda machine made a particular point of demonising the British prison hulks, but it is true that they were very cramped, damp and rat-infested, with some hulks being commanded by vicious petty-minded tyrants. They did, however, overstate the conditions, the Transport Board being at great pains to feed and clothe the prisoners adequately, but the great propensity to gamble

Prison hulks moored at Portsmouth.

among the prisoners, even to the clothes on their back and their food, was certainly a significant factor in the death rates on board. Two wrongs do not make a right, but it must be emphasised that the French treatment of British prisoners of war, held in cold, damp fortresses, could not be described as any better.

Guarding these prisoners was also a major drain on naval resources, with each hulk usually staffed by just over thirty officers and seamen and a party of about forty Marines or army veterans to guard between 500 and 700 prisoners.

A lieutenant commanded the hulk, and each had a master, gunner, boatswain, purser, cook, surgeon, steward, two midshipmen, a master's mate and a clerk assigned to it, all of whom the Navy could ill afford to spare. Some attempt to house prisoners of war in better conditions had begun with the construction of the first purpose-built prisoner of war camps in the world at Norman Cross in 1796 and others soon existed at Millbay in Plymouth, Forton and Stapleton near Bristol, but the numbers of prisoners simply continued to overwhelm the system.

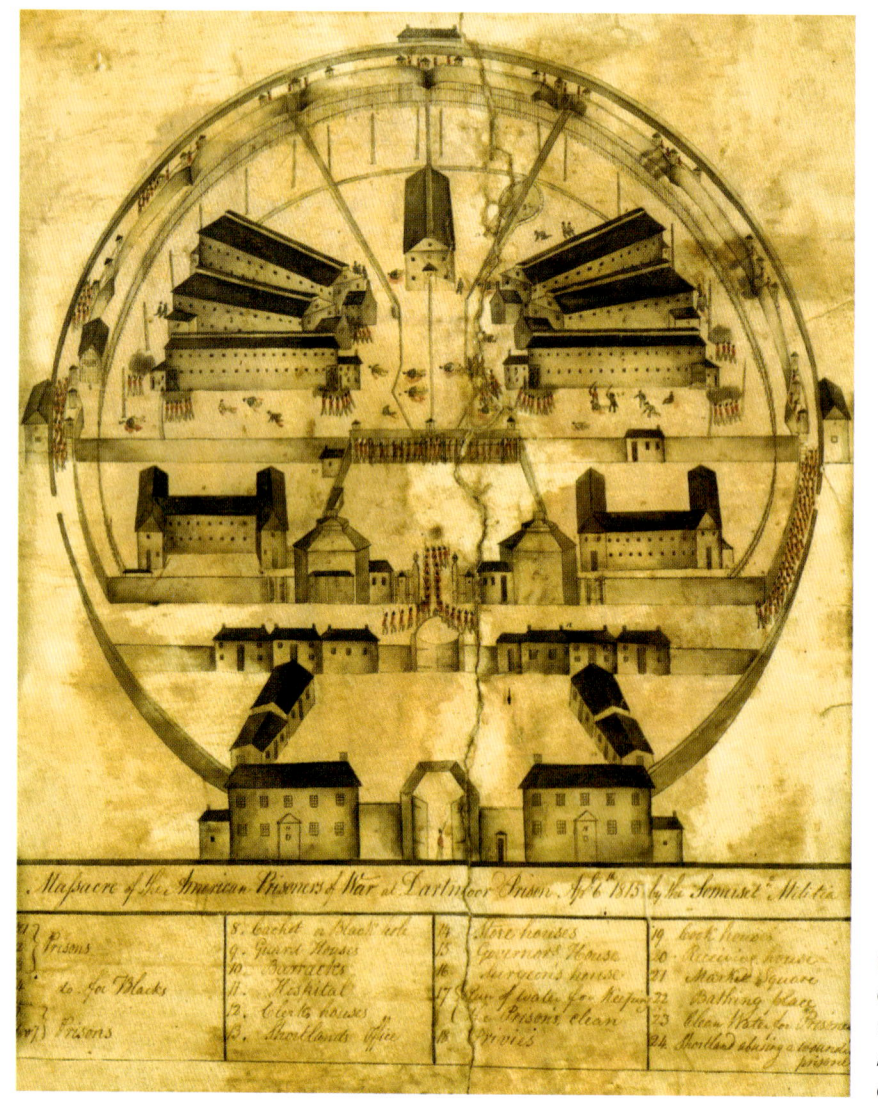

Dartmoor Prison, depicting the massacre of American prisoners on 6 April 1815.

VICTORIAN PHOTOGRAPH OF THREE HULKS MOORED AT PLYMOUTH

A prison hulk in Victorian times.

A plan had also been put in hand to provide better longer-term accommodation for prisoners ashore and Dartmoor was completed in 1809, Rochester and Edinburgh Castles were utilised from 1810, while further new prisons were established at Esk Mills and Valleyfield in 1811 and Perth and Liverpool in 1812, but still demand continued to outstrip the supply of places and the notorious hulks remained in operation throughout. The advantage to the Navy of land-based prisons was that although still the responsibility of the Transport Board, they were staffed by regular and militia troops rather than naval personnel.

All of the European prisoners were returned home by ship in late 1814, leaving only American prisoners at Dartmoor as that war continued into 1815. Heightened tensions over the delay in repatriating the American prisoners after peace had been ratified led to a riot and an overzealous response from the commander of the prison. The militia guards opened fire on the American prisoners, killing nine and wounding a number of others. However, such a serious incident was a rare occurrence.

Just as the prisons finally emptied in July 1815, war had broken out once again and within days Dartmoor was opening its doors again for over 4,000 French prisoners taken at the Battle of Waterloo, who were held there until February 1816, when the prison was locked up and abandoned. Later, as with Perth, the prisons were reopened in Victorian times for civilian prisoners and remain as such to this day.

84
Stern Windows of HMS Trincomalee

Once a ship was within cannon range, the tactics available to defeat an enemy warship were numerous, with different countries having a strong preference for different methods of attack.

The first concern was usually to gain the weather gage as this allowed the ship to be the aggressor and greatly facilitated surprise manoeuvres or alternatively aided flight. Ships could begin firing at distances of up to 300m to gain an advantage over enemy ships with lighter guns and damaging the rigging to prevent being outmanoeuvred or outsailed. British and American ships preferred to bring the ships in very close and fire into the hull, often double or triple loading their initial broadside for maximum effect. Firing on the hull was designed to degrade the fighting ability of the enemy crews and hopefully disable some of their cannon, with the odd shot even striking a mast or below the waterline, to damage the enemy ship's speed and manoeuvrability. The French preferred to concentrate their fire on the enemy's masts and sails in an effort to make the

Two frigates exchanging murderous broadsides at close range.

enemy ship uncontrollable and completely at their mercy.

Close-quarters broadsides were murderous, with cannonballs ripping through the wooden hulls and causing a shower of razor-sharp splinters to fly across the deck, scything through any flesh it came into contact with. Despite the horror, these broadside slugging matches could go on for up to an hour, with both sides suffering terrible losses, until one side had had enough and fled or surrendered.

Without masts, ships lost all ability to manoeuvre or to move at all and were then susceptible to attack from a position from which few of their own cannon could fire back, when the unequal contest would draw to its inevitable conclusion.

If a ship could manoeuvre so that it crossed the bows or stern of an enemy ship, it could unleash its entire broadside at the most vulnerable part of the enemy, while they were unable to fire many guns in reply. This was known as 'raking' fire and it could be particularly devastating. The cannonballs, after piercing the bow or smashing through the glazed stern windows, had free rein to fly the whole length of the deck killing and maiming dozens in its path and disabling any number of cannon in its way. Few ships could withstand more than a couple of raking broadsides, before their gun decks were a charnel

A dismasted French frigate at the entire mercy of the enemy.

A warship being raked through the stern windows.

BOARDING and TAKING the AMERICAN SHIP CHESAPEAKE, by the Officers & Crew of H.M. Ship Shannon, Commanded by Capt. Broke, June 1813.

Boarding an enemy vessel.

house and their firepower decimated. Surrender or flight were virtually the only options.

Often, despite horrendous losses of men and guns, crews continued to fight on heroically and to bring things to an end, it became necessary for the ships to crash alongside each other, when one of the ships would send boarding parties, armed with pistols, cutlasses, knives and even marlinspikes and axes, streaming onto the deck of the enemy ship. Furious and vicious hand-to-hand combat would ensue, until either the boarders succeeded in overrunning the ship or they were repelled and the ships parted again to fight on.

Naval warfare was little short of brutal and dehumanising, the injuries inflicted being absolutely horrendous and the dead plentiful. Eventually the morale of one crew would eventually collapse in the gore of their comrades and the lowering of the colours brought the fighting to an end, although it was only the beginning for the suffering of the wounded. There was very little glory in a naval battle, the prize being only the battered remnants of a once-proud warship.

85
Greenwich Royal Naval Hospital

The Royal Hospital for Seamen at Greenwich was established by order of Queen Mary II in 1692 although a naval report the previous year had already proposed turning the unfinished palace of Charles II on the site into a hospital. It was designed by Sir Christopher Wren for no charge, although it was completed by Sir John Vanburgh after his death.

The original plan for a single building would have ruined the view of the Thames from the Queen's House (centre) and the plans were modified to retain the view by splitting it in two. The building formed four large courtyards and was designed to house some 2,044 seamen pensioners, four times the size of Chelsea Hospital built for the Army. Mary died in 1694, but her husband William saw the project through for the express purpose of 'the reliefe and support of Seamen serving on board the Ships and Vessells belonging to the Navy Royall … who by reason of Age, Wounds or other disabilities shall be uncapable of further service … and unable to maintain themselves'.

Work began on converting the unfinished palace into King Charles's Court, but it was not until 1751 that the entire edifice was complete, when the fourth square, Queen Mary's Court, was finished. The funds to build this hugely expensive building came from numerous sources. King William promised £2,000 per year but struggled to pay it, so in 1696 sixpence was levied from every sailor's wages; £10,500 paid in fines for smuggling were given to the project; over £6,000 was handed over from the confiscated property of the pirate Captain Kidd; all unclaimed prize money was allocated to the fund; Parliament granted £6,000 per annum from the coal tax; a local gentleman bequeathed over £20,000 of property to the fund; the vast lands of the Earl of Derwentwater, a Jacobite supporter, were gifted to the hospital (huge amounts of coal were later found there) but even after all of this Parliament had to grant £10,000 per annum to complete the project.

The hospital complex contained an infirmary and a Royal Hospital School for orphans of seafarers. It closed its doors as a hospital in 1869. The pensioners were allocated a uniform, many years before naval seamen had one. Originally grey, it changed to brown, before finally settling on blue as portrayed in the second half of the seventeenth century. Each court or quarter of the hospital was divided into individual wards usually named after famous naval men. The wards were partitioned into cabins usually for single occupation, although a few held small groups, bringing the total number of persons that could be accommodated up to 2,710 'In Pensioners'.

Their food rations were plentiful with 1lb (0.5kg) of meat on five days per week, 4 ounces (125g) of cheese per day, 1lb of bread per day and half a gallon (2.25 litres) of beer per day. On the two non-meat days, they received pease pottage, double the cheese and 2 ounces (62.5g) of butter.

A senior pensioner was appointed to each ward with two mates, who ensured that the pensioners shaved each day, kept their clothes clean and generally behaved. They also ensured that any sick pensioners were attended to. Difficult pensioners could be forced to wear yellow coats as a mark of shame and were known as 'canaries', fined or expelled. Wives could visit the pensioners but they were never allowed to reside with them in the hospital and the men were allowed to 'chalk off' meals, being paid an allowance in lieu of the generous diet which they could use to support their wives who usually worked locally as domestics.

Clearly, the Navy had a great number of pensioners leaving the service beyond those that Greenwich Hospital could accommodate, these were known as 'Out Pensioners'. From 1763 these pensioners received the sum of £7 per annum, which was not a huge amount of money to live on. In 1814 with the war ending, a new scale of pension was established based on the number of years of service, added to an additional

A Greenwich Pensioner.

An ex-sailor playing a fiddle for money.

allowance for the wounds suffered. Under 7 years' service received between 5 and 10 pence per day and those with 21 years' service received 1 shilling and 6 pence per day. Many found the pension inadequate, especially if they were married with a family, and were forced to work or beg to make ends meet. In 1820 there were some 30,000 'Out Pensioners' on the hospital books and the cost eventually becoming too much for hospital funds, in 1829 the government took over responsibility for paying the pensions.

Very few officers could take up residence in Greenwich Hospital with only places for four captains and four lieutenants, while all others received half pay as a retainer, which officially could be stopped if they refused to accept a commission. However, a blind eye seems to have been turned to the issue as many officers remained on half pay for the rest of their lives. Sometimes officers were promoted purely to place them on a higher rate of half pay and a number of 'superannuated and retired' officers remained on the Navy List. Wounded or invalided officers could also receive specific pensions for their hurts.

The Admiralty also set that each ship carried a 'widow's man' on the books for every 100 men in the crew. These fictitious men were paid, the funds being allocated centrally for the relief of widows and dependents of officers killed in service as they rarely received any pension.

Print of a midshipman on half pay earning a living as a shoe-shine.

86

Contemporary View of Port Royal, Jamaica

The West Indies Station was formed following the capture of Jamaica in 1655 to protect British-held islands from the attacks of Spanish and French forces from their own islands. The West Indian islands were renowned for their general unhealthiness from tropical diseases which were little understood. Indeed in the 1720s three successive commanders on the station succumbed to tropical diseases and it was quite normal for up to 50 per cent of the naval personnel on this station to be incapacitated at any one time. A naval hospital was built in 1745 in an effort to contain the diseases, but it was so badly sited that it was reported to be 'rather a hurt to the service than a relief'.

Sugar plantations worked by slaves were the main draw for Europeans to the West Indies and as Britain sought a greater influence in this part of the world, the opportunities for mercantile trade grew exponentially. Between 1803 and 1812 sugar accounted for 21 per cent of all British trade, with the amount of sugar shipped annually increasing four-fold in some 60 years. Trade also expanded greatly in the opposite direction as well, with exports to the West Indies of luxury goods increasing by nearly 30 per cent in the same period.

The Royal Navy was essential to maintain the safety of British possessions in this area of the world, where islands belonging to other European countries, often enemies to Britain, were interspersed. Jamaica was far removed from the other British islands in the east of the Caribbean including Barbados, Antigua, Grenada, St Kitts and Nevis and was constantly threatened by the vast islands of Cuba and Hispaniola (now Haiti and the Dominican Republic) owned by the Spanish and French. Jamaica was by far the most important island commercially, being estimated to be worth around £27 million in 1774 (around £2.5 billion today). The British Windward and Leeward Islands also found the French islands of Guadeloupe and Martinique between them, acting as a constant thorn in their side, harbouring as they did numerous privateers which homed in on British merchant shipping. Therefore a second large naval base was established on Barbados and a small base at St Lucia, the latter changing hands too often to ever become a major base. There were then two Commanders-in-Chief in the West Indies, based at Jamaica (the Jamaica Station) and Barbados (the Leeward Station).

The American War of Independence was when this station was at its peak, with the serious threat posed by American commerce raiders. However, a typical force on the Jamaica Station between the wars was a 50-gun flagship, three frigates and five sloops and schooners.

Much of the work in these waters involved the suppression of enemy privateering and general patrolling, but also included a frequent demand to ferry army units from island to island and

A View of Kingston and Port Royal circa 1820.

also to support attacks on enemy-held islands. However, at times major fleets appeared in Caribbean waters, causing consternation and fear everywhere.

The Napoleonic Wars became a real opportunity for Britain to increase its control of this region, but was also too valuable to leave unprotected, indeed throughout the Seven Years war and Napoleonic Wars around 15 per cent of the entire Royal Navy was stationed in the West Indies. In 1797 the Jamaica Station had grown to seven ships of the line, fifteen frigates and seven sloops. In 1805 it had risen further in the number of ships but was now more suited towards anti-privateer actions, with only three ships of the line, fourteen frigates and no less than twenty-four sloops. However, once Britain was at peace with Spain in 1808, numbers on the station fell dramatically.

The Leeward Station was always viewed as more vulnerable to a visit from an enemy fleet and in 1797 the squadron consisted of nine Third Rates, sixteen frigates and eleven sloops, however after this, as most of the enemy islands were captured, the number of ships on the station dwindled. With many of the islands being handed back at the Peace of Amiens in 1802, the squadron increased in size again on the resumption of war in 1803 to six of the line, thirteen frigates and thirteen sloops. By 1810 the majority of the enemy islands were again in British hands and the threat had diminished greatly, the squadron having fallen by 1812 to only one ship of the line, five frigates and thirteen sloops.

In 1830 the West Indies Squadron was amalgamated with the North American one although the Navy continued to use its dockyard at Port Royal until it closed in 1905.

The Old Naval Hospital at Port Royal.

87

Admiralty House, Trincomalee, Purchased in 1810

The East Indies Station had been created in 1744 as the British possessions and merchant convoys operating in the Far East grew exponentially. In 1792 this squadron only had four frigates and three sloops, but by 1797 this had risen to thirty-two ships, including ten of the line, seventeen frigates and four sloops. However, particularly after the permanent capture of the Cape of Good Hope in 1806, the only threat remaining in the East was from piracy and commerce-raiding French frigates. Because of this, the number of naval vessels in the East dwindled and in 1812 there were only twenty-four warships of which only two were of the line.

It has to be borne in mind, that the Bombay Marine, the East India Company's own navy, also had ships patrolling these waters, whilst the East India Company merchant ships were also armed to the level of smaller frigates for self-defence and when in convoy were capable of forming line and defending themselves against quite powerful enemy vessels. Indeed, the Navy utilised the bases and port facilities of the East India Company in the early days, Fort William alongside Bombay harbour offering dry docks capable of accommodating a 74-gun ship from 1807. For this reason warships of a larger size were not deployed on this station. Shipbuilding facilities were also developed at Bombay and naval ships began to be constructed here, made of teak. The Navy did also use Madras as a base, but this lacked dockyard facilities and at certain times of year the anchorage was dangerous. Calcutta had dockyard facilities but was not used extensively by the Navy.

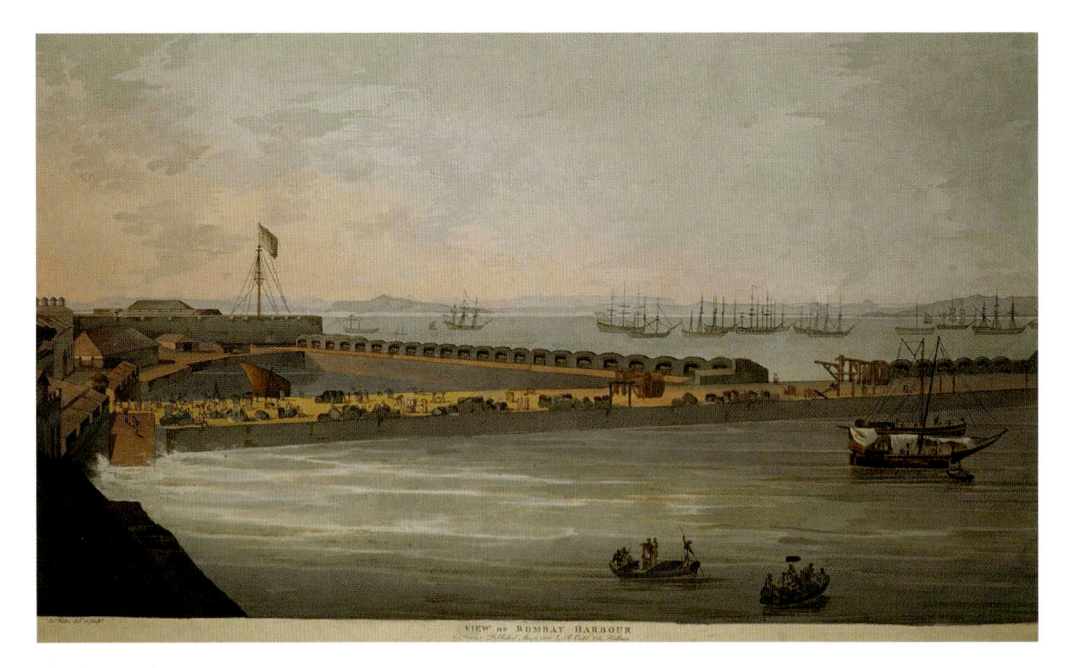

Bombay Harbour.

Fort St George, Madras.

A naval base had been planned on Great Andaman Island, but this was abandoned with the capture of Trincomalee in 1795. Plans were then put in place to establish this as the primary base for the East Indies fleet, despite the fact that there were no facilities there beyond a wide

ADMIRALTY HOUSE, TRINCOMALEE, PURCHASED IN 1810

Port Jackson (Sydney), Australia.

bay, but by 1810 work had begun, and the base was operational by 1815, with the admiral and his headquarters being established here.

The Navy did not extend their naval bases as far as Port Jackson in Australia until after 1815. Although it is known that some dockyard facilities had been established by 1796, it was deemed by the Navy as simply a safe anchorage at this time.

This relatively easy-going station was severely shaken up in 1803, however, when the French Admiral Linois was ordered with his squadron, comprising the *Marengo* of 74 guns and three frigates, into the Indian Ocean to destroy British commercial shipping, establishing a base on the Isle de France (Mauritius). Because of the wide expanse of ocean that the Royal Navy was attempting to control, it proved difficult to bring together a squadron strong enough to defeat Linois and eradicate the problem. However,

despite some early successes against individual merchantmen, Linois' first encounter with an East India Company convoy of sixteen of their heavily-armed merchantmen and fourteen other merchant ships at the Battle of Pulo Aura in February 1804 led to a defeat, having to retreat without capturing any ships. A second attempt at Vizagapatam Bay in September again led him to be driven off having only captured one merchant ship. Having failed, Linois sailed for Europe, but ran into a Royal Navy squadron at the Cape of Good Hope and was forced to surrender. This was the end of any serious threat to British trade in the East Indies.

Utilising their naval supremacy, the British looked to eradicate many of the possessions of their European neighbours in the Far East to give them complete domination in the region. The Dutch holdings in India had been taken in 1807 and Mauritius, that perpetual thorn

The Battle of Pulo Aura.

The taking of Banda-Neira in 1810.

in the centre of the Indian Ocean, providing a safe harbour for French privateers, was finally taken in 1809. Turning further afield, a joint expedition by Crown forces and the East India Company overran the Dutch island of Amboyna in 1809 and the Spice Islands of Ambon, Ternate and Banda-Neira the following year.

88

An Original Bombay Marine Flag

The Honourable East India Company (HEIC) had existed since 1600 but because of problems with the Portuguese Navy and with pirates, the Marine Department was established in 1612, and by 1686 this force had moved to Bombay and became known as the Bombay Marine, which even had its own Marine detachment. These ships were Company-owned warships designed specifically to protect the merchant fleet and also to survey the coastline to aid navigation. Many of the seamen on board were Indian lascars, but the ships were entirely commanded by British officers. The Marine became known by the nickname of the 'Bombay Buccaneers'.

The ships of the Bombay Marine were small coasting vessels but included the *Hastings* (32 guns), *Mornington* (22), *Malabar* (20), *Ternate* (16), *Teignmouth* (16), *Benares* (14), *Aurora* (14), *Nautilus* (14), *Crappier* (14), *Mercury* (14), *Prince of Wales* (14), *Thetis* (10), *Ariel* (10), *Psyche* (10), *Vestal* (10), *Fury* (8), *Jessy* (brig) and *Stromboli* (bomb).

In 1809 a joint Royal Navy and Bombay Marine squadron acted against Persian Gulf pirates operating out of Ras al-Kaimah but with only limited success. The *Aurora*, shown in the painting defending a British convoy from pirate ships, was captured by two French frigates in 1810 but was recaptured later that year when

Aurora attacked by pirates.

the British took the Isle de France (Mauritius). The Navy and Bombay Marine also cooperated in 1811 for the invasion of Java, which was captured successfully. The Bombay Marine is seen as the precursor of the modern Indian Navy.

East India Company ships had always been relatively heavily armed for merchant vessels, because of the length of their voyages in often hostile waters and the ever present fear of pirate attacks. During the wars, the company arranged for all of their ships to be granted 'Letters of Marque'. This was not to allow them to use their cannon in self-defence, but to allow their ships to make legal prizes of enemy ships they encountered on their routes. The merchant ships had many more gunports painted on their hulls than they actually had as a subterfuge but they did often carry quite a respectable arsenal. The Royal Navy did purchase a number of HEIC ships to bolster their own numbers and they were rated as Fourth Rates.

Sailing to India in large fleets, the large East Indiamen were called on to protect the convoys. In February 1804, French Admiral Linois with the *Marengo* of 74 guns, two frigates and a corvette, on a commerce-raiding mission, spotted a convoy of sixteen East Indiamen accompanied by thirteen merchant ships and a small brig. Commodore Nathaniel Dance realised their extreme danger, but was also aware that the East India Company ships were large enough to look like warships at distance. Forming his Indiamen into a line to protect the other merchants, he convinced Linois that the convoy was heavily protected and the French squadron sailed away. In reality Linois' squadron was much more powerful than the East Indiamen and they missed the opportunity of capturing a huge prize.

The East Indiaman *Warley*.

East India fleet at sea.

The numbers of ships employed at any one time by the HEIC is quite difficult to calculate as they constantly hired and fired ships. Indeed, between 1790 and 1830, some 400 ships were employed, but at any one given time the average number of ships in their service (not including the Bombay Marine) was between 100 and 150 ships.

89

Surgeon's Amputation Saw circa 1800

The health of the crew was seen as a critical factor in the success of naval operations and therefore the subject did receive quite a bit of attention by the Admiralty. In the early eighteenth century a number of major expeditions to the West Indies had seen thousands of deaths and subsequent failure and it was an imperative to find ways to improve general health, although unfortunately the cause and methods of prevention of many diseases had yet to be discovered. Even in 1809 a joint expedition of naval and army units to the island of Walcheren off Holland saw thousands falling sick and dying from a type of malaria. Protracted periods of patrolling off enemy ports in all weathers to maintain a blockade also took its toll on the crews.

Even with this significant effort, it was still true that the Navy lost more men to disease or accidents than it ever did by enemy action. In 1810, it has been estimated that half of all losses were caused by disease and about a third of the total was by accidents while a further one in ten died in shipwrecks, major fires or explosions on board ships, which often caused huge casualties among their crews. This leaves less than one in ten who suffered by enemy action. In total some 5,000 men died in the service that year.

This would appear to show that little had improved, but that is far from the truth. Improvements to the diet and the successful treatment of such diseases as scurvy and smallpox had seen a marked drop in the loss of men by disease, but there was still a long way to go. Typhus was still prevalent and yellow fever and malaria common problems in the West Indies particularly.

A surgeon was supposed to be supplied to all warships and they were allocated surgeon's mates at the rate of one per gundeck, which roughly equated to a medic for each 200 men on board. Until 1806, however, pay was poor and many ships were below regulation levels for medical staff. Improved pay and conditions implemented that year saw the situation improve dramatically and in later years complaints of a shortage of medical staff declined noticeably. Surgeons did not hold a position of high status on board naval vessels. Indeed they were generally looked down upon and best avoided, until their expertise became invaluable in hopefully saving their lives.

Naval surgeons generally had a very bad reputation, many being drunkards and of the worst character, only capable of performing amputations and stemming bleeding, everything else being beyond them. However, it is undoubtedly true that some individual surgeons were conscientious and did all they could for the men.

SURGEON'S AMPUTATION SAW CIRCA 1800

Surgeon's saw for amputation of smaller bones.

Surgeon's trepanning set.

253

Surgeons provided their own equipment and medical chest, which was checked and sealed before boarding a vessel to ensure they hadn't simply borrowed bits. From 1804 onwards the Navy reimbursed them for the medicines they had to purchase, which greatly helped matters. The surgeon was responsible for visiting the sick twice a day and producing a sick list for the captain daily. He also kept journals recording surgical cases and medicinal cases separately which could be inspected. The surgeon also inspected every new recruit brought on board as a volunteer or by the press and had to certify that they were fit and healthy. Most of his time however, was spent administering to the sick and providing lotions or medicines to combat the symptoms.

Sick berths or bays were sited in the most airy part of the ship, the old belief that being smoked by the ovens was the best location having lost favour in medical circles. These berths were, however, generally simply composed of a row of hammocks where the sick were placed and lay until they recovered or died. By the late 1790s the importance of fresh air became universally recognised and the berths were placed on or near the upper deck in most ships, although no instruction to do so emanated from the Admiralty.

However, in combat, such an exposed position was completely unacceptable and the surgeons and the sick were taken down into the depths of the ship into the 'cockpit', where they were below the waterline and were largely safe from enemy shot, this was where the surgeon's cabin was also located. In action the cockpit became the operating theatre, with the wounded being brought down and operated on in turn, regardless of rank, if they did not bleed out while waiting for their turn (triage was not practised at this time). Often the cockpit became too crowded and as soon as operated upon, the

The cockpit with surgeon's knives already laid out on the table.

patients were spread throughout the orlop deck and rarely attended to again for many hours. The surgeon and his mates mechanically continued the task of assessing the injuries, placing those without hope to one side to die and immediately amputating any shattered limbs. In the Army at this time a debate still raged as to whether it was better to amputate immediately, or whether to delay and decide later, in an effort to preserve the limb if possible. That argument had been settled for some time in the Navy, amputations being performed instantly while the patient was naturally anaesthetised by shock and hopefully avoided the dangers of gangrene setting in. The 'loblolly boys' brought the patients forward in turn for treatment and then placed them in wherever they could, before going for the next one. Any women on board usually helped by providing water or solace and companionship to the wounded and dying.

Most of the major naval bases at home and abroad had been provided with hospital facilities by 1760, but some lesser ports which did not have one utilised old ships hulks as hospital ships. Patients could be transferred to these hospitals for long-term illnesses or recovery after serious wounds, before being discharged from the service, but they had also started being used to isolate patients away from the rest of the crew to avoid major outbreaks. This was particularly useful in cases of typhus and yellow fever in an attempt to protect the healthy crew members.

The Naval Hospital at Malta.

90
Death Mask of Richard Parker

Mutinies, at least on a small scale, involving small numbers of deeply unhappy men on a single ship, were commonplace in the Navy throughout the entire period, with twelve occurring in 1805 and fifteen in 1813 and there is no reason to believe that these were unusual years. What was less common and something the Admiralty constantly watched for with great nervousness was a fleet mutiny, as occurred in 1797.

In the Army, intolerable conditions often led to significant numbers of desertions, but at sea, that was rarely an option and therefore mutiny was the only course for seeking redress. However, the term mutiny in naval law was a bit of a 'catch-all' offence, from an individual act of disobedience to a complete crew overthrowing the authority of the captain. Indeed the law actually recognised four categories of mutiny. 'Mutinous Assembly' and 'Mutinous Language' were included in one offence, 'Concealment of mutinous designs' was a separate offence and there was 'Mutiny' itself, the most serious of all. Striking or attempting to strike a superior officer was also viewed as tantamount to mutiny but not stated as such in the Articles of War. All of these various offences carried a maximum sentence of death.

Individual mutiny was by far the most common offence and during the Revolutionary Wars, even the hint of republican sympathies or radical talk could see a man charged. As late as 1805 a captain's clerk suffered 150 lashes for expressing republican views. Even the offence of trying to sink the ship was counted as mutiny.

For decades, crews had mutinied frequently, refusing to go to sea under a particularly harsh captain or over lack of pay, and the Navy had frequently treated them sympathetically and listened to the demands and sometimes gave in to them, all without any violence offered on either side. However, by the 1780s this kind of action was more frequently accompanied by violence from the crew and harsh disciplinary action by the Admiralty, slowly upping the ante. Finally in April 1797, this pent-up anger broke out in a fleet-wide mutiny at Spithead. A number of petitions had been sent by the crews to the Admiralty complaining about their lack of pay, but these had been ignored. Frustrated, when the *Queen Charlotte* was ordered to weigh anchor, the crew refused and gave a great cheer. This was the prearranged signal for a mass mutiny. All sixteen ships refused to weigh and a list of grievances was sent to the Admiralty, including better pay, more and improved food and better treatment for the sick. Almost all of their demands were granted within the week including the first pay rise for nearly 150 years. Unfortunately, a fight between the Marines and sailors on HMS *London* in which five sailors were killed caused the mutiny to intensify, even so, the crew merely incarcerated the ship's officers despite the deaths of their colleagues. Lord Howe was sent to negotiate and the men's demands were quickly conceded. By mid-May the fleet was back at sea defending the coast, with discipline fully restored.

Immediately afterwards, however, a second large-scale mutiny broke out at The Nore (off Sheerness), but this time it was a much more radical affair, pushing for far greater reforms on the back of those concessions gained at Spithead. They demanded more shore leave, regular payment of wages, a fairer distribution of prize money and the removal of some unpopular officers. In order to cause the maximum disruption, the mutineers also attempted to stop all trade on the Thames, but were prevented from achieving this. Meanwhile, in order to stop the Dutch fleet taking advantage of the situation, Admiral Duncan patrolled the Dutch coast with his only two loyal ships, whilst signalling to an imaginary fleet over the horizon, which succeeded in keeping the Dutch ships quiet. This time Parliament took things much more seriously, forbidding all contact with the fleet, with shore batteries erected to threaten the ships. Realising that there was not going to be an easy victory this time, ships slowly gave up one at a

Contemporary print of the delegates of the mutiny at The Nore.

Signatures of the crew of HMS *Mars* apologising for joining the Nore mutiny.

time and sailed to join Duncan at sea. Eventually the mutiny collapsed and the ringleaders, including Richard Parker, were hanged, others being flogged or transported to Australia for life.

A further attempt at a mutiny by the Mediterranean Fleet the following year was put down harshly and thereafter fleet mutinies stopped. However, single ship mutinies continued at a regular pace, but they were generally put down rigorously with the ringleaders being sentenced to hang and gradually the problem subsided, not perhaps because the crew were more content, but it is more likely that the harsh measures by the naval authorities dissuaded many.

Violence was always a part of mutinies to a greater or lesser extent, but usually both sides tried to avoid deaths. Even in the notorious case of the mutiny on the *Bounty*, the majority of the officers were allowed to leave in the ship's boat. However, one mutiny became notorious for its violence, that aboard HMS *Hermione* in 1797. The mutiny arose because of the harsh treatment meted out by Captain Pigot and his officers and nine officers including the captain were murdered. Realising their fate if captured, the crew then sailed into a Spanish port, handing their ship over to the enemy. The mutineers were relentlessly hunted for years and eventually most of them were captured and hanged.

Desertion, which also carried the death penalty, although rarely administered, was also a constant problem, with estimates by contemporary officers averaging up to 10,000 men per year. Desertion was particularly prevalent when a warship was in harbour just as a large merchant fleet was sailing. With better pay and conditions and an easy escape route if the desertion was only discovered once the fleet had sailed made it an attractive option, with little danger of being recaptured. Some particularly unhappy ships found it difficult sending any sailors ashore. In 1810 HMS *Alfred* lost thirty-six men from three separate watering parties in the West Indies in four days! To limit opportunities for desertion warships rarely berthed alongside, but usually anchored in the bay and controlled boat movements to restrict the opportunities and even mounting guards at night, and shore leave was also very rarely given. The dangers of recapture were infinitesimal and therefore there was little that could be done to stop it.

Portrait of Richard Parker.

91
Superb Diorama of a 'Cutting Out' Expedition

Prize money was a huge incentive for both ships' captains and their crews, with command of a frigate on an independent patrol, with no senior officers to oversee the operation, being seen as a golden opportunity to gain great wealth. Not surprisingly, such appointments were eagerly sought after and their attraction even for the crews can be seen by the relative ease they appear to have had crewing their ships fully, many volunteering to serve with a successful frigate captain. Indeed, the fame of some of these captains became legendary, with their numerous tales of dramatic operations and significant financial gain. Some captains such as Thomas Cochrane, Edward Pellew, Henry Blackwood, William Hoste and Philip Broke became household names and their actions were retold in the journals of the day.

However, these small-ship operations were not only daring and sometimes astounding in their audacity, but downright dangerous and took a heavy toll on crews. Capturing a merchant ship at sea was relatively straightforward, although even an innocent-looking merchant vessel could actually turn out to be a strongly manned privateer and capturing an enemy warship was certain to be a hard-fought battle.

However, as the war progressed and British mastery of the seas was affirmed, enemy vessels sought the protection of heavily-fortified harbours and also prepared strong defences on board as soon as a British vessel came within sight. To launch night attacks on such strong defences required a great deal of pre-planning and determination to succeed, with a high probability of defeat and suffering significant

Boarding an enemy warship.

A naval dirk used in close combat.

losses. Literally thousands of such 'cutting out' operations were undertaken during the latter years of the war and a number were defeated with heavy loss by a stiff defence. However, many succeeded, against formidable opposition and with only the slimmest chances of success, simply because of the audacity, sheer courage and determination displayed by both officers and men and a stubborn refusal to be defeated.

Action ashore was not confined to capturing prizes, however, despite its inherent attraction. A perusal of the actions of Cochrane or Hoste during these wars will soon discover a whole host of shore-based operations undertaken to disrupt enemy capabilities. Signal or lookout posts were routinely destroyed, as were shore batteries and harbour facilities, but beyond these, enemy troops travelling the coastline were bombarded, fortresses were attacked and then defended to disrupt enemy communications, sieges of island fortresses were routinely undertaken with cannon being hoisted by naval teams to the very pinnacles of seemingly impossible crags to fire over the defences of fortress towns to force their surrender.

The 'Navy Spirit' engendered by the frequent reports of these successes published in the newspapers led to a belief both within the Navy and the general public at large that British sailors could achieve virtually anything they set their mind to. It is something that every person who has joined the Royal Navy in the two succeeding centuries has aspired to emulate.

92

A Pair of Slave Shackles

The trade in slaves from West Africa to the West Indian islands and to North America had been very lucrative for all concerned for more than a century. From the African warlords who sold their prisoners, the shipowners who packed the slaves in to an intolerable level to maximise profits and the plantation owners who made great profits from their labours, everyone had a vested interest in the continuation of this awful trade.

The Royal Navy had no interest in this trade, being a purely commercial venture, until Parliament voted to end the slave trade in British ships in 1807. This did not end slavery for the hundreds of thousands of slaves already in the Americas but it banned any more slaves being sent there from Africa. Clearly many nations were involved in this trade and the British ban had no effect on ships of other nations, so in 1808 the government ordered the Royal Navy to establish a West Africa squadron by which a blockade of West Africa was established to end the trade. However, with such great profits to be made it is not surprising that many chose to ignore or flout the ban. Because Britain was at war with France and her allies, the Navy could detain any ships of those nations carrying slaves as enemy ships, but that could not apply to the ships of allies.

Initially the Navy did not give this role much attention, establishing a squadron of only two vessels, the 32-gun frigate HMS *Solebay* and the brig sloop HMS *Derwent*, not a large force to patrol the entire west coast of Africa, particularly when the home base for the ships was at Portsmouth, ensuring that one of the two ships was almost certain to be away from the station at any particular time.

Britain made strenuous diplomatic efforts to persuade other European powers to ban the slave trade and Portugal, one of the biggest slave trading nations, was persuaded to allow the British ships to detain Portuguese slave ships in 1810, but the trade was not banned in their own African possessions.

Two private ventures equipped ships to bolster the British blockade by capturing slave ships under the authority of a Letter of Marque. However, the privateers *Dart* and *Kitty* did not last long and no others joined this trade, indicating that it was not a profitable venture. A Vice Admiralty Court had also been established at Freetown, Sierra Leone in 1807 to make the prize money procedure for captures more efficient.

After the wars, other European nations gradually abandoned the trade, but a new faster type of Baltimore clippers outran the naval vessels until captured clippers were turned against them, but even in the 1840s the Navy was employing 25 vessels and over 3,000 men on this blockade.

Because of tropical diseases causing a high death rate in the crews, the West Africa Station was the least popular posting in the Navy. America added ships to the Atlantic patrols informally in 1820 and they formally became part of a joint West Africa squadron in 1842. Between 1808 and 1860 it is estimated that 1,600 slave ships were captured and 150,000 Africans released. Despite these successes, it is estimated that well over a million Africans were transported to America as slaves during the same period.

Unfortunately the British captains could not arrest slave ships that had no slaves onboard, causing some dreadful incidents where captains of slave ships threw their cargo overboard when threatened with arrest, the poor Africans being unable to swim in their shackles.

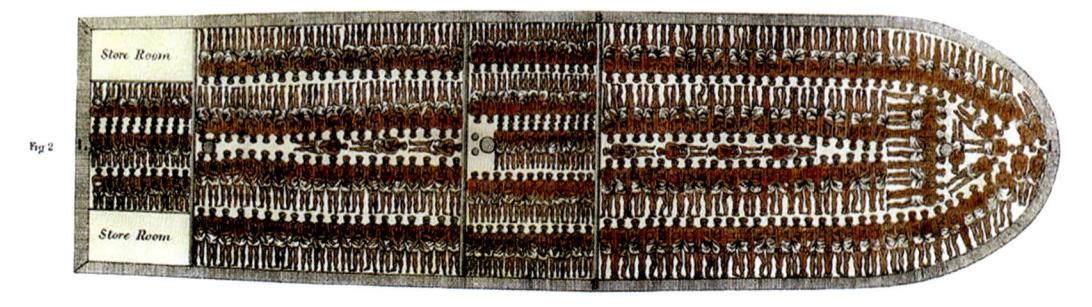

Layout of a slave ship.

93

A Cat of Nine Tails

Naval discipline was, as it still is today, controlled by the Articles of War, originally drawn up in 1650 but amended in 1749 and 1757. Altogether, there were thirty-six Articles defining crimes and their punishment; four dealt with Sunday services and profanity with indeterminate sentencing, but the next twelve which detailed crimes against the monarch and the state, including spying, consorting with an enemy or neglect of duty were to be severely punished with death an option in all cases. The third section covered such things as murder, theft and assault, all of which could again receive the death penalty. The final section were specifically military in nature, including crying for quarter, withdrawing from a fight or failure to chase an enemy, these were to be very severely punished, with literally only the death penalty being available as an option. A final 'catch all' clause allowed captains to punish any crimes not mentioned in the Articles, in accordance with custom at sea. A copy of the Articles of War must always be on shown on a Royal Navy ship.

As the Articles could not offer advice and instruction on many issues in naval life, a separate tome known as the Admiralty Regulations and Instructions listed the duties and restrictions in each role in the ship and included copies of all of the forms required to be completed. These were updated regularly with new issues published in 1787, 1806 and 1808.

In the event of a crime, the captain was able to administer his own punishments for minor crimes, but he was not able to administer large numbers of lashes as is often portrayed. In fact the captain could not order a sailor to receive more than three dozen lashes.

For any serious offence potentially requiring a greater punishment, a court martial had to be held, particularly in almost any case against a petty officer or an officer, as he could not dismiss from the service or reduce in rank or seniority except by a court martial. A court martial had to be requested by the captain, which had to be approved by the admiral on station and consist of between five and thirteen captains, as the admiral ordered. He could, however, order a stoppage of 'grog' or a spell in chains in the depths of the ship for lesser offences.

A range of punishments was available to the court martial. The death penalty was always carried out by hanging for sailors, petty officers and Marines, if possible on the offender's own ship, from the yards. With a noose round his neck and a cloth bag over his head, the condemned man was hastily raised to the yard by a team running with the rope and he was left there for one hour to ensure his death. Any announcement of a death sentence had to be approved by the Admiralty when in home waters, allowing the monarch to grant clemency if they desired. However pardons were only announced at the very last moment possible before the guilty party was hoisted to the yard. Officers convicted of a capital crime were usually shot by firing squad.

Flogging round the fleet was thought to be even worse than death by many. The courts sentencing floggings of anywhere from 100 to 1,000 lashes

A flogging.

was permissible. Usually floggings occurred on the offender's own ship, but in the most serious cases, he could also be flogged around the fleet, when he was rowed to each ship in turn and received a portion of his sentence on each. As the prisoner was rowed around the ships, he was accompanied by a Marine drummer, who constantly beat the 'Rogue's March'. It was not uncommon for men to die during this extended ordeal.

Flogging was carried out using the 'Cat of Nine Tails' with knots in the nine lines to add to the injury suffered. The crew was assembled to see the flogging carried out and the Marines formed as a guard with loaded muskets to prevent any attempt to disrupt the punishment. For theft, a heinous crime in the eyes of sailors, an even heavier cat known as the 'Thieves' Cat' was used, which had heavier knots and caused much greater injuries to the back. Indeed at least one ship mutinied because the captain used the 'Thieves' Cat' for ordinary offences, which the crew believed to be excessive. When flogged the man was tied to a grating placed upright and each boatswain's mate struck him with the cat every six to twelve strokes to ensure that the strokes did not slacken in intensity.

Another punishment inflicted, was 'Running the Gauntlet', when the accused was dragged around the deck tied to a chair or barrel, between two lines of crewmen, who all flailed him with three rope yarns which they all held.

'Starting' the men with a cord or cane to urge them along at their work was commonplace despite the court martial of an officer in 1809 and forcing the men to drink a half gallon of salt water was another regular punishment, but the Admiralty rarely viewed such practices as acceptable if brought to trial.

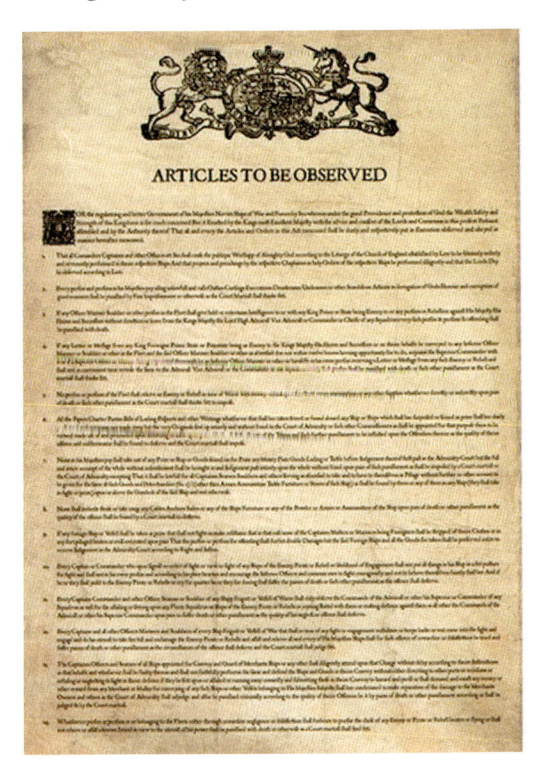

The Articles of War.

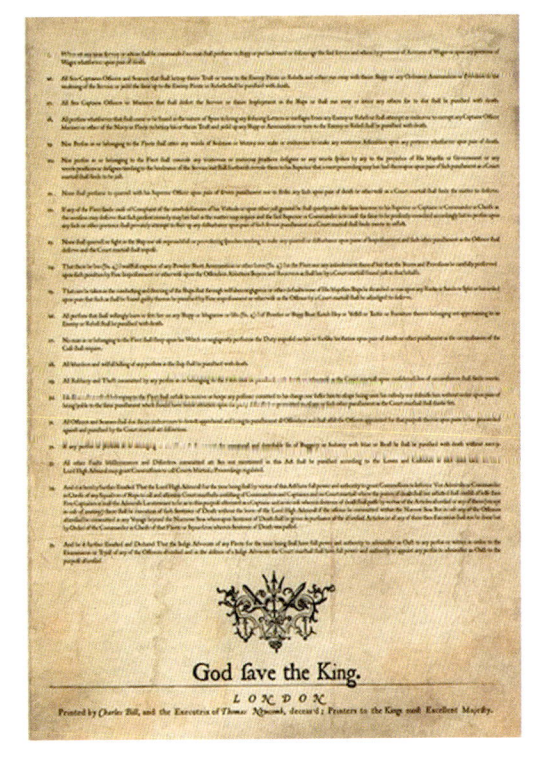

British Letter of Marque issued in 1813

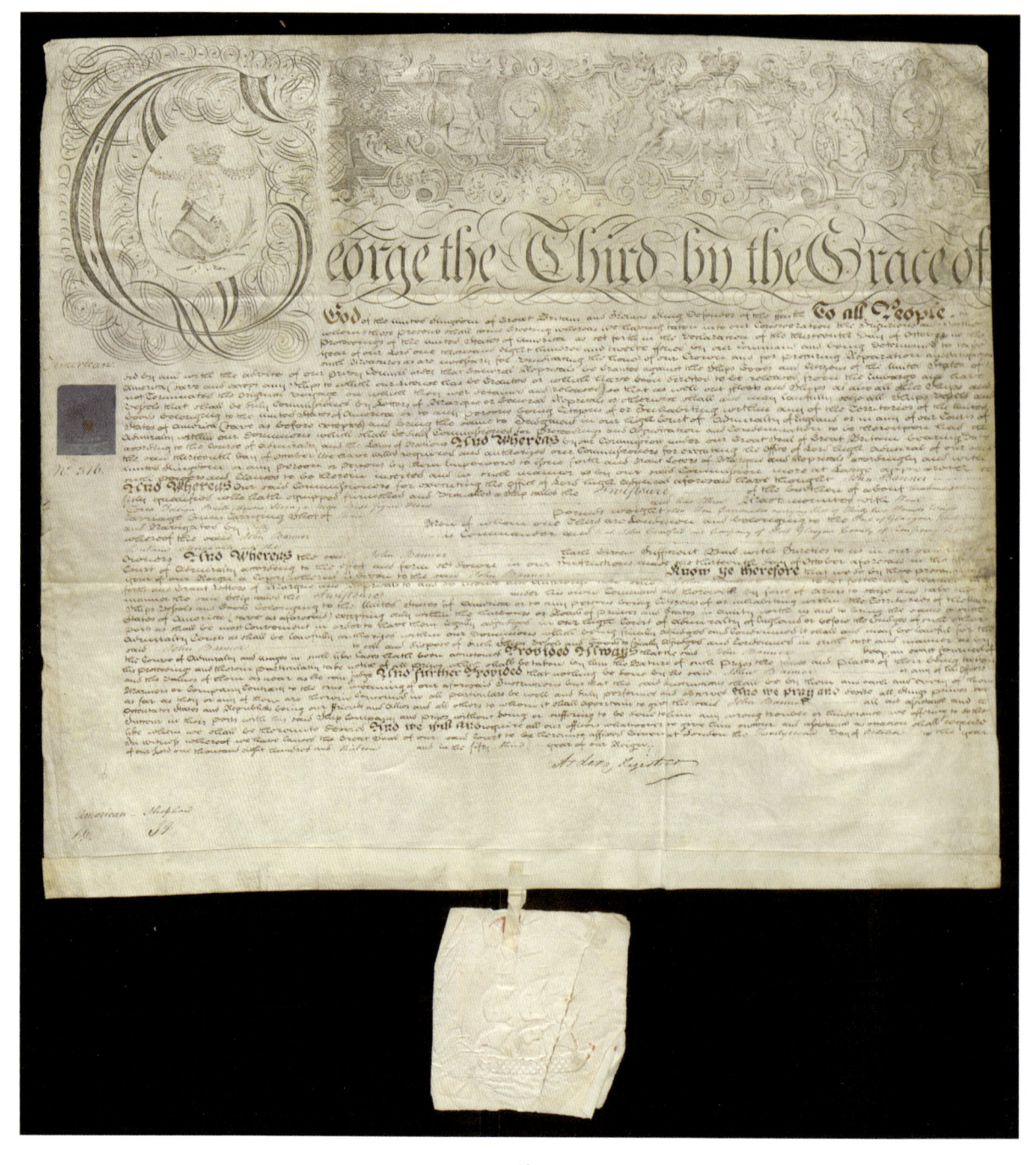

Piracy was still a major problem in many areas of the world and the Royal Navy was regularly tasked with attempting to stamp it out, but with too many other priorities in wartime, pirates were pretty well able to operate without interruption. Piracy had been eradicated in much of Europe, but in wartime governments now turned to legalised piracy, which was sanctioned by a Letter of Marque from the Admiralty. Letters of Marque had been used since 1293 and they continued to be used in wartime until they were abolished in 1856. Armed with this legal charter, a private shipowner could organise a heavily-armed crew and venture out on the high seas, capturing any enemy merchant ships they encountered. The crews of these privateers were rarely paid a wage, but they earned a share in the profits made and they therefore fought hard to capture enemy ships, even against strong opposition. All East India Company ships also sought a Letter of Marque as company policy, allowing them to take any prizes that they might come across. By the internationally-accepted rules of war, the crews of privateers were treated as prisoners of war if captured, whereas pirates received the death penalty. The British and Americans particularly encouraged privateers as a cheap way of damaging the enemy's trade in the American War of Independence and in the War of 1812. However, the greatest proponent by far was Napoleon and those states under his control, France, Denmark (including Norway), Holland, Spain and Italy encouraged vast numbers of vessels to become privateers and to prey on British merchant shipping. These privateers were therefore a constant thorn in the Navy's side and a large proportion of the 'cutting out' operations carried out in the ship's boats were against these heavily-armed privateers, who often put up a very determined defence.

Beyond European waters, piracy was still a huge problem and a great deal of effort was required to at least keep it under some form of control. The Caribbean, the ancient lair of pirates, was still of concern, whilst merchant shipping passing along the eastern coastline of Africa, the Middle East or in any part of the Indian Ocean remained under constant threat of attack by sizeable groups of pirate ships attacking together. Because of this, merchant vessels carried a number of cannon and personal sidearms to protect themselves while the East India Company vessels were armed as strongly as small frigates to protect their valuable cargoes and often sailed together in convoys to give mutual protection.

The Navy were occasionally able to put together a force to destroy these pirate fleets and their bases, one such large-scale operation being the attack on the Qawasim tribal federation based

A Corsair pistol.

Attack on Ras Al Khaimah in 1809.

Attack on Algiers in 1816.

in the Straits of Hormuz at Ras Al Khaimah in 1809, but despite this strong admonishment, the problem persisted for more than another decade.

The greatest pirate problem, however, had been in the Mediterranean for some centuries, from the Barbary Pirates or Corsairs, who operated out of the North African ports of Tripoli, Algiers and Tunis. These pirates were the scourge of merchant shipping of all nations and even Italian coastal towns received their unwelcome visitations. These Muslim pirates also took Europeans into captivity, releasing the rich for huge ransoms and selling the rest into slavery, many men being put to work on the oars of their galleys and the women sold into harems.

European countries had begun to combine in periods of peace to compel the pirates to release numbers of slaves and to honour their country's flag. However, in times of war the European navies had little time for dealing with piracy and the corsairs were persuaded to grant free passage to ships flying the flag of that particular nation for an annual 'tribute' in gold, such as the French and Danes paid. Others, like Britain and later America, refused to pay a tribute and kept their merchant vessels relatively safe by the threat of heavy retribution. America went to war with the Corsairs after they refused to pay the tribute any longer, the war continuing from 1801–5, before the pirates agreed to end attacks on American shipping in return for payment of a ransom to release American prisoners.

Following the end of the Napoleonic Wars the Americans were forced into action again to release prisoners and a further ransom paid. Meanwhile in 1816 a Dutch and British squadron under the command of Lord Exmouth was sent by their governments to finally sort the Barbary pirates out once and for all. The Beys of Tunis and Tripoli quickly agreed to the release of all slaves, but the Bey of Algiers refused. A heavy bombardment of the city by the ships soon persuaded him to change his mind and over a thousand Christian slaves were released and the American ransom money returned. However, the Barbary Pirates were not fully eradicated until the 1830s when France took control of the North African countries.

Medal commemorating Exmouth's action in 1816.

95
Contemporary Depiction of the Landing at Aboukir Bay, 1801

For many years, the Navy and the Army had been at loggerheads over control of joint operations and it is painfully obvious that in many instances the Navy deposited their unwanted guests quickly and with the least difficulty for themselves.

The island-hopping expeditions of 1794 and 1795 are a good example of this, with the army being deposited ashore on a very good landing beach where there was minimal opposition, allowing them to successfully gain a foothold without much loss. However, it was not uncommon for the troops to have to then march for many miles over steep mountains thickly covered in jungle to reach the enemy fortresses which had to be captured to gain control of the island. This led to an inordinate amount of work bringing up cannon and supplies in their wake and led to high losses from tropical diseases, when landings near the enemy works were feasible, but required greater preparation and planning to overcome the opposition.

However, the British landing in Holland at Calantsoog in 1799 was opposed by a strong French force, which lined the sand dunes with infantry and artillery. The landing was covered by a heavy cannonade from the warships, forcing the French to take cover behind the sand dunes and allowing the first wave of boats carrying 2,500 men to land without much opposition initially. Once ashore a strong French attack was beaten off with the help of a number of gunboats lying close to the shore, which fired grape at close range and drove the French columns off. Soon further waves of troops were landed which overwhelmed the defenders. It had been a significant success and the British commander, Sir Ralph Abercromby was to put this experience to great use a few years later.

In 1801, when General Abercromby commanded a large force for the invasion of French-held Egypt, he made concerted efforts to prepare for all eventualities, fully expecting a strong defence aimed to deny him a beachhead.

CONTEMPORARY DEPICTION OF THE LANDING AT ABOUKIR BAY, 1801

Landing on Martinique in 1794.

Calantsoog in 1799.

In the months prior to the invasion, the fleet rested in the sheltered harbour of Marmorice Bay, where constant landing drills were performed to ensure that the men knew exactly what to do in the real thing. Finally the fleet sailed for Egypt, but unfortunately the element of surprise was lost when stormy weather prevented any possibility of a landing for a full week. It was therefore obvious when the landing did go ahead on 8 March 1801, that the French would put up a stout defence in an attempt to deny them a way off the beach.

Preparations included landing engineer officers to study the beach and access to the countryside beyond, but unfortunately two of them were captured, although reconnaissance continued in small boats. The landing was to be performed in three waves, the first of fifty-eight flatboats carrying fifty soldiers each, the second consisting of eighty-one cutters and the third of thirty-seven launches. Boat crews were to keep in line, taking their position from a boat flying a flag in each wave as a marker to ensure that the boats landed simultaneously. Some of the flatboats even had a drop-down bow to allow artillery to disembark easily on the beach. As each boat dropped its men ashore, they would pull back to the fleet and embark

The landing at Aboukir in 1801.

CONTEMPORARY DEPICTION OF THE LANDING AT ABOUKIR BAY, 1801

Landing on Mauritius in 1810.

another wave. The boats were protected by a line of gunboats carrying a cannon loaded with grape. Further out bomb vessels continually targeted the sand dunes held by the French defenders.

Naval officers were tasked with a role akin to a modern beachmaster, getting the men and equipment off the beach as quickly as possible. On landing, the troops rapidly formed up, loaded and drove forward to get beyond the beach. It was a textbook operation, and one that would be recognised as using the same broad principles utilised in modern amphibious landings.

The French, numbering around 2,000 infantry, with ten cannon firing deadly bursts of canister from the sand dunes, stoutly defended the beach and were even aided by cavalry who charged up to the waterline in an attempt to destroy the infantry as they struggled out of their boats, but they were eventually driven off by heavy musket fire. The determined landing succeeded but with some loss, the British suffering in excess of 900 casualties, whilst the French lost some 300 men before they were driven from the sand hills and forced to retreat.

Later amphibious landings were to follow Abercromby's principles and Army and Navy cooperation became much more professional, with better understanding of each other's capabilities and limits. Indeed, in the Adriatic in 1811–14, it almost became a competition between the two services as to who could come up with the most daring operation to capture a neighbouring island or port, with everyone working together superbly to succeed in the common goal.

Of all amphibious operations conducted by the Royal Navy during the period, perhaps the

The fleet evacuating General Moore's army at Corunna 1809.

most important of them all was not a landing but an evacuation. Had a large fleet of warships accompanying a convoy of transport ships not arrived at Corunna in Spain in December 1809, then Britain's largest army abroad may have been lost and without it, it is difficult to see how the Duke of Wellington could have fought the ensuing Peninsular War effectively. It was the Napoleonic version of the evacuation of Dunkirk.

96

A Patriotic Fund £100 Sword

Founded at Lloyd's Coffee House in July 1803 by a group of Lloyd's underwriters and London merchants, the Lloyd's Patriotic Fund continued until 1825. It was to be capitalized by a public subscription, which raised £100,000 (about £5 million today) in one month. The fund was administered by a committee which was connected with, but wholly independent of, Lloyd's itself.

It was set up primarily to give grants to the naval wounded and pensions to the dependants of those killed in action, but it also awarded prizes to those who had demonstrated great valour at a time when official gallantry awards did not exist. The rewards varied between ornate swords, silver plate or other decorative items through to cash payments, and all came with a certificate to commemorate the occasion for the reward. These awards were highly prized and were celebrated widely as a boost for national morale. A meeting in May 1809 decided to discontinue these awards to focus all of the available funds on providing help to the severely wounded and dependents of those killed, although some officers purchased a sword rather than take a cash sum, such was the esteem attached to them.

Swords of different values were issued for certain ranks: midshipmen and Royal Marine lieutenants received one valued at £30 (about £1,500 today), lieutenants and Royal Marine captains received one valued at £50 (£2,500 today) and naval commanders and captains received a sword valued at £100 (£5,000 today). A total of 172 swords were awarded, with 16 of £30, 88 of £50 and 39 of £100, the other 29 being a specially-designed £100 sword granted to all 29 captains commanding ships at the Battle of Trafalgar in 1805. Similar swords were also awarded by the Corporation of the City of London, but these were not of a uniform design or value.

A further sixty-six vases were presented during the period, often but not solely to widows of an esteemed officer. The Fund also sought to help the impoverished children left behind and a large amount of money was paid

Patriotic Fund silver vase with cover.

to educational establishments to pay for their education. They also made a large donation of £61,000 (around £3 million today) to help fund the Royal Naval Asylum or Greenwich Hospital School allowing the trust to nominate children to be pupils.

Between 1805 and 1812, the fund was also actively employed in forwarding money for the support of British prisoners of war held in France, when Napoleon's government refused to continue the age-old practice of paying for their upkeep. The money was forwarded to the committee of prisoners at Verdun, which oversaw its distribution and did allow them to support a hospital and a school for the children of prisoners as well as providing funds to the prisoners directly.

Although the fund ceased taking on new cases in 1825, it began again in 1841 and continues to this day, supporting armed forces' charities.

Patriotic Fund certificate.

97

Contemporary Image of the Revenue Cutter Greyhound *in Chase*

Because of high import duties, smuggling was endemic during the seventeenth and eighteenth centuries, with large numbers of people in the coastal regions of most European countries being involved in these clandestine activities.

One estimate puts the figure for smuggled tea into Britain in the decade after 1782 at two-thirds of all tea imported, but this particular trade stopped when the taxes were slashed on tea imports. Import duties were one of the government's largest sources of revenue and they therefore made great efforts to stop smuggling, even using the Army and the Navy to help. The incentives for smuggling became even more lucrative during wartime, when supplies of goods from enemy countries (often Spain and France) were officially banned. This was particularly a problem after Napoleon banned British imports ino Europe with the Milan Decree of 1806

280

CONTEMPORARY IMAGE OF THE REVENUE CUTTER *GREYHOUND* IN CHASE

and Britain retaliated the following year with a ban on all trade with the French Empire in their 'Orders in Council'. This opened up a huge market for illicit trade in both directions and the smugglers were certainly not slow to increase their business dramatically.

The government response to this explosion in smuggling was not well coordinated, mainly because no single entity had responsibility for it. The Board of Customs' staff levied taxes on imported goods, but the Board of Excise staff, who generally looked after internal taxes, also had responsibility for levying the taxes on imported tea and cocoa beans and spirits. Therefore both departments provided patrols to catch smugglers, but they did not cordinate their efforts. The situation was further confused by the fact that Scotland had its own boards who operated independently of England and Wales, while Ireland had a much more practical setup with one board covering all import taxes, but again failed to coordinate with efforts on the mainland. This meant that there were five separate organisations involved, plus the Royal Navy and Army and, as can be imagined, it was a complete mess.

Each port generally had two customs officers pernmanently on site, with a number of staff, who would inspect the ships coming into port. Riding officers were employed separately to scour the coast for smuggling boats or hideouts, but this was extremely dangerous business, many smugglers being prepared to kill to preserve their business and the Army was often called in to provide men to protect them in carrying out their duties.

Smuggler's cave in the cliffs at Dover.

Smuggling became very big business and large organised gangs went to great lengths, including digging out caves in the rock or even tunnels allowing the goods to be taken far inland without being seen. The men carrying out the smuggling rarely owned their boats or were financially dependent on their cargoes, almost all of these smuggling operations being funded by local merchants or city speculators, who could expect a huge return on their capital if not caught.

The Customs Service operated a fleet of cutters, with thirty-six of them being in service in 1799, the ones based in the English Channel near Dover only covering a 10 or 20-mile section of coastline, such was the intensity of smuggling operations. The average cutter was 130 tons and carried fourteen cannon with a crew of forty men. The Excise Board only ran seven cutters of their own. Eventually in 1809 a unified Preventive Water Guard Service was set up amalgamating these different units bringing together a force of thirty-nine cutters and sixty-two boats, however smuggling remained a problem throughout the war.

However, other government departments found the smugglers useful for their own operations. Both France and Britain undoubtedly used smugglers to spy on their enemy and also as a route to smuggle agents, communications and weapons into enemy-held territory. Later, Napoleon positively encouraged the smugglers, opening the port of Dunkirk to 'ships known under the name of Smugglers', extending this to the port of Wimereux in 1811 at the same time as the original licence moved from Dunkirk to Gravelines. It is known that at least 300 English

A cartoon claiming that the high cost of food in Britain was due to the smugglers selling produce to the French. In fact the gold was going in the other direction.

smuggling boats operated out of these ports, making no less than 606 visits to the port of Gravelines alone in 1813. The products mostly smuggled into Britain were spirits (especially cognac), lace, silk and leather goods, whilst gold was by far the most sought-after goods going the other way.

Another area of business the smugglers got involved in was the transportation of escaped French prisoners of war back to France, for a significant fee. Another valuable asset smuggled to France and one regularly used by Napoleon himself, were newspapers, British papers not being as heavily controlled, often giving more up to date news from the far edges of Napoleon's Empire than he had received via official means.

Despite the best efforts of the Revenue men, arrests were infrequent and it was claimed that between 300,000 and 400,000 gallons of spirits were smuggled into the country in the year of 1813 alone.

Smuggling continued way beyond the end of the war in 1815, although better coordinated prevention services and a virtual blockade of the south coast saw it dwindle through the 1820s. It did not end fully, however, until Free Trade agreements came into force in the 1840s, which finally killed the trade.

Smugglers at work.

98
Naval Officer's Gold Medal 1794–1815

It was unusual during this period to issue medals for gallantry. In fact it was generally only the captain of a ship of the line who would be awarded a medal of any kind. Between 1794 and 1815 the Navy issued a large named gold medal to admirals, commodores and captains of the fleet and a smaller version was issued to individual captains for a particular action. As they were specifically named for a certain action, it was possible for officers to have more than one of the medals. However, during the entire Napoleonic Wars only 22 large medals and 117 smaller medals were issued. After 1815 the issue of the medal was discontinued with the enlargement of the number allowed into the Order of the Bath. The rules for the issue of the medal were so restrictive that when Lieutenant Cuthbert commanded HMS *Majestic* throughout the majority of the Battle of the Nile after Captain Westcott was killed as the action began, he was refused a medal as he was not a captain by rank.

With no official medals being produced, a number of commercially-produced medals were struck for those who served or simply patriotic civilians could purchase at a price. The medal shown commemorating Admiral Duncan's victory over the Dutch fleet at Camperdown in 1797 is a very good example of this type.

However, such was the elation following Nelson's great victory against the French fleet at the Battle of the Nile in 1798, it prompted the admiral's friend, Alexander Davison, to finance the production of a medal to commemorate the battle. He had gold medals distributed to all of the captains, but he went much further, issuing a silver version to the ships' officers, bronze gilt to the petty officers and a bronze version to every sailor in the action. This was the first medal produced for all ranks in an action although it was produced in different metals. Unfortunately, Davison kept to the Admiralty rules on distribution and only those serving on ships of the line received one.

NAVAL OFFICER'S GOLD MEDAL 1794–1815

Battle of Camperdown Medal 1797.

Davison's Battle of the Nile Medal 1798.

Nelson's second victory at Copenhagen was not to see any medals issued at all, but following his third and final victory at Trafalgar in 1805, Mathew Boulton produced a tin Trafalgar medal and issued it to all ratings, believing that the officers would be well looked after by others. Davison also produced a larger tin medal purely for the crew of HMS *Victory*. However, although most were proud to receive a Trafalgar medal, a few sailors are reported to have been unhappy that the medal was made in cheap tin rather than brass and threw their medal overboard in disgust.

These medals clearly only covered the major fleet actions, but very many smaller actions gained no recognition until 1848. It was then that Queen Victoria ordered the issue of the Naval General Service Medal, which was identical to the Military General Service Medal issued at the same time to the Army, both being issued in silver to all ranks, with the recipient's name being engraved on the rim of the medal. Only one medal was issued for each recipient, but named bars attached to the medal ribbon showed the actions which that recipient had actually served at, many being individual ship actions, such as the one in the photograph showing a bar for HMS *Victorious* capturing the French warship *Rivoli* in 1812. The Naval General Service Medal allowed claimants to obtain medals and bars for any action since 1793, although very few were still alive to claim for these earlier actions. However, this was more generous than the provisions for the Army in the Military General Service Medal which only provided bars for actions as far back as the Egypt campaign in 1801, earlier actions not receiving a bar.

Boulton's Trafalgar Medal.

Naval General Service Medal.

99
Staffordshire Ceramic Figurines of the 'Sailor's Farewell' and the 'Sailor's Return'

'Jolly Jack Tar' was to become a major character in popular culture of the eighteenth and nineteenth centuries, represented as a straight-talking, boisterous, hard-drinking all-round fine fellow who bravely laughed in the face of death. He stood full alongside the other great figure of the time, stout 'John Bull'.

His emergence as a fictional national icon was intimately tied to the huge expansion in the Royal Navy and Britain's eventual dominance of the high seas around the world, enabling the huge expansion of both colonisation and trade. However, it was a softening of attitude from a people greatly averse to the deep unfairness of the press gangs snatching people and taking them to sea and often irritated by the drunken loutishness of groups of sailors let free on a run ashore.

Jack Tar's image was softened with the heavy drinking and loutish drunken behaviour portrayed simply as a lust for life and such phrases as 'a girl in every port' hung oddly with the often-repeated image of the heartrending farewell of a sailor off to sea, parting with his loved one and his children. This image did not always fully reflect public attitudes to the Navy, however, the mutineers of 1797 and 1798 often being portrayed as men with genuine grievances eventually hijacked by evil revolutionaries, but these were seen as a few bad eggs and the images of the honourable and patriotic Jack remained.

Both contemporary fiction and theatre were the main proponents of the growth of the image of the plain-speaking, direct and simple sailor, who was very masculine, had a strong nationalism coursing through his veins and, perhaps most importantly, a real 'authenticity'. Numerous plays, musical pieces and comedies invariably included the character of the loyal

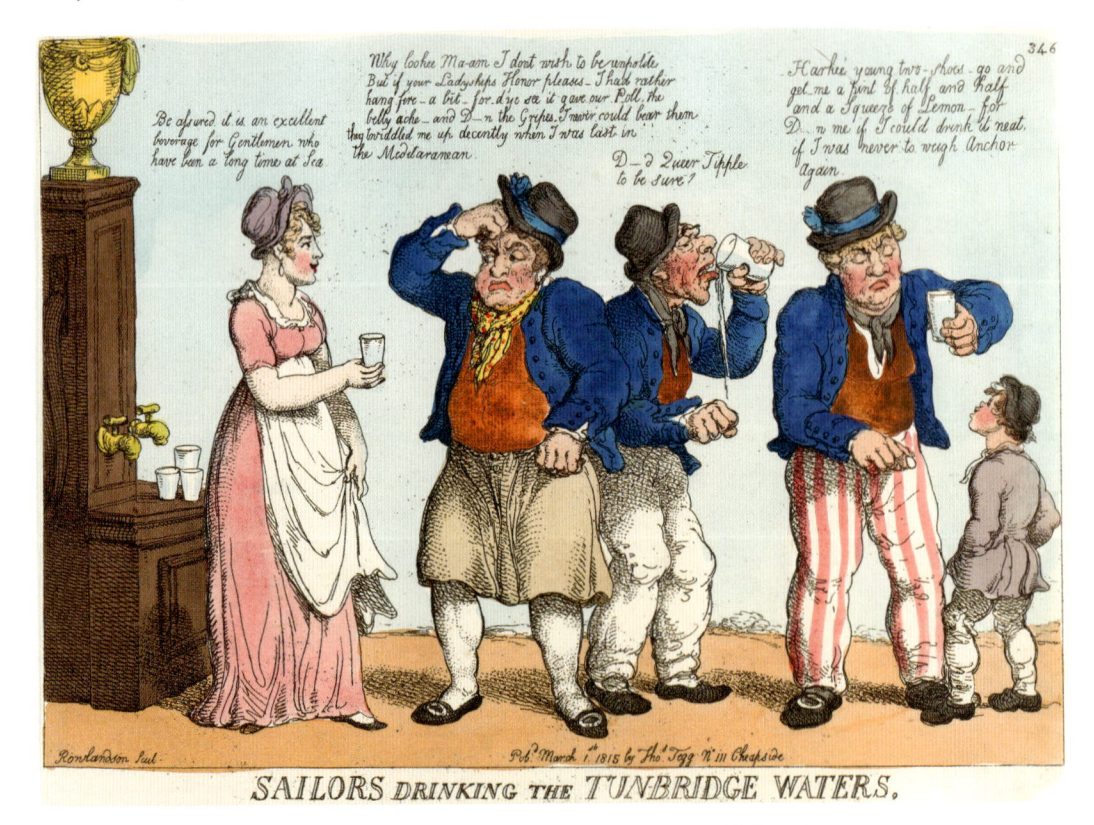

Rowlandson cartoon of sailors unable to drink the waters at Tunbridge Wells 'neat'.

patriotic Jack Tar, with his incomprehensible speech full of nautical jargon and it is certain that the general public took Jack to their hearts. Even Jane Austen was to portray Jack in *Persuasion*.

Jack also featured heavily in political cartoons and in numerous songs of the period, which were regularly sung by families at home. Through the depiction of Jack Tar, the Navy was portrayed as a social meritocracy, masculine and very moral, it was not perhaps a very true reflection.

One well known song of the period shows this self-belief perfectly – 'Hearts of Oak'

> To honor we call you, not press you like slaves;
> For who are so free as the sons of the waves.
> Hearts of oak are our ships; hearts of oak are our men;
> We always are ready; Steddy boys, steddy:
> We'll fight, and we'll conquer again, and again.

Perhaps another less well known song from a play of the time, perhaps portrays the public attitude to the Navy better

> We who brave the stormy main,
> Lead lives of pleasure free from pain;
> Let the welcome then go round,
> May our Ship ne'er run ground,
> May our grog pot ne'er ebb dry,
> Nor British tars from Frenchmen fly.

It has to be pointed out, however, that Jack as popularly portrayed was always white Caucasian, whereas studies have shown that many black African freed slaves were incorporated into the Navy, where they were treated to some racist jibes, but it was a world where your worth was judged by your abilities and experience far more than colour or ethnicity. Some estimates put the

Contemporary cartoon of Jack out in Wapping.

John Bull – ever more hungry for enemy ships.

number of black sailors in the Navy towards the end of the wars at nearly a quarter, although this estimate may be a little high.

What the image of Jack did do was to make ordinary Britons, who had no real idea of the hardships of a life at sea, feel very much at one with him. Jack was brave to the point of foolhardiness and no matter what the odds, he would always overcome all dangers and difficulties to gain a victory. This became an obligation and an expectation, one that was very hard to always live up to, but Britons had taken their sailors to their hearts and elements of that positive image remain to this very day.

100

Colourised Photograph of Nelson's Foudroyant which Ran Aground at Blackpool in 1897

It is often imagined that the age of the wooden warship ended quickly after the end of the Napoleonic wars in 1815, with the rapid rise of steam propulsion, but that is very far from the truth. Steam had actually begun to be used by ships as early as 1807, but in these early days, it was confined to smaller ships such as tug boats. This was because the only technology available to propel a steam ship was a large revolving paddle which would be extremely vulnerable to damage in battle, therefore warships continued to rely on wind power.

The late 1840s really was the end of the wooden sailing warship, with the invention of the screw propeller and then the introduction of explosive shells. Steam-powered frigates with screw propulsion were at sea by the mid-1840s and ships of the line soon followed, the French launching the first as the *Napoleon* in 1850. Within a decade the Royal Navy had built eighteen brand-new steam warships and had also converted forty-one sailing ships to steam, although retaining their sails as well. The French Navy were in an arms race with the Royal Navy, but they could not keep up with the British rate

Photograph of HMS *Vernon* of 50 guns, built in 1832, being towed to be broken up in 1923.

HMS *Queen Charlotte* built in 1810, but renamed *Excellent* in 1859 and broken up in 1892.

HMS *Excellent* 1860

of producing steam warships and they therefore looked elsewhere for an advantage.

Explosive shells had begun to appear in the 1840s and this required ships to have far greater protection than the old wooden walls. Initially, navies converted their wooden-hulled warships by cladding them in iron sheeting, the French developing the first ironclad warship over a wooden hull in 1859 named the *Gloire*. This, however, did not offer the protection that fully-armoured iron hulls did and the Royal Navy launched the first two ironclad and iron-hulled warships in the next two years, named HMS *Warrior* and *Black Prince*. This was effectively the end of the wooden warship, although the first warship to be built without masts for sails and totally reliant on steam power was HMS *Devastation*, launched in 1871.

As the wooden sailing warships became obsolete, they were either sold to be broken up or moored in the various harbours around the country as hulks and used as training ships or floating prisons until they became so rotten that they had to be dismantled.

Perhaps the most famous painting which invokes this feeling of an end of an era is J.M. Turner's *The Fighting Temeraire, tugged to her last berth to be broken up, 1838*, which depicts the ghostly hull of the 98-gun HMS *Temeraire* built in 1798, being towed to the breakers yard by a steam paddle tug whilst the sun sets poignantly in the distance.

A number of these wooden hulks survived until the late nineteenth and early twentieth century, when unfortunately there was little sympathy for these rotting hulls and no thought given to their preservation. A number were scrapped, including HMS *Queen Charlotte* in 1892, HMS *Clyde* in 1904 and HMS *Vernon* in 1923. Others being used as training ships came to a sad end, running aground, deemed not worth trying to refloat and broken up. HMS *Foudroyant* ran aground on Blackpool Beach in 1897 and was wrecked beyond repair, the only saving grace being that HMS *Trincomalee*, then destined to be broken up, was saved as her replacement, taking her name. Another warship used as a training vessel, was HMS *Wellesley*, which was completed in 1815. She was luckily saved from a serious fire in 1914 and even survived a German air raid in 1940 and was refloated.

HMS *Clyde* built in 1828 as a drill ship for the Royal Naval Reserve at Aberdeen. She was sold to be broken up in 1904

HMS *Wellesley*, built in 1815, on fire in 1914. She later sank after being bombed in 1940 but was refloated. She was eventually broken up in 1948.

HMS *Implacable* (originally the French *Duguay Trouin* captured in 1805), taken out of Portsmouth Harbour and sunk in 1949

COLOURISED PHOTOGRAPH OF NELSON'S *FOUDROYANT*

HMS *Unicorn* in the 1950s.

Following the end of the Second World War there was again no appetite for the expense of saving the last of these hulks and HMS *Wellesley* was broken up in 1948. Perhaps the greatest loss however was that of HMS *Implacable*, a French prize. Originally named the *Duguay Trouin* and built in 1795, she had been captured in 1805. In 1949, she was towed out to sea by the Navy and scuttled in one of the worst cases of historic vandalism in the last century. Her sad demise was recorded by a Pathé newsreel and can be viewed online today.

Thankfully a handful of ships of the great period of Nelson's Navy have been left to us today. The fame of HMS *Victory* and the fact that she remained the flagship at Portsmouth for so long ensured her survival, although no longer afloat. However, the only two other warships from this period left to us today came to us almost by accident.

HMS *Trincomalee*, launched at Bombay in 1817, was only saved from the breaker's yard when she replaced *Foudroyant* as the training ship at Falmouth and later at Portsmouth. In 1986 she was taken to her new home in Hartlepool and renamed *Trincomalee*. She has been fully refurbished, and is the oldest Royal Navy vessel still afloat.

HMS *Unicorn*, a sister-ship of the *Trincomalee* being built to the same design, was constructed at Chatham and launched in 1824. Because she was launched in peacetime, she was never fully rigged, but a superstructure was built over her deck and she was laid up 'in ordinary' (mothballed) serving as a hulk and depot ship for the next 140 years. Initial plans in the 1960s were to complete her and she would have looked like the *Trincomalee*. However, it was then realised that much of the roofing over the deck was original as was the entire hull. It has therefore been decided to leave her as she is, retained as the most complete and only example left of a ship 'in ordinary' still in existence.

These are the last legacies of the magnificent ships of Nelson's Navy.

Index

49th Regiment of Foot, the, 156

Abercromby, General Sir Ralph, 272, 275
Abergavenny, HMS, 82
Active, HMS, 227
Admiralty Regulations and Instructions, 197, 211, 265
Agamemnon, HMS, 30, 38
Ajax, HMS, 30, 60
Alarm, HMS, 40
Alaska, 216
Alfred, HMS, 259
Algiers, 270–1
Ambon, 248
Amboyna, 248
Amiens, Peace of, 208, 230, 244
Anson, Admiral, 174
Anson, HMS, 86
Antelope, HMS, 82
Antigua, 22, 25, 208–9, 243
Antwerp, 203
Archer, HMS, 92
Articles of War, the, 256, 265
Asia, HMS, 81
Atlas, HMS, 79
Australia, 214–15, 247, 259

Banda Neira, 248
Barbados, 210, 243
Barbary Pirates, the, 271
Barfleur, HMS, 78
Barham, Lord, 15, 30
Barrow, John, 16
Basque Roads, 202
Baudin, Captain Nicolas, 214–16

Beaver, Captain, 213
Bedford, HMS, 165
Bell Rock Lighthouse, 138
Bellerophon, HMS, 119
Bermuda, 25, 207–8, 222–4
Bermuda, HMS, 222
Bigot, Sebastian de, 189
Black Prince, HMS, 293
Blackwood, Captain, 261
Blenheim, HMS, 78
Blomefield, Thomas, 18, 57
Bloodhound, HMS, 92
Board of Admiralty, the, 111
boatswains, 19, 23, 111–12, 116, 118–19, 120, 232, 267
Bombay, 210, 245–6, 249, 295
Bombay Marine, the, 245, 249–51
Boulogne, 185, 190, 203–4
Boulton, Mathew, 285–6
Boyne, HMS, 79
Brest, 35, 135, 200–2
Bridport, Admiral, 97
Britannia, HMS, 76
Brodie Stove, 170
Broke, Captain Philip, 261
Brown, William, 212–13
Bustamante, Admiral, 229

Cadiz, 10, 218, 228
Cadmus, HMS, 61
Caesar, HMS, 79
Calantsoog, 272–3
Calcutta, 245
Calcutta, HMS, 82
Calder, Vice Admiral, 10, 202

296

INDEX

Caledonia, HMS, 77
Caledonian Ship Canal, the, 178
Cambridge, HMS, 79
Cape of Good Hope, 23, 25, 208, 210, 245, 247
Cape St Vincent, Battle of, 7, 191–2, 200, 217, 218, 219
Cape Town, 208
Carron Iron Works, 57, 72
Cartagena, 218, 229
Carysfort, HMS, 87
caulker, 111, 121, 208
caulking, 48–50, 70, 121
Channel Fleet, the, 97, 200–2
chaplains, 122–3, 166
Chappe, Claude, 129
Charon, HMS, 213
Chatham, Earl of, 15
Cherbourg, 200
Civilian Officers, 111
Clyde, HMS, 293
Cobh, 25, 36
Cochrane, Captain Thomas, 85, 186, 202, 261–2
Collingwood, Admiral, 11, 217
Congreve, William, 185
Cook, Captain, 174
cooks, 19, 111, 167, 169–72, 182, 232
coopers, 25, 117, 121
Copenhagen, 10, 93, 96, 185,
Copenhagen, Battle of, 103, 115, 156, 191, 194, 205, 285
Cornwallis, HMS, 210
Coromandel, HMS, 82
Corsica, 7, 208, 218
Cotton, Admiral, 217
Croker, John, 16
Cuba, 243
Culmer, Billy, 139
Cumberland, HMS, 216
Cumberland House, 18
Customs Service, 282
Cuthbert, Lieutenant, 284

Dalrymple, Alexander, 16, 133
Dance, Commander Nathaniel, 250
Dart privateer, 264
Dartmoor Prison, 23, 232–3
Dasher, HMS, 222
Davison, Alexander, 284–5
Deal, 22, 25, 130, 203
Decaen, General, 216
Derwent, HMS, 263
Derwentwater, Earl of, 239
Devastation, HMS, 293
Devonport (Plymouth), 18, 31, 35, 36
Diomede, HMS, 82
Dominican Republic, 243
Dover, 5, 34, 138, 281, 282
Downs, The, 22, 34, 138, 204
Dreadnought, HMS, 79
Driver, HMS, 222
Duguay Trouin, 294–5
Duke, HMS, 79
Duncan, Admiral, 257, 259, 284
Dunkirk, 276, 282

Eddystone Lighthouse, 137
Edinburgh Castle, 233
Egypt, 9, 10, 213, 272, 274, 285
Elba, 208, 218
Encounter Bay, 215
Erebus, HMS, 187
Esk Mills Prison, 233
Etaples, 204
Excise Board, the, 280
Exmouth, Admiral Lord, 271

Falmouth, 25, 130, 295
Favourite, HMS, 227
Ferrol, 200, 201, 202
First Lord of the Admiralty, the, 14–15, 30
Flinders, Captain Matthew, 213
Flushing, 96, 186
Formidable, HMS, 78

Fort McHenry, 96, 187
Fort William, Bombay, 245
Forton Prison, 232
Foudroyant, HMS, 79, 291, 293, 295
Foxhound, HMS, 114
Fremantle, Captain, 205
Fury, HMS, 96, 249

Galgo, HMS, 186
Gambier, Admiral, 94, 122, 202, 205
Ganges, HMS, 197
Gascoigne, John, 72
Généreux, 9
Géographe, 215
Gibraltar, 9, 22, 25, 92, 98, 208, 217, 218, 219, 221
Glascock, Captain, 211
Glatton, HMS, 73, 82
Gloire, 293
Glorious First of June, Battle of the, 191, 192, 201
Glory, HMS, 79
Goliath, HMS, 213
Grampus, HMS, 82
Gravelines, 282–3
Greenlaw (near Edinburgh), 23
Greenock, 23
Greenwich Royal Naval Hospital, 11, 53, 238–40, 278
Grenada, 243
Guadeloupe, 243
gunners, 23, 59, 111–12, 116, 120, 140, 159, 232

Haiti, 243
Halifax, Nova Scotia, 7, 21, 25, 81, 133, 210, 222
Hamilton, Emma, 10
Hamilton, Sir William, 10
Harrison, John, 145
Haslar Hospital, 21, 22
Hawkins, Sir Richard, 174
Hecla, HMS, 96

Heligoland, 210
Hermione, HMS, 259
Hermione (Spanish), 227
Hibernia, HMS, 77
Hindostan, HMS, 82–3
Hispaniola, 243
Honourable East India Company, the, 82, 133, 177, 178, 245, 247, 248, 249, 250, 269
Hood, Admiral, 217
Hoste, Captain William, 11, 85, 261, 262
Hotham, Admiral, 217
Howe, Admiral Lord, 189, 257
Hull, 25, 32
Hydrographic Department, the, 133

Implacable, HMS, 60, 80, 294, 295
Impregnable, HMS, 31, 77, 79
Impress Service, the, 108, 151
Indefatigable, HMS, 86
Investigator, HMS, 215–16
Irish Station, the, 202
Isis, HMS, 82
Isle de France, 216, 247, 250

Jamaica, 22, 25, 208, 242–4
Japan, 216
Java, 250
Jervis, Admiral Sir John – see the Earl of St Vincent, 218

Kent, HMS, 77
Key, Francis Scott, 187
Kidd, Captain, 238
Kitty privateer, 264

L'Orient, 200
Lancaster, Captain James, 174
Langsdorff, Baron von, 216
Le Havre, 200
League of Armed Neutrality, the, 10, 204
Leith, 25, 204, 213

INDEX

Leopard, HMS, 83
Letters of Marque, 264, 268–9
Lind, James, 174, 175
Linois, Admiral, 247, 250
Lissa, Battle of, 219–20
Liverpool Prison, 233
Lloyd's Patriotic Fund, 277
London, HMS, 257
London, Tower of, 17, 18
Louis XVI, King, 7

Mackenzie, Murdoch, 133
Madras, 22, 210, 245, 246
Madras, HMS, 82
Magiciene, HMS, 32
Magnanime, HMS, 86
Mahé, Bertrand Comte de la Bourdonnais, 189
Mahon, 22, 208, 209, 218
Majestic, HMS, 284
Malabar, HMS, 82–3
Malta, 9, 25, 208, 218, 219, 220, 221, 255
Marengo, 247
Marine Artillery, the, 96, 153
Marine Society, the, 148, 198
Mars, HMS, 160, 258
Martinique, 210, 243, 273
master at arms, 111
masters, 19, 109, 110, 111, 113–14, 133, 135, 138, 141, 152, 166, 226, 232
Mauritius – see Ile de France
Mediterranean Fleet, the, 217–18, 259
Melville, Lieutenant General, 72
Melville, Viscount, 15
Melville Hospital, Chatham, 22
midshipmen, 139–41, 142, 143, 151
Milan Decree, the, 280
Milford Haven, 36
Millbay Prison, 232
Minotaur, HMS, 136
Moore, Commander Graham, 227, 229
Murray, Lord George, 129–30

Nadezhda, 216
Napoleon, 291
Napoleon Bonaparte, 9, 10, 30, 32, 92, 119, 185, 201, 205, 215, 230, 231, 269, 278, 280, 282, 283
Naturaliste, 215
Naval General Service Medal, the, 285–6
Navy Board, the, 19–20, 21, 99, 111, 113, 138, 152
Nelson, Horatia, 10
Nelson, Admiral Lord Horatio, 7–11, 28, 98, 99, 115, 126, 145, 190, 194, 202, 205, 217, 218
Nepean, Sir Evan, 16
Neptune, HMS, 77, 79
Neva, 216
Nevis, 7, 243
New Holland, 215
Newcastle, 25, 178
Newfoundland, 178, 222
Nile, Battle of the, 9, 191, 194, 213, 218, 284, 285
Nisus, HMS, 213
Nore, The, 34
Nore Mutiny, the, 257–8
Norman Cross, 23, 232
North Sea Fleet, the, 203–4,
Nuestro Senora de la Mercedes, 226, 229

Ocean, HMS, 78
Orders in Council, 281
Ordnance, Board of, 15, 17–18, 23, 57, 59, 152
Owen, Commodore, 185

Paignton, 22
Panther, HMS, 82
Parker, Admiral Sir Hyde, 9
Parker, Richard, 256, 259
Parys Mountain, Anglesey, 41
Pasco, Lieutenant, 190
Paul I, Tsar, 10
Pellew, Admiral, 11, 217, 261
Perry's Yard, Blackwall, 30
Perth Prison, 233

Phelan, Louise, 213
Pickle, HMS, 88, 89
Pigot, Captain, 259
Pilots, Society of, 138
Plymouth Sound, 36
Pomone, HMS, 85
Popham, Sir Home, 130, 189–90, 205
Port Jackson, 215, 247
Port Royal, Jamaica, 22, 208, 242–4
Portsmouth, 8, 18, 21, 22, 23, 24, 25, 30, 33, 35, 130, 138, 142, 154, 200, 212, 229, 231, 263, 294, 295
Prince, HMS, 79
Prince George, HMS, 78
Prince of Wales, HMS, 79
prison hulks, 22, 24, 148, 205, 230, 231, 233, 255, 293, 295
privateers, 176, 177, 178–9, 204, 224, 226, 243, 244, 248, 261, 264, 269,
Prometheus, HMS, 93
Pulo Aura, Battle of, 247, 248
pursers, 19, 111, 116–17, 159, 160, 166, 232

Queen Charlotte, HMS, 77, 212, 256, 292, 293
Queensboro, HMS, 89
Quota Act, the, 149

Rainbow, HMS, 73
Ramillies, HMS, 106
Ras-al-Kaimah, 249, 270, 271
Redoubtable, 11
Reynard, 213
Rivoli, 285
Rochefort, 200, 201, 202
Rochester Castle, 233
Romney, HMS, 82
Rosily, Admiral, 10
Royal George, HMS, 77
Royal Hospital School, Greenwich, 239
Royal Naval Academy, the, 142–3
Royal Sovereign, HMS, 76

sailmakers, 52, 111, 118
Salisbury, HMS, 82, 174
San Josef, 7, 191
San Nicolas, 7
Santa Cruz, Tenerife, 9
Santissima Trinidad, 77
Scanagalla, Francesca – see William Brown
Selsey Bill, 200, 203
Seppings, Robert, 39
Serres, John, 135
Sheerness, 25, 35, 36, 130, 257
Sicily, 10, 221
Sick and Hurt Board, the, 19, 21, 22, 23
Smeaton, John, 138
Smeaton Tower, 137
Smith, Commodore Sir William Sidney, 185
Snell, Hannah, 211
Solebay, HMS, 263
Somerset House, 19–20
Spence, Graeme, 133
Spencer, Earl, 15
Spitfire, HMS, 94
Spithead, 35
Spithead Mutiny, the, 256–7
St George, HMS, 79
St Kitts, 243
St Lawrence, HMS, 77
St Lucia, 243
St Petersburg, 205, 216
St Vincent, HMS, 77
St Vincent, Battle of, 7, 191, 192, 218, 219
St Vincent, Cape, 200, 217
St Vincent, Earl of, 15, 29, 143, 217, 201, 217, 218
standing officers, 111, 118
Stapleton Prison, 23, 232
Stevenson, Robert, 138
Stonehouse Hospital, 22
surgeons, 9, 19, 21, 22, 27–9, 111, 156, 166, 174, 211, 213, 232, 252–5
Surprise, HMS, 87
Swallow, HMS, 213

telegraphs, 15, 129–31, 190
Temeraire, HMS, 78–9, 293
Temple, HMS, 30
Teredo worm, 40
Ternate, 248
Torbay, 22, 35, 36
Toulon, 9, 10, 208, 218–19
Trafalgar, Battle of, 9, 10, 11, 30, 50, 56, 59, 64, 73, 89, 98, 104, 130, 190, 191, 193, 194, 202, 221, 277, 285–6
Transport Department, the, 22
Tribune, HMS, 160
Trincomalee, 41, 42, 74, 84, 85, 108, 128, 159, 234, 245, 246, 293
Trincomalee, HMS, 41, 42, 43, 74, 84, 85, 108, 128, 159, 234, 245, 246, 293, 295
Trinity House, 138
Tripoli, 271
Triton, HMS, 166
Tunis, 270, 271

Unicorn, HMS, 295
Union, HMS, 79

Valleyfield Prison, 233
Vanburgh, Sir John, 238
Vernon, Admiral, 184
Vernon, HMS, 292–3

Victorious, HMS, 284
Victory, HMS, 8, 10, 39, 40, 41, 44, 45, 47, 50, 52, 56–7, 58, 59, 61, 62, 64, 68, 69, 70, 73, 76, 98, 102, 120, 121, 124, 127, 130, 157, 166, 167, 170, 171, 182, 188, 285
Victualling Board, the, 25–6, 180
Ville de Paris 77
Villeneuve, Admiral, 10
Vizagapatam Bay, 247

Walcheren Expedition, the, 186, 252
Walker, Samuel, 57, 68
Warrior, HMS, 293
Wellesley, HMS, 293–5
West Africa Station, the, 263–4
West Indies, the, 7, 10, 36, 177, 183, 184, 208, 217, 242–4, 252, 259
Westcott, Captain, 284
Weymouth, HMS, 82
Whitehaven, 25
William IV, King, 141, 142
Wimereux, 282
Windsor Castle, HMS, 79
Woolwich, 18, 36, 57, 154, 185
Wren, Sir Christopher, 238

Yarmouth, 18, 22, 23, 36, 130, 204